PELLI

I see my buildings as pieces of cities, and in my designs I try to make them into responsible and contributing citizens.

—Cesar Pelli

Architecture adds dimensions
to my life that would be impossible to
acquire if I retired.

The beautiful thing about
architecture is that every project
is brand new.

I am forced to renew myself with
every project. Isn't that wonderful?

I realize that having a style would be very beneficial for my practice from a marketing standpoint, but I can't do it.

I believe my responsibility as an architect is to design the most appropriate building for the place.

Each place has a distinct culture and function, which for me requires an appropriate answer.

Published in Australia in 2018 by
The Images Publishing Group Pty Ltd
ABN 89 059 734 431
6 Bastow Place, Mulgrave, Victoria 3170, Australia
Tel: +61 3 9561 5544 Fax: +61 3 9561 4860
books@imagespublishing.com
www.imagespublishing.com

The Images Publishing Group Reference Number: 1246

National Library of Australia Cataloguing-in-Publication entry

Title: Cesar Pelli: Life in Architecture / Michael J. Crosbie (Ed.).
ISBN: 9781864706932 (hardback)

Notes: Includes bibliographical references and index.

Subjects: Pelli, Cesar (monograph). 1926–
Architects—Argentina.
Architects—Brazil.
Architects—Chile.
Architects—China.
Architects—Hong Kong (China).
Architects—Indonesia.
Architects—Italy.
Architects—Japan.
Architects—Malaysia.
Architects—Mexico.
Architects—The Netherlands.
Architects—Singapore.
Architects—Spain.
Architects—United Kingdom.
Architects—United States.
Architects—Vietnam.
Architecture—Modern—20th century.
Architecture—Modern—21st century.
Architectural design.

Book design: Pablo Mandel
www.circularstudio.com
Typeset in URW Geometric and Minion Pro.

Production manager | Group art director: Nicole Boehringer
Senior editor: Gina Tsarouhas
Cover photography: © Jeff Goldberg

Printed on 130gsm Yulong Pure creamy and 128gsm Kinmari matte art paper by Everbest Printing Investment Limited, in Hong Kong/China

IMAGES has included on its website a page for special notices in relation to this and our other publications. Please visit www.imagespublishing.com

PELLI

LIFE IN ARCHITECTURE

MICHAEL J. CROSBIE

images
Publishing

Contents

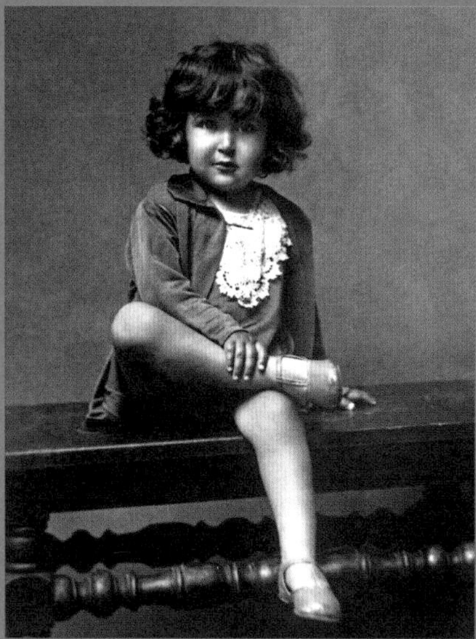
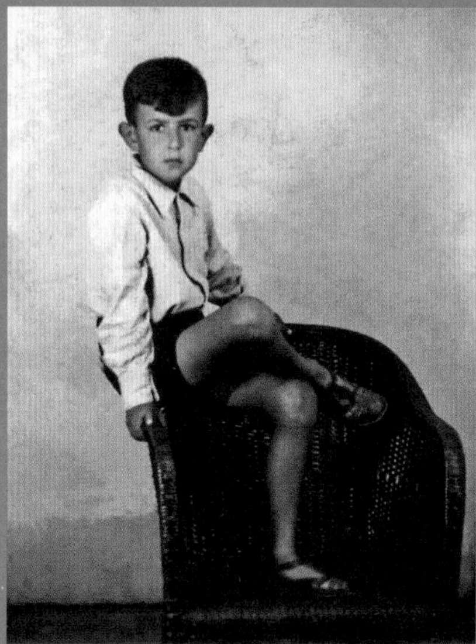

Life in Architecture
by Michael J. Crosbie

It is a brisk March morning in New Haven, Connecticut. Cesar Pelli, the founder and a senior principal of Pelli Clarke Pelli Architects, leafs through some correspondence as he sits in his small private office, one story up, directly above the front door to the firm, located since it began in 1977 near the corner of Chapel and High Streets. It is just down Chapel from Rudolph Hall, home of the Yale School of Architecture, which Pelli headed as dean for seven years.

The office contains ample evidence of the public prominence of this man and his contributions to the field of architecture. There is a wall in the front office that is lined with several decades' worth of international magazine covers featuring Pelli and his work. Design award certificates cover other walls, including one for the Gold Medal of the American Institute of Architects, bestowed upon Pelli in 1995, and another citing the practice as the AIA Firm of the Year in 1989. In 1991 Pelli was named one of the ten most influential American architects living. There are models everywhere, a veritable museum of cardboard, wood, and plastic of some of the most recognizable landmarks in architecture over the past half-century-plus: the Petronas Towers, New York's World Financial Center, the Museum of Modern Art tower, laboratories, skyscrapers, airports, and concert halls by the score.

Pelli emerges, lanky and tall, from his office for our meeting. Dressed neatly and conservatively in black pants, a navy sweater vest, and an open-collar white shirt, he is gracious in his salutation, which is punctuated with a rollicking laugh. He offers to pour us each a cup of coffee. For Pelli, architecture is like breathing. On the cusp of his tenth decade, he comes to the office on a daily basis. He clearly enjoys being there, he enjoys being an architect. Pelli exudes the relaxed yet courtly charm and ease of a man so perfectly suited for his life's work, his life in architecture.

So, let's begin.

Cesar Pelli was born on October 12, 1926 and raised in San Miguel de Tucumán, Argentina, capital of Tucumán province in the west of the country. Pelli describes himself as bookish as a child, not particularly athletic or competitive, but the favorite with his parents among his two younger siblings. His mother and father, also from Tucumán, had grown up poor. Pelli seems to be an amalgam of his parents, as he describes them. His mother was one of the first women to graduate from the Universidad Nacional de Tucumán and had a fierce commitment to education as a social benefit, "the key to everything," as Pelli notes. She became a progressive teacher in the public school system, teaching geography and French. Pelli's father

TOP Cesar Pelli, at center of group shot with his Tucumán classmates, the 'Gauchos'. BOTTOM, LEFT TO RIGHT Cesar at the center with his mother and brother, Victor, in 1939; Cesar's parents, Teresa B. Suppa and Victor V. Pelli, in 1925; Cesar's mother in 1965.

was not a college graduate, and had worked as a reporter for the local newspaper (he met his future wife while profiling the local women's basketball team) and also as a civil servant. Pelli recalls that his father liked to draw, to sculpt in clay, and to do woodworking. A change in the political party in power resulted in his father losing his job. Pelli remembers him working at home a lot, and he would watch him as he worked. "He took great pleasure in creating things," recalls Pelli, transforming materials, "like planing a piece of wood. He taught me how to use tools." His mother's passion for education was paired with his father's interest in craft.

A career in architecture was not an obvious choice for Pelli. There were no architects in his family and no architect role models in his city. As Pelli was completing high school he planned to attend college but he had no means to or intention of leaving Tucumán. While speculating on what he might study (philosophy was an interest), his father gave him a catalog from the Universidad Nacional de Tucumán, which included a program in architecture. "I had never heard of architecture," says Pelli, "never known an architect." But the curriculum in drawing, art, and history was appealing. Finishing high school at the age of 16, Pelli figured that if architecture turned out to be a mistake he could always change his mind without losing too much time.

And at first, it looked like the wrong road. While Pelli loved the architectural history courses, the design studio projects seemed completely disconnected with the reality of life in Tucumán in the early 1940s. The architecture program was in the Beaux-Arts tradition, with hours spent studying the classical orders, ancient precedents, and carefully composing plans and façades, rendering them with ink washes and watercolors. "We were designing temples, urns, and tombs," Pelli recalls. "I was good at this, but I had my doubts. What do I do with this when I graduate?" A change of faculty at the school, including the arrival of young professors from Europe fleeing World War II, gave the program a new direction. Suddenly, the studio design assignments changed. "They gave us a bus stop, and I thought it was fantastic," laughs Pelli, "because it was real and it was something that could be used in my hometown!" Pelli notes that the program's more relevant focus on the connections between modern art and architecture (Pelli enjoyed doing analyses of Matisse paintings), the emphasis on the tactile nature of materials, the openness to blue-sky speculation, along with awareness of architecture's social agenda, created a climate of excitement and passion for his choice of a profession. It was a moment in his life, says Pelli, akin to Saul's on the road to Damascus. "Architecture could have a social purpose," Pelli

ARCHITECTURAL RECORD
4

Progressive Architecture

INTERIORS
FEBRUARY 1987

summa+ 47

THE BOTTOM LINE

はざま11/12'96

a+u

César Pelli
EL GENIO DE TUCUMAN

Yale
Designed for Science
Musical Memories
When Cars Were Banned

ARCHITECTOR

BLUEPRINT
CHIPPERFIELD IN JAPAN
DESIGN WITHOUT DESIGNERS

營建世界
CONSTRUCTION & ENGINEERING

DINOSAUR TRACKS THE MARTIAN FOSSILS
SCIENTIFIC AMERICAN
DECEMBER 1997
SPECIAL REPORT:
BUILDING THE BIGGEST
How the tallest skyscrapers and other giant projects took shape

AyC
LA REVISTA
CESAR PELLI
Entrevista Exclusiva

日経アーキテクチュア
NIKKEI ARCHITECTURE
2001 11-12
試される「監理の自立」
こだわりの家づくり名人

at
Architecture Magazine
シーザー・ペリ

says in describing how the profession opened for him. “For the place you live, you could do something. We could learn from the other arts, and if we were very good we could reach a level of art. It still keeps fueling me.” The social/civic aspect of architecture and its role in shaping the way people live their lives became a constant in Pelli’s practice throughout his career. As he prepared to finish architecture school, Pelli relates that he can remember a point where he knew that he wanted to devote his life to architecture and why he wanted to be an architect: “To do something for society, and something that could be art at the same time,” says Pelli. “That feeling still exists for me, it hasn’t changed.” He had made the right decision.

After graduating Pelli taught studio design for two years at the Universidad Nacional de Tucumán while also working in a government office designing and building low-cost public housing for sugarcane workers. He freelanced, too, designing small private homes. In 1952, an opportunity to study in the US presented itself at the University of Illinois at Urbana Champaign School of Architecture, in the graduate program, where he was offered a $95 monthly stipend from the US Department of State for nine months of international education. Pelli moved with his wife, Diana Balmori, a fellow architect who had also studied at Tucumán. Upon graduating from Illinois, two job offers presented themselves: one for a large firm in Detroit for $3.50 an hour, and the other an opportunity to work for Eero Saarinen’s office in Bloomfield Hills, Michigan, for $2.50 an hour. The Detroit offer meant forty percent more income compared to working for Saarinen. Pelli, Diana, and the first of their two sons were living in a very modest rental home, and they had no family money to fall back on. But the chance to work for one of the world’s greatest living architects carried an incalculable value, and the young Pelli family headed to Bloomfield Hills. It is a decision Pelli has never regretted.

Pelli started with Saarinen’s practice in 1954. Over the next decade (except for a short, eight-month return to Argentina in 1960 to teach and work on a competition) Pelli was involved in a wide variety of iconic Saarinen projects, most notably the TWA Terminal at JFK airport in New York (Pelli focused on shaping the columns along the lines of force); the Morse and Stiles residential colleges at Yale (which occasioned Pelli’s first trip to the East Coast); and for a short time the US Embassy in London (a project that Saarinen thought the most important of his life, according to Pelli).

Pelli considered his time with Saarinen akin to a post-graduate experience. Working with Saarinen impressed upon Pelli an approach to architectural problem analysis and design

TOP AND MIDDLE Cesar working with Eero Saarinen on the TWA terminal in the late 1950s. BOTTOM At a mock-up of the exterior wall for Yale’s Morse and Stiles residential colleges in the 1950s.

TOP A gathering of top American architects in 1977, from left to right: Frank Gehry, Michael Graves, Charles Moore, Cesar Pelli, Philip Johnson, Charles Gwathmey, Stanley Tigerman, Peter Eisenman, Robert A.M. Stern.
BOTTOM Cesar with family in 1977.

that was specific to each project—"the style for the job"—as Saarinen liked to say. Pelli remembers Eero as not particularly talkative. Unlike his father, Eliel, Eero was quiet, introverted, focused, hardworking, no nonsense. "Eero was a different kind of being," says Pelli, "one focused and incredibly directed. He was not very vocal. You learned by observing him. He would sit next to you and design with you. You could see his dedication and concentration." Saarinen's office worked primarily in physical models, a design technique that Pelli carried with him when he started his own firm (which continues to rely on modeling to design, although more of the models today are done by computer).

Pelli continued with Saarinen's office after Eero's death in September 1961 until 1964, when he completely shifted gears, taking the post as Director of Design at Daniel, Mann, Johnson and Mendenhall (where he stayed for four years), and then Partner for Design for nearly a decade at Gruen Associates (both in Los Angeles, where teaching at UCLA permitted Pelli to keep a foot in the world of academia). While Saarinen would lavish time on a design until he felt it was just right (he amazingly scrapped the client-approved design for the TWA terminal and started over, taking another year to redesign it), the DMJM and Gruen offices prized speed and meeting budgets. Pelli cultivated a discipline about how to quickly analyze a design problem, interact with clients, and deliver a project within its financial constraints. "At DMJM I learned to be very flexible," says Pelli. "You needed to be fast. DMJM would give you an allotted number of hours for design, so the project would make a profit." At Gruen—a more architecture-dominated office than DMJM's engineering focus—Pelli wed his interests in architectural design responses to contemporary construction techniques to operating within large project teams. Gruen also introduced him to working with developers and the collaborative nature of such relationships, allowing him to hone interpersonal skills that would serve Pelli well in growing his own firm. Pelli has developed a capacity to see the client as a potential collaborator. He notes that the most fruitful collaborations with clients happen with those who have "...a very clear idea of what they want, and participate constructively," Pelli explains. "They are well organized, give clear responses and directions, have reasonable budgets. They give you direction, but they don't draw for you." Pelli notes that a collaborative client is not necessarily the key to creating a great building, but it can make the process more rewarding and efficient for both the architect and the client. Perhaps most importantly, at the end of the process Pelli wants the client to see the building as his or hers, not just the architect's.

The California years encouraged Pelli to develop an approach to architecture as "the art of the possible" (an orientation also found in Saarinen's work). Architecture as the art of the possible means that the architect accepts the facts and limitations of the project brief head on—without ignoring them, trying to change them, or circumventing them—so that the result is an authentic response to the reality given, while it aspires to some greater end (Pelli has said that no building is more important than the place it is part of, and that no architect is more important than the building and its role—the antithesis of "signature" style architecture prevalent today). He has described the limits and constraints of a particular project as architecture's "lifeblood." It defines a "practical center" within the project at hand, the direction it wants to go in, which Pelli believes permits the architect greater latitude for creativity.

Notable works from Pelli's California period indicate two dominant themes: the exploration of circulation spines as generators and organizers of the plan, and the refinement of exterior glass skins as pure expressions of building construction and form. The Urban Nucleus project on Sunset Mountain Park, COMSAT Laboratories, and the competition-winning scheme (although never built) for the United Nations City in Vienna were among the most inventive of the spine schemes. Spines cascading down a mountainside organized the ambitious Urban Nucleus project—a veritable city on a hilltop. COMSAT's plan allowed it to continue to grow across its rural Maryland site, while the UN City design increased the complexity by weaving a series of towers of different heights into the horizontal spine plan geometry. The spine as an organizing element continued to appear in Pelli's later work, such as a private residence he designed in the Western US and the North Terminal at Reagan National Airport in Washington, D.C.

Pelli's early and sustained interest in Joseph Paxton's 1851 Crystal Palace in London as pivotal in the history of architecture, and the ensuing separation of enclosure from frame in early 20th-century buildings, led directly to projects such as Teledyne Laboratories, Century City Medical Plaza, San Bernardino City Hall, and the first phase of the Pacific Design Center. In all of these projects, Pelli literally pushed the envelope in his use of glass as an all-enclosing, homogenous material that did not rely on the structural system for expression. Narrow mullions, sleek profiles, ceramic fritted glass that obscured distinction between vision and spandrel units, and elemental yet powerful building forms distinguished these buildings and (for better or worse, in less-capable design hands) provided a strong direction for glass curtain wall buildings of the 1960s and '70s.

TOP AND RIGHT Cesar with collaborators and client with models for the Four Leaf Towers development. ABOVE Cesar with wife and partner, Diana Balmori. OPPOSITE TOP Cesar with Diana. MIDDLE With the client at the Gewirz House. BOTTOM Talking to clients on the Museum of Modern Art project.

Two late projects from the California oeuvre in particular reveal Pelli's maturing interest in gauging his architecture to the particular circumstances of "place," and architecture's civic role in creating identity. In the 1972 design for the US Embassy in Tokyo, Pelli explored the use of a taut concrete panel skin instead of glass as an enclosure because the State Department required that the exterior wall be 15-centimeter-thick (6-inch-thick)—concrete as a reference to the local tradition of *shoji* screen architecture. In this project, Pelli signaled a direction leading to groundbreaking projects more than a decade later, such as Herring Hall at Rice University. In a tangent to his work in glass enclosures (and his interest in Paxton), Pelli designed the Commons of Columbus in 1970 and the Niagara Falls Winter Garden in 1975. These glass-enclosed "great rooms," scaled to accommodate the celebration of life in a city, became a repeating theme throughout Pelli's later work in creating urban places for civic exchange, echoes of which can be seen in the design of the Salesforce Transit Center, currently under construction in San Francisco.

When he was named Dean of the Yale School of Architecture in 1977, Pelli expected to carve out a modest practice as an appendage to the life of an architectural don.

But the awarding of the expansion and renovation of the Museum of Modern Art in New York City in addition to the design of the MoMA residential tower, just as Pelli arrived in New Haven, necessitated the creation of a practice that could respond to such high-profile projects. From California, Pelli brought long-time collaborator Fred Clarke, who with Balmori and Pelli formed the nucleus of Cesar Pelli & Associates (CP&A). A key strategy in undertaking the MoMA commission was to associate with Gruen Associates as Executive Architect, which allowed CP&A to focus on design while Gruen handled technical aspects and construction documentation. In the process Pelli and his collaborators developed a way of working that would have far-ranging influence on their own practice and the profession at large. The structure of a design firm working with an associated firm that would provide technical and documentation support would become the backbone of Pelli's practice, allowing CP&A to undertake large projects without a corresponding large staff. The structure well served CP&A and later Pelli Clarke Pelli Architects (with an office in New York City that opened in 2000 and headed by Cesar's son, Raphael). However, the past dozen years have seen the practice take on more aspects of project documentation and construction administration. The practice has earned a well-deserved reputation for design documentation and communication, detail development and refinement, and follow-through, making the resulting finished work seamless.

TOP LEFT Cesar visiting on-site during construction.
TOP RIGHT Cesar and son Rafael Pelli in 2004. BOTTOM Pelli in Shanghai, 2010.

Pelli's teaching at several architecture schools and his seven-year tenure as architecture dean at Yale reverberate through the practice today in the way projects are managed and move forward. Structured a bit more like an academic design studio than the project assembly line that most firms resemble, the method seems to have evolved naturally from Pelli's proximity to academe. Projects continue to be managed and staffed by teams that do not change as the project moves from concept to refined detail. Alternative design responses and ideas are studied collectively, and younger team members are encouraged to critique as well as to present. One of the keys to making this work is to set project goals at the beginning, clearly communicate them, and reference them as the project proceeds.

This is another technique that Pelli learned from Saarinen. He recalls that design ideas that emerged from Saarinen sketching at home in isolation were never as strong as those that evolved collectively. In fact, during his practice Pelli has resisted the inclination to sketch first. "Most other architects would go first to the pencil, but for me, it is verbal," explains Pelli. "I have always seen architecture as an act of collaboration, which is essential. I only draw if I need to. I appreciate the ideas that young architects can propose, making it a more sensitive, richer response to the site and the city we are building in."

The ethos of creating a "teaching office" has always been part of Pelli's practice. He sees it not only as a continuation of his role as an academic; it touches something very deep inside him as a human being. Pelli wrote in his 1991 book, *Observations for Young Architects*: "My love for teaching is older than my love for architecture," [Observations, 139] and I suspect that through the act of teaching he reaches back to his mother. When I asked Pelli to talk about the place of teaching in his life in architecture, he reflected, "I don't need to be building, I could be teaching and feel just as satisfied. I have taught most of my life. That is why I could leave the School of Architecture at Yale. I could teach here," meaning his practice. "Teaching young men and women to become very good architects is part of my obligation, and we prepare them," explains Pelli. "That is part of our responsibility here." The core of academic training, as Pelli sees it, is to fill future architects with a sense of idealism, a sense of purpose, and a social consciousness. But actually acquiring the tools in order to perform as an architect is difficult to accomplish in school, like learning to swim. "You can't pretend that you are in the water in school."

The products of more than 50 years' practice, the collection of projects presented in this volume is vast in its breadth. The landmarks are those that push ideas and areas of interest that Pelli defined earlier in his architectural life, enriching and refining them as he matured as a designer and opened wider circles of collaboration with colleagues. The condition of the enclosure continued as a focus of attention, most notably in the residential tower at MoMA, where Pelli played with light, minimal surface texture, and subdued color that resonated with the Midtown Manhattan context. There's an anthropomorphic character to the pattern of glass that has been pointed out by such critics as John Pastier and Gavin Macrae-Gibson, and historian Lee Edward Gray, and which Pelli pursued in later skyscraper projects.

Herring Hall at Rice University, mentioned earlier, is a melding of Pelli's interest in the thin skins of contemporary construction and his deepening sense of obligation to respond to the context of color, pattern, material, and form—although not in a historicist way common in many buildings of the mid-1980s. Pelli told me that his clients at Rice were pushing him to design more of a revivalist piece of architecture with literal references to Rice's landmark 1910s brick buildings by Ralph Adams Cram. He pushed back with a work that exists on its own contemporary architectural terms, enriched by the campus's architectural past. A similar approach is seen in the Carnegie Hall Tower in New York. As Pelli moves into stainless steel cladding with a variety of delicate surface finishes, the towers become more resonant with the atmosphere of the place they live in—the cool grays and blues of London in the One Canada Square tower at Canary Wharf, and the mellow yellows, pinks, and purples of Plaza Tower in Costa Mesa, California. By the time the Petronas Towers were built in Kuala Lumpur, the skin becomes fully animated in depth (Joseph Giovanni described this as "spatializing" the façade) [Sections, 59], responding to the climate, the city, and national culture of Malaysia.

Other tall buildings offer another line of Pelli's inquiry into architecture responding to place, history, and local context. Historian Lee Gray in his book, *Pattern and Context,* and the late Vincent Scully in an essay for a 2000 Yale exhibit of the architect's work, both observed that Pelli resuscitated the moribund "high-rise" building type of the 1970s, with its monotonous wrapper and flat top, by reviving and re-purposing the older terminology of "skyscraper" to remind us that these creations were meant to inspire as cathedrals once did (and still do). Pelli created a new appreciation for the work of such architects as Raymond Hood, William van Alen, Hugh Ferris, and Eliel Saarinen (particularly the latter's entry to the Chicago Tribune Building competition), and infused projects such as the Norwest Tower (now Wells

Fargo Center), the Bank of America Headquarters, and the Salesforce Tower with a sense of aspiration and romanticism. Pelli notes that Eero Saarinen had said that the ultimate architectural design assignment for any architect would be a cathedral. Pelli managed this by revitalizing the skyscraper as the cathedral's modern-day surrogate.

Pelli believes that every work of architecture needs to become a piece of the city, town, or community that it is in, and it is the architect's responsibility to design for these contextual conditions. The best examples of this in Pelli's work are the scores of public spaces that he has created in projects large and small. Some of these public spaces were not in the client's program, but Pelli made a case that they would contribute to the life of the community beyond the functional requirements of the building project. The Winter Garden at New York's World Financial Center (now Brookfield Place, which has a new glassy entry Pavilion designed by Pelli Clarke Pelli), is perhaps Pelli's greatest civic gathering place, an architectural element he inserted into the program. It is a direct descendent of the Commons of Columbus and the Niagara Falls Winter Garden, and a progenitor of crystalline chambers that came afterward, such as Founders Hall at the Bank of America Building, the West and East Winter Gardens at Canary Wharf, and Kurayoshi Commons in Japan. All of these are marvelous hubs of human activity, and they have "cousins" in Pelli's oeuvre. The distant relations to these great rooms are the lobbies of many of Pelli's performing arts centers, such as the Schuster in Dayton, the Segerstrom Concert Hall in Costa Mesa, and the Overture Center for the Arts in Madison—all grand and generous gestures of welcome and hospitality. I would argue that even the entry to the National Museum of Contemporary Art in Osaka, the grand concourse of the Reagan National Airport North Terminal (a breathtaking space of the caliber of New York's Penn Station and Grand Central), and the Docklands Light Railway Station in London can all trace their lineage to the World Financial Center Winter Garden.

The civic and public spaces that Pelli has designed around the world share with the Winter Garden the architect's passion for creating settings in urban places where the lives of citizens can play out. The Thomson Plaza for the Arts at the Arsht Center is such a place. It responds to the mild climate of Miami with a cradle of outdoor public space that bridges Biscayne Boulevard—a locale for promenades and performance. Piazza Gae Aulenti in Milan is another example of a vibrant public space embraced by surrounding buildings, canopies, and pools. The Salesforce Transit Center and Salesforce Tower promises to be a new kind of public space that will extend along a rooftop garden for four blocks in downtown San Francisco. All of these projects affirm the importance of city spaces where the everyday can be celebrated.

The central importance in Pelli's work of great gathering spaces—both openly orchestrated to the life of the metropolis and those carefully gift-wrapped in a tissue of glass as offerings to the city—has been cultivated throughout Pelli's life in architecture, and nourished by the places that inspire him. Many of his own descriptions in this book of his work are forthright affirmations of architecture's need to move the human heart. Although an intellectual, Pelli does not intellectualize his craft, coolly abstracting it to satisfy some arcane architectural agenda. He approaches it with the goal of creating places that will make a difference in the lives of those who live with them, that they will be memorable, edifying, genuine, well-made—but most importantly, moving. For these reasons, Pelli impresses one as an architectural phenomenologist: he cares about how buildings are perceived and experienced (not just by architects) and how they affect people.

This is how he himself contemplates architecture.

"The value of art reaches you deeply," says Pelli of his life in experiencing and creating architecture. "If it has no art, it doesn't touch you. That is the only measure I know." What places have made an indelible mark on Pelli? He says that the building that has moved him most is Chartres Cathedral. "The combination of the form," explains Pelli, "the space, the sounds, the art in the windows, the sculptures, capture all of your senses. You are one with the building. It is the most extraordinary work of architecture that has captured me."

Recalling the moving experience of a spiritual place like Chartres is one way that Pelli recharges his creativity. Another is time in a city. "I love walking in cities, almost any city," says Pelli, as he ticks off some of his favorites: New York, London, Buenos Aires, Venice. But "the wild" places, as Pelli calls them, are also restorative: gardens, forests, landscapes. His preference for nature both within and outside urban places is fitting for a man who sees the work of the architect as akin to that of a gardener. It is a model that Pelli learned from Eero Saarinen, and it sums up Pelli's belief that the best architecture always seems natural to its place. He describes the work of the architect gardener this way: "The gardener understands the nature of a particular site, its climate, soil, shade, and nurtures each plant so that it can become the best possible example of its species. Buildings, with their changing needs and their attachment to site, are more like living trees than inert blocks of stone." [Observations, 164]

Good gardeners know that nature cannot be forced, will not be hurried. It is best to coax it, tend it gently, content in the knowledge that its full blossoming may take years of careful attention, feeding, pruning, care—the cumulative accretion of small moves. For Cesar Pelli, that is precisely what makes the best kind of architecture.

Cesar with family, from left to right, Diana Balmori, son Dennis Pelli, grandchild Iris, Cesar, grandchild Dhalia, son Rafael Pelli.

Mimi Styne
274·8601

Cesar Pelli's California Decade

by John Pastier

California has been a powerful magnet for architects and designers for well over a century, and once these newcomers arrived, they almost invariably stayed. Bernard Maybeck, the Greene brothers, Irving Gill, R. M. Schindler, Richard Neutra, Erich Mendelsohn, John Lautner, Charles and Ray Eames, Victor Gruen, Anthony Lumsden, Frank Gehry, and Thom Mayne are among the most celebrated of those permanent transplants.

Cesar Pelli would surely have been on this elite list of relocated talents, had he chosen to remain a Californian. He emigrated from Argentina with stops at the University of Illinois and the office of Eero Saarinen, and then moved to the West Coast in 1966 to direct design first for DJMM and later Gruen Associates, two large Los Angeles architectural firms. At that time, serious contemporary design in California primarily revolved around the single-family house, a building type that lay outside Pelli's range of interest. His commissions were primarily commercial and institutional, and he treated them as opportunities to explore interior circulation patterns and the visual qualities of the then-new material of reflective glass curtain walls, sleek and tautly detailed. But in 1977, on the heels of the Pacific Design Center (his finest realized design at that point), he chose to become, in his own words, an East Coast architect. This involved serving as Dean of Architecture at Yale, participating in a more complex architectural culture, working with more adventurous and substantial clients, and enjoying the freedom that came with a fully independent architectural practice.

Clearly, this uprooting worked out well, allowing Pelli to design an impressive collection of buildings over the next four decades: performing arts centers, museums, airports, libraries, academic buildings, and, most notably, skyscrapers. His East Coast design practice produced dozens of the 's tallest and most refined skyscrapers, including the twin towers in Malaysia that, for a time, held the world record for the tallest buildings in the world and, with their Islamic-derived geometries, may be the most original and culturally sensitive tall buildings anywhere.

In retrospect, the Los Angeles portion of Pelli's career was relatively modest compared to what followed. But three epic designs from that period more than hold their own. Unfortunately, only one was built. The first, dating from the mid-1960s, was the urban nucleus for Sunset Mountain Park, a dramatic yet graceful concrete megastructure for several thousand residents in western Los Angeles' Santa Monica mountains. Entered from the top, (where social and commercial spaces were concentrated and all cars would be stored), its terraces cascaded down the rugged hillsides by as many as 40 stories. In effect, it was a single-faced skyscraper anchored to an undulating geological substructure. The conception was graphically breathtaking, winning a first-prize design award from *Progressive Architecture* magazine, but also economically problematic in a for-profit context (the client was a small oil company).

Pelli's design for UN City was the product of a 1969 design competition for a United Nations facility in Vienna embracing over 370,000 square meters (4 million square feet) of offices, auditoria, conference spaces, and a rapid transit rail connection. It was not just a building, but also an embodied strategy for vertical and horizontal phasing and expandability along a generously scaled circulation spine. The visual result was a dynamic, self-explanatory expression of a complex program. The megastructure earned first prize in a pool of 280 competition entries from 50 countries, but the Viennese powers that be connived to block its construction, in favour of a lesser design of local origin. In the process, the architectural world missed out on a major icon.

The Pacific Design Center opened in West Hollywood in 1975 to serve the interiors and furnishings industries, and is the final great product of Pelli's Los Angeles years. This 69,675-square-meter (750,000-square-foot) extruded behemoth, clad in ultramarine glass, rises out of an otherwise low-scaled neighborhood, and constitutes a bold and quirky urban gesture that reflects the sprawling metropolis itself. Its completion drew a mixed public reaction. It was soon named 'The Blue Whale,' and eventually gained a good if not total degree of public acceptance. The Pacific Design Center has been expanded by Pelli twice since then, with a green element added in 1988 and a red one in 2014. The two components more than doubled the project's original size, and there is talk of further expansion. What was originally Pelli's *adieu* to Los Angeles has turned out to be only an *au revoir*.

Sunset Mountain Park

1965

Santa Monica, California, US

The Urban Nucleus project at Sunset Mountain Park was to be sited on a protruding spur within the Santa Inez, a valley with a view of the Pacific Ocean. A network of inclined elevators provided access at all levels. The project had fifty levels but was never more than three stories high in any one place. It was a revolutionary and beautiful design which enhanced the form of the valley, which would retain its lush greenery.

The design came about because conventional cut-and-fill to create pads for single-family homes proved too expensive, as the site had too many flaws. The Urban Nucleus project was affordable and the developer, Sunset Oil, was ready to go ahead with it but it was over-invested in multiple other properties and eventually went bankrupt. Much of the land became a state park.

This design won First Prize in Progressive Architecture—it was my first published design and the first opportunity I had to express my ideas in my name, and because of this it was a very important chapter in my career.

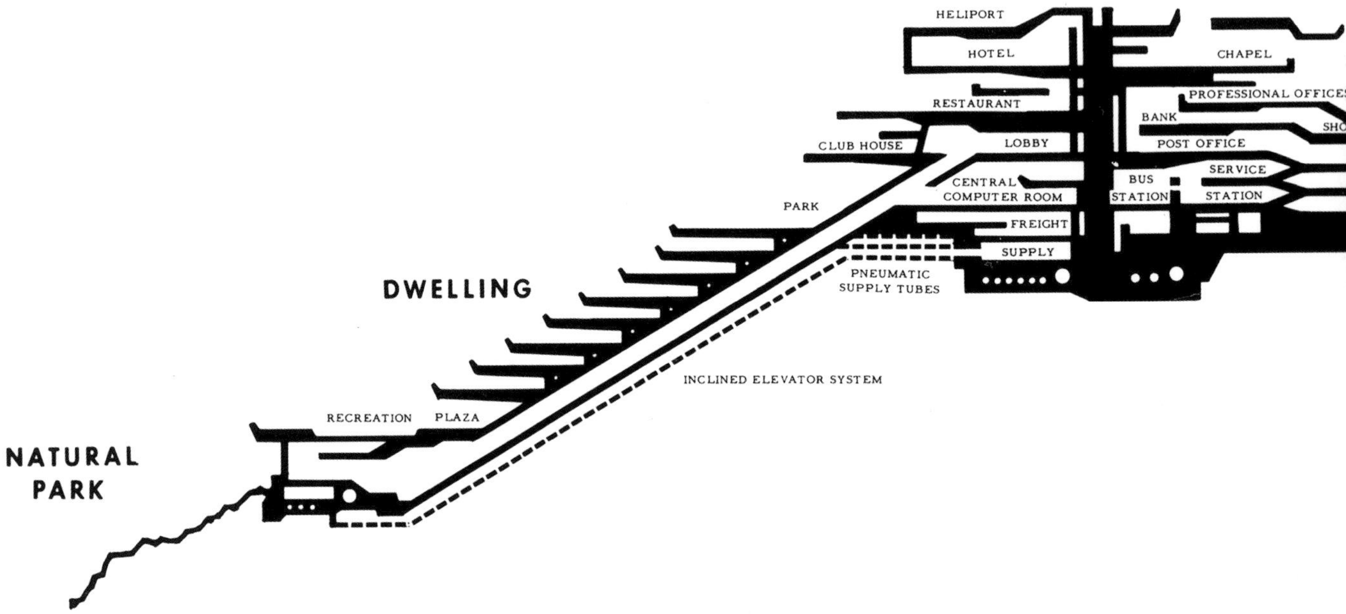
HELIPORT
HOTEL
CHAPEL
PROFESSIONAL OFFICES
RESTAURANT
BANK
SHO
CLUB HOUSE
LOBBY
POST OFFICE
SERVICE
CENTRAL
COMPUTER ROOM
BUS
STATION
STATION
PARK
FREIGHT
SUPPLY
PNEUMATIC
SUPPLY TUBES
DWELLING
INCLINED ELEVATOR SYSTEM
RECREATION PLAZA
NATURAL
PARK

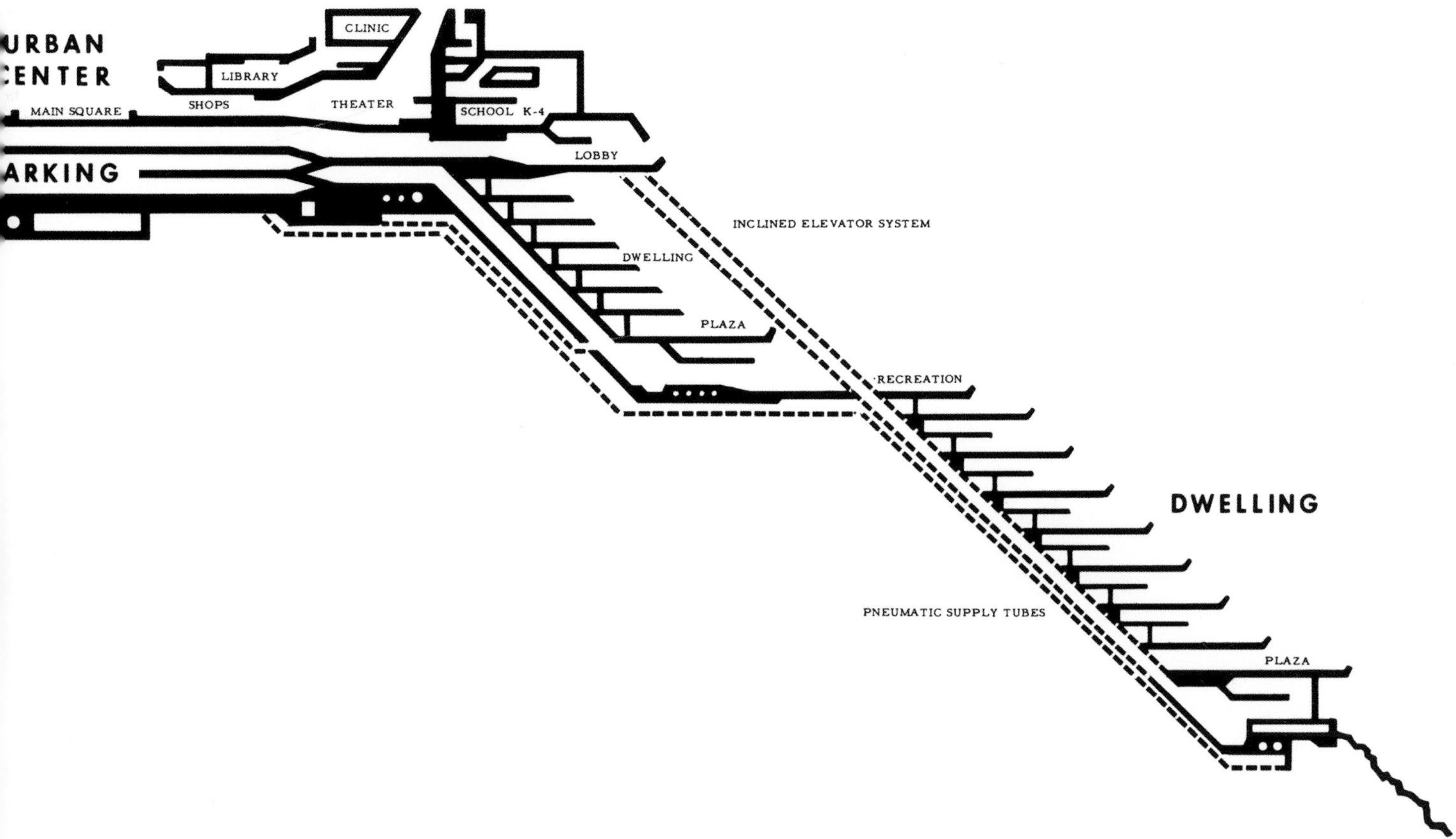
URBAN
CENTER
CLINIC
LIBRARY
SHOPS
THEATER
MAIN SQUARE
SCHOOL K-4
ARKING
LOBBY
INCLINED ELEVATOR SYSTEM
DWELLING
PLAZA
RECREATION
DWELLING
PNEUMATIC SUPPLY TUBES
PLAZA

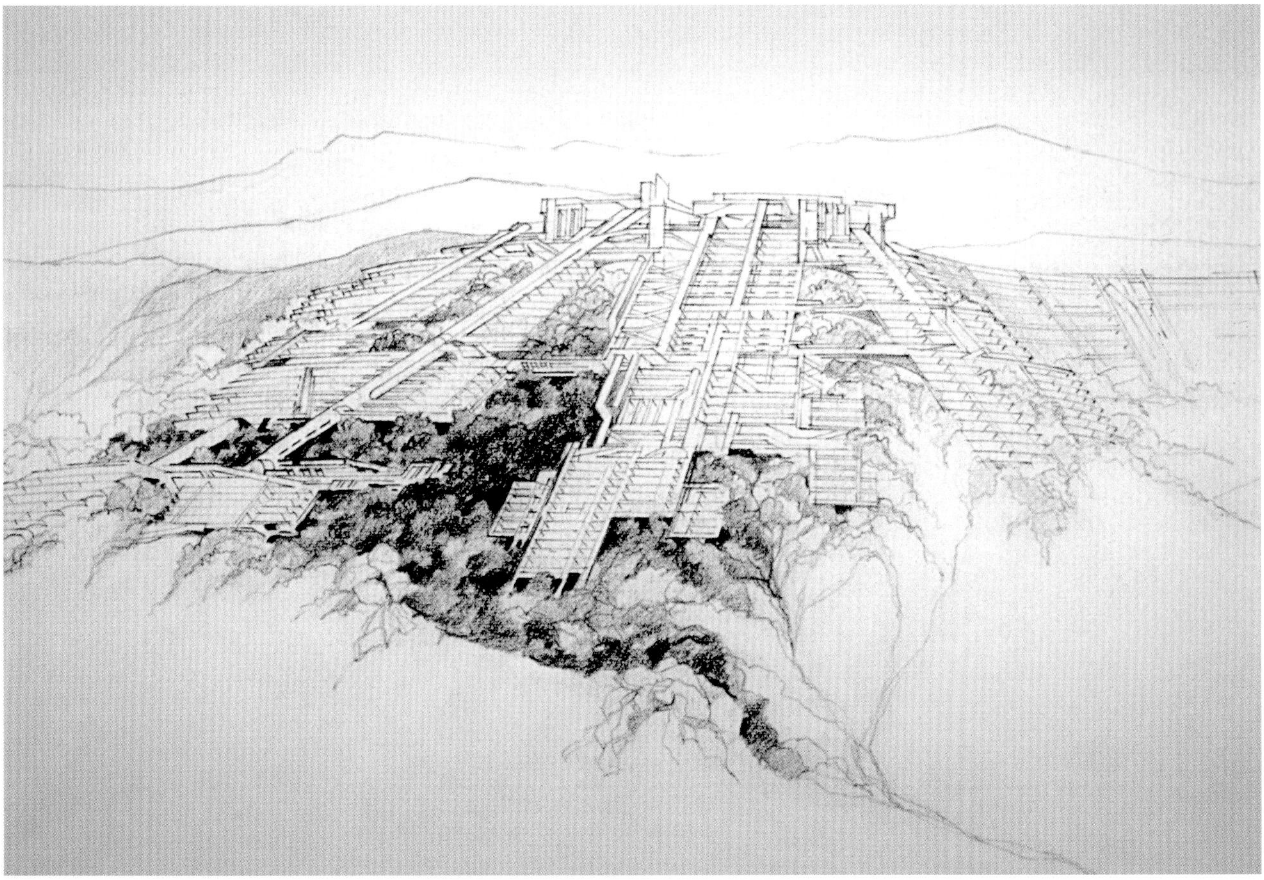

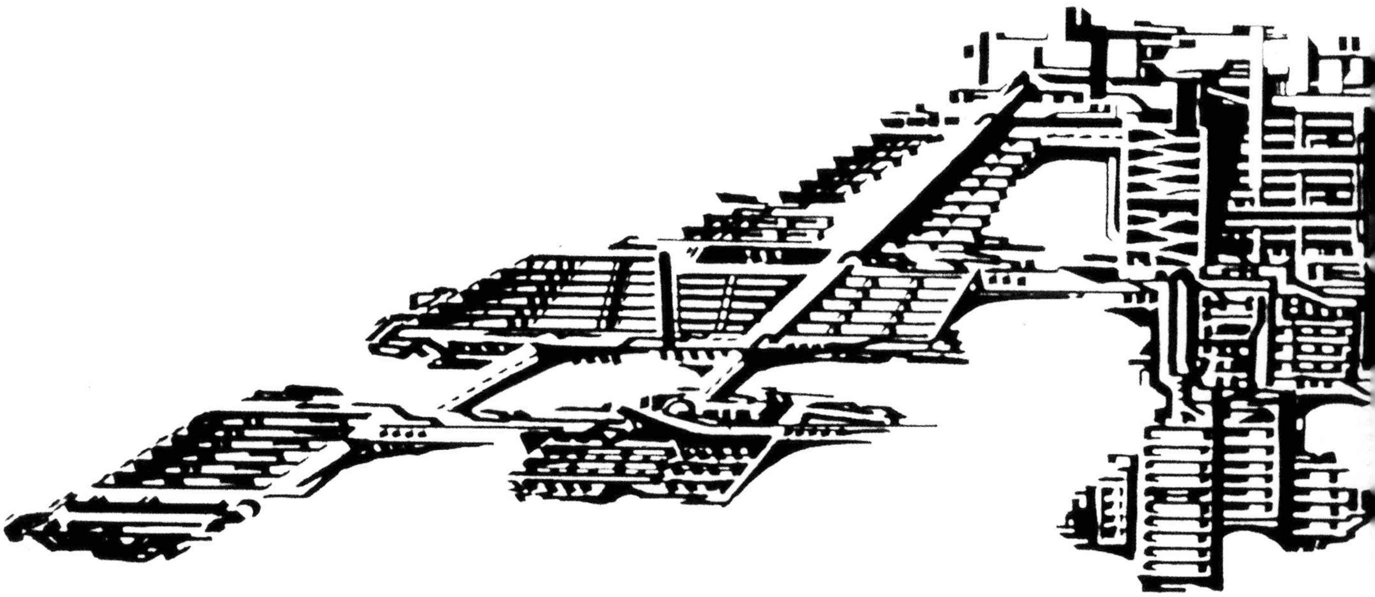

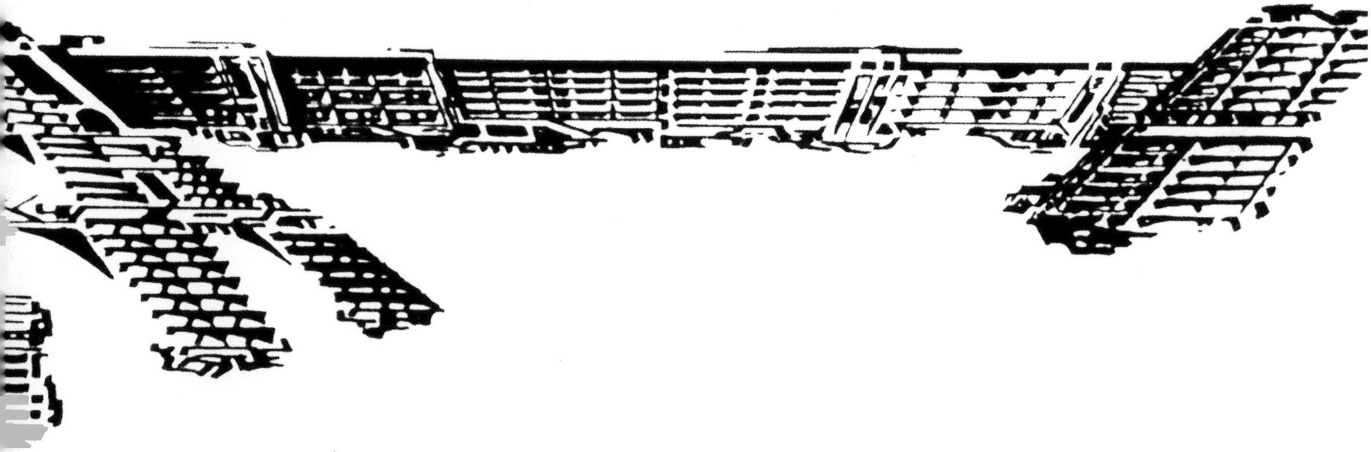

Teledyne Labs
1966
Los Angeles, California, US

I wanted the Teledyne Systems building to be very advanced, in the way it worked and in the way it looked. In the 1960s, when this plant was built, it was the age of heavy concrete Brutalism in architecture. This made this building even more exceptional.

The plant was planned along an artery of movement: the main circulation. This spine distributed people, goods, and utilities. The circulation is the place where life is most intense for all occupants, and I made it the most exciting place in the complex: two walking levels, continuous windows to the assembly and laboratory areas, and large glass walls to the main court and the preserved orange groves.

The exterior is clad entirely in glass and metal: bronze glass and gray-brown metal—shiny surfaces half-hidden behind orange trees.

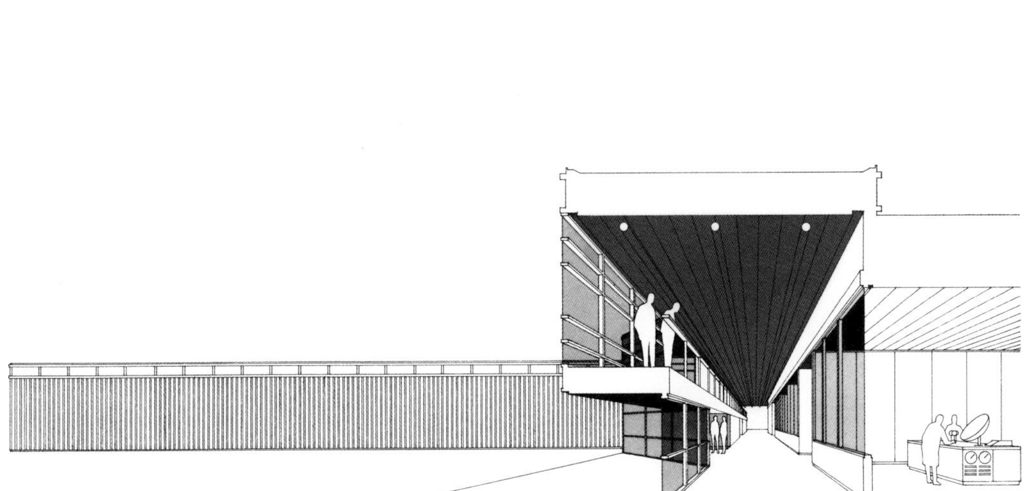

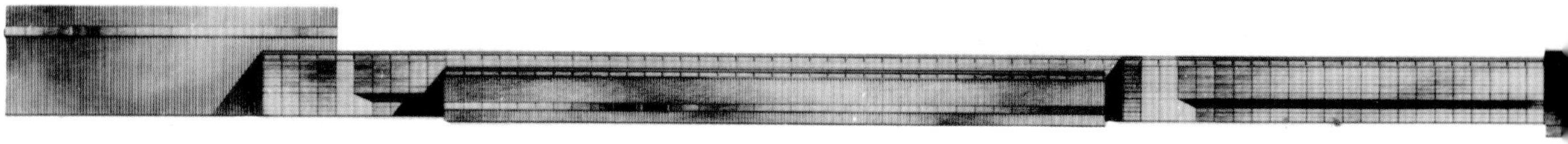

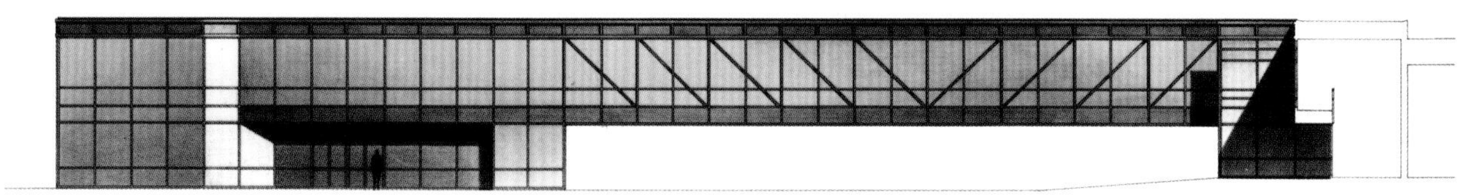

SPAN South elevation. BOTTOM Elevation detail of bridge.
OPPOSITE Site axonometric.

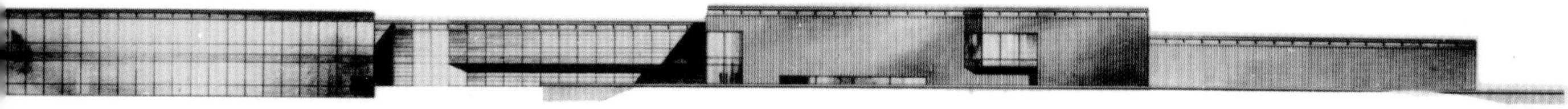

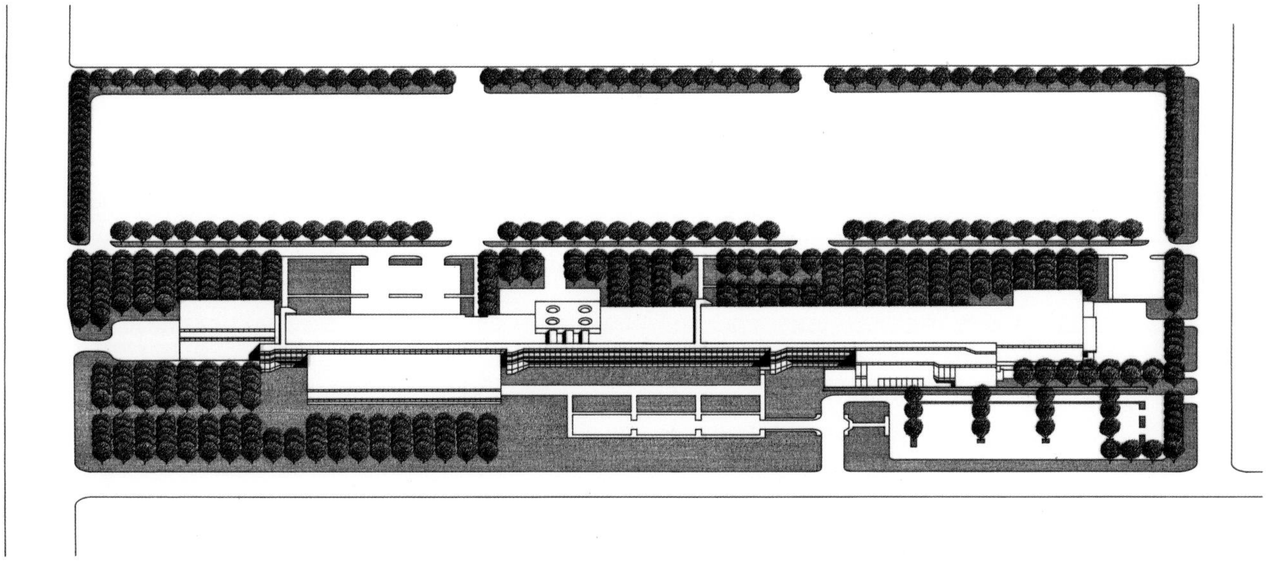

COMSAT Laboratories
1969
Clarksburg, Maryland, US

Located on a 85-hectare (210 acres) wooded site in Montgomery County, Maryland, I designed the complex to appear as a daring man-made metallic object carefully placed within a natural setting. It incorporated ideas dear to me: a metal skin, a machine-made look, and a diagrammatic linear plan. The plan gathers spaces off a central spine, which serves as the common room or meeting place and offers great flexibility.

The building is clad in aluminum panels which curve around the edges of the structure, emphasizing the feeling of an object sitting on the grass. It was a very advanced design, much ahead of its time.

In 1968, COMSAT Laboratories received a Design Award from *Progressive Architecture.*

I am interested in theories that organize a building. The COMSAT Laboratories plan is highly expressive of my beliefs of how people move in the building and enjoy it. It is all about the spine.

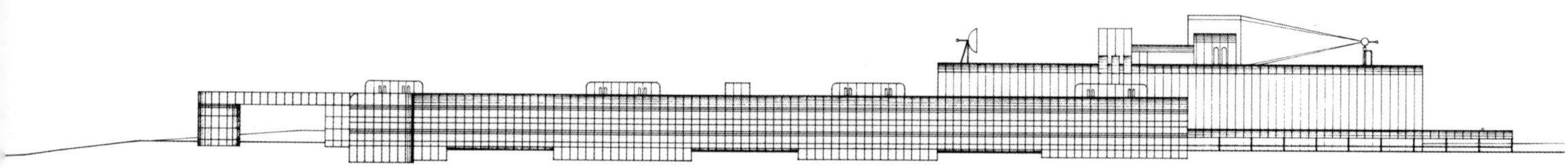

West elevation

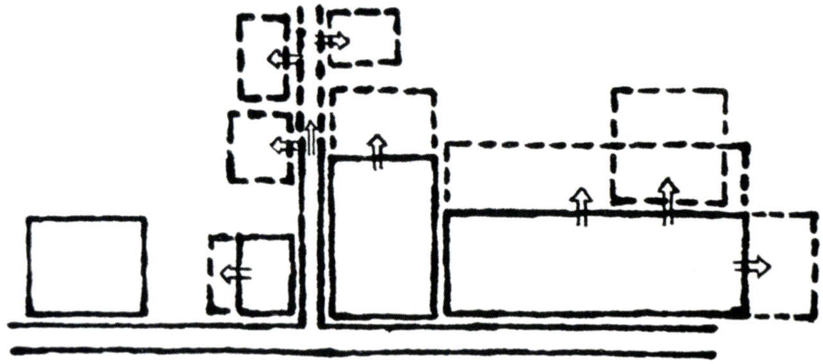

Undetermined growth

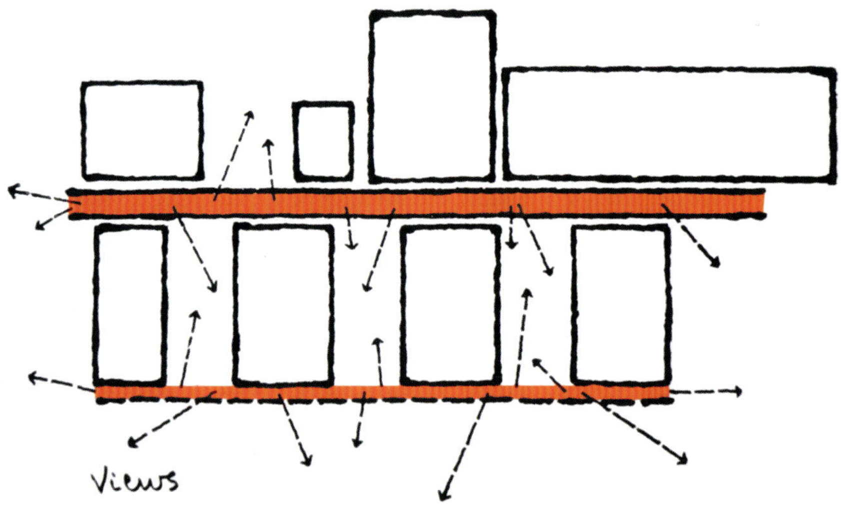

Views

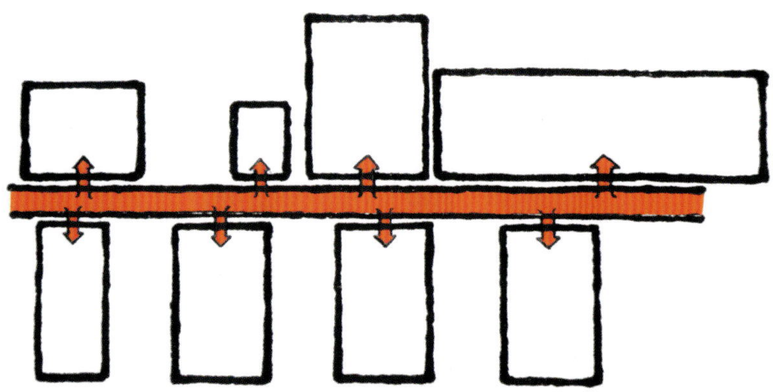

Corridor and Spaces

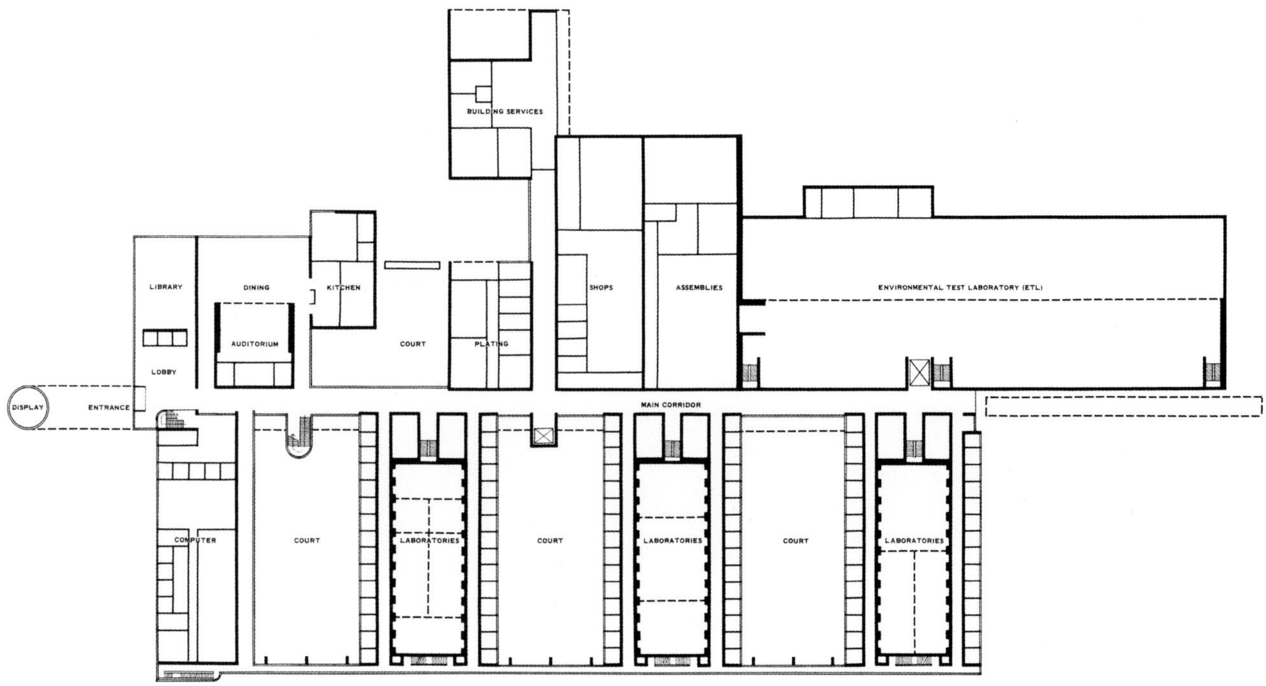

First-floor plan

TOP North elevation. BOTTOM West elevation. OPPOSITE Detail of the aluminum-panel exterior curved around the edges of the structure.

Kukui Gardens
1969
Honolulu,
Hawaii, US

Kukui Gardens is a public housing project for the Clarence T. C. Ching Foundation, which we won in a competition while I was partner for design for Gruen Associates. I tried to make it the most welcoming, most and attractive group of houses I could imagine. I wanted the buildings to communicate happiness and confer dignity on their occupants.

The project is a community of 820 low-cost public dwellings in Honolulu. Pedestrian streets, which widen to form courts in some places, link peripheral parking areas to a large playground and park at the center of the site. The streets are defined by three-story row-type housing. The rows (and blocks and chevrons) are not made up of simple houses; instead they are composed of several different types of building modules. Each of these typically contains three dwellings, a full-width apartment below, and two half-width duplexes above. There are no corridors in these units. Each building module has an exterior staircase which is shared by the two upper dwellings. The construction system comprises concrete block walls measuring 3.9 meters (12 feet, 8 inches) at the center, made from precast concrete slabs. Each building module is two structural modules wide.

All units have through exposures. Most have a private outdoor space, a yard in the ground-floor units, and a lanai (a type of Hawaiian veranda) in the upper units. The number of modules and the many different ways in which they can be combined give a rich variety to the streets. The exterior stairs form small, semi-private pools of space along the streets.

The site was successfully designed to ensure vitality and community.

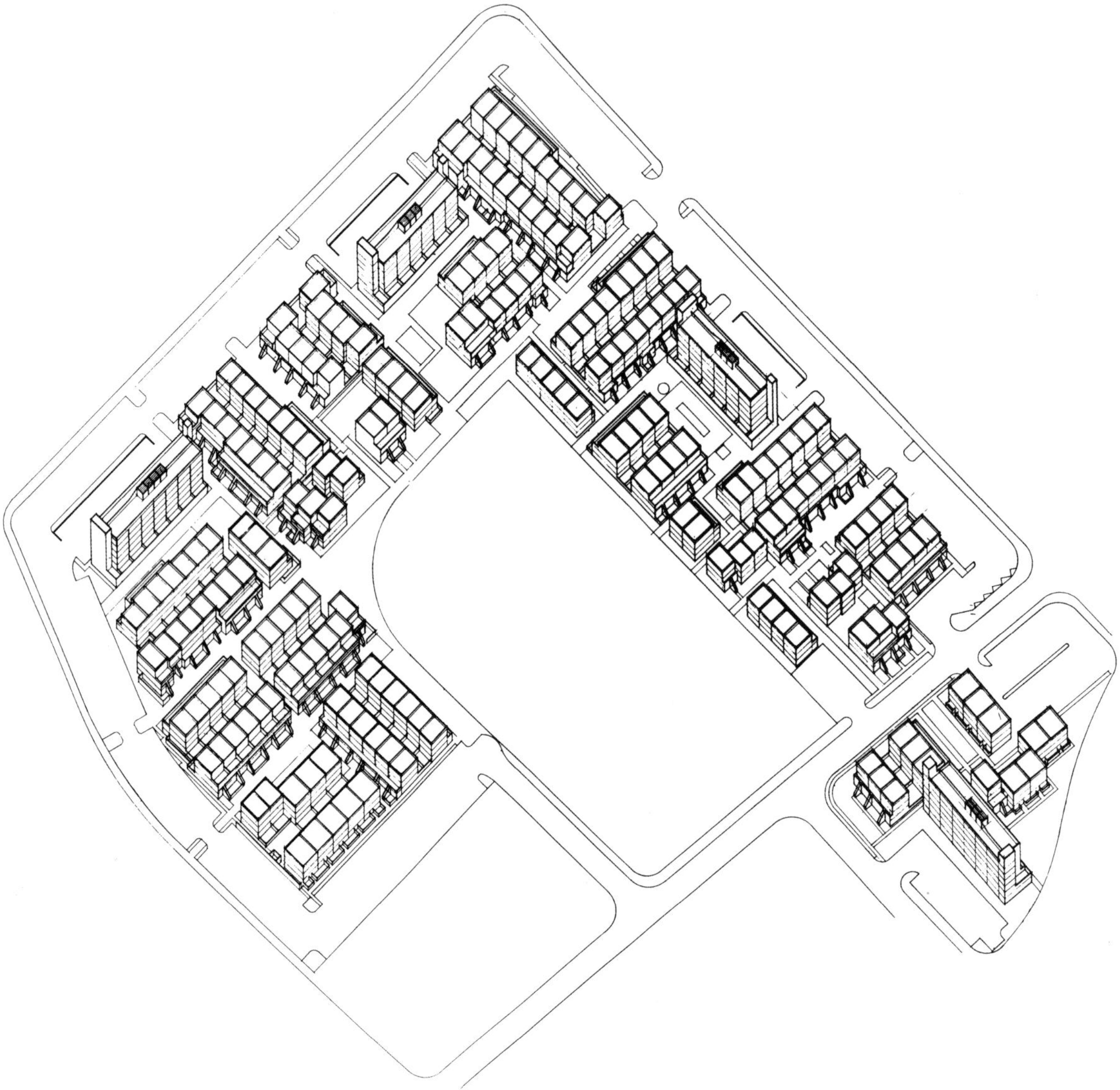

UN City
1969
Vienna, Austria

I led a design team that won first prize in an open international competition for the design of the United Nations International Organizations Headquarters and Conference Center in Vienna, but this design was not the one Austria chose to build.

Notwithstanding this, the project was widely published and was an important milestone in my career. It led directly to the US State Department commissioning me to design the US Embassy in Tokyo, which, in turn, when I opened my own firm, led me to design many projects in Japan.

UN City was designed to change and to grow. The headquarters could be expanded at any stage, and it would have given Vienna a modern, fresh, and exciting image.

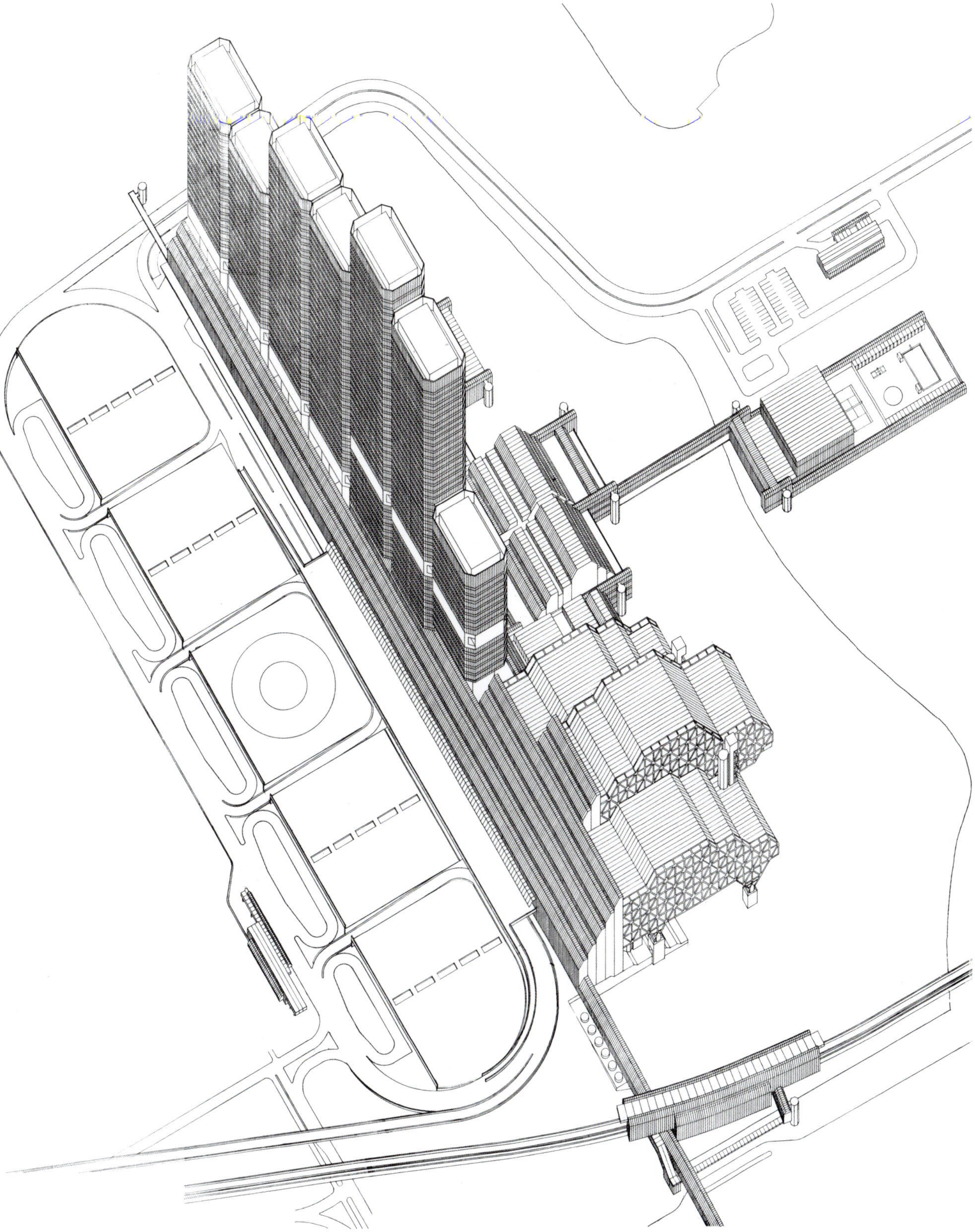

Isometric drawing

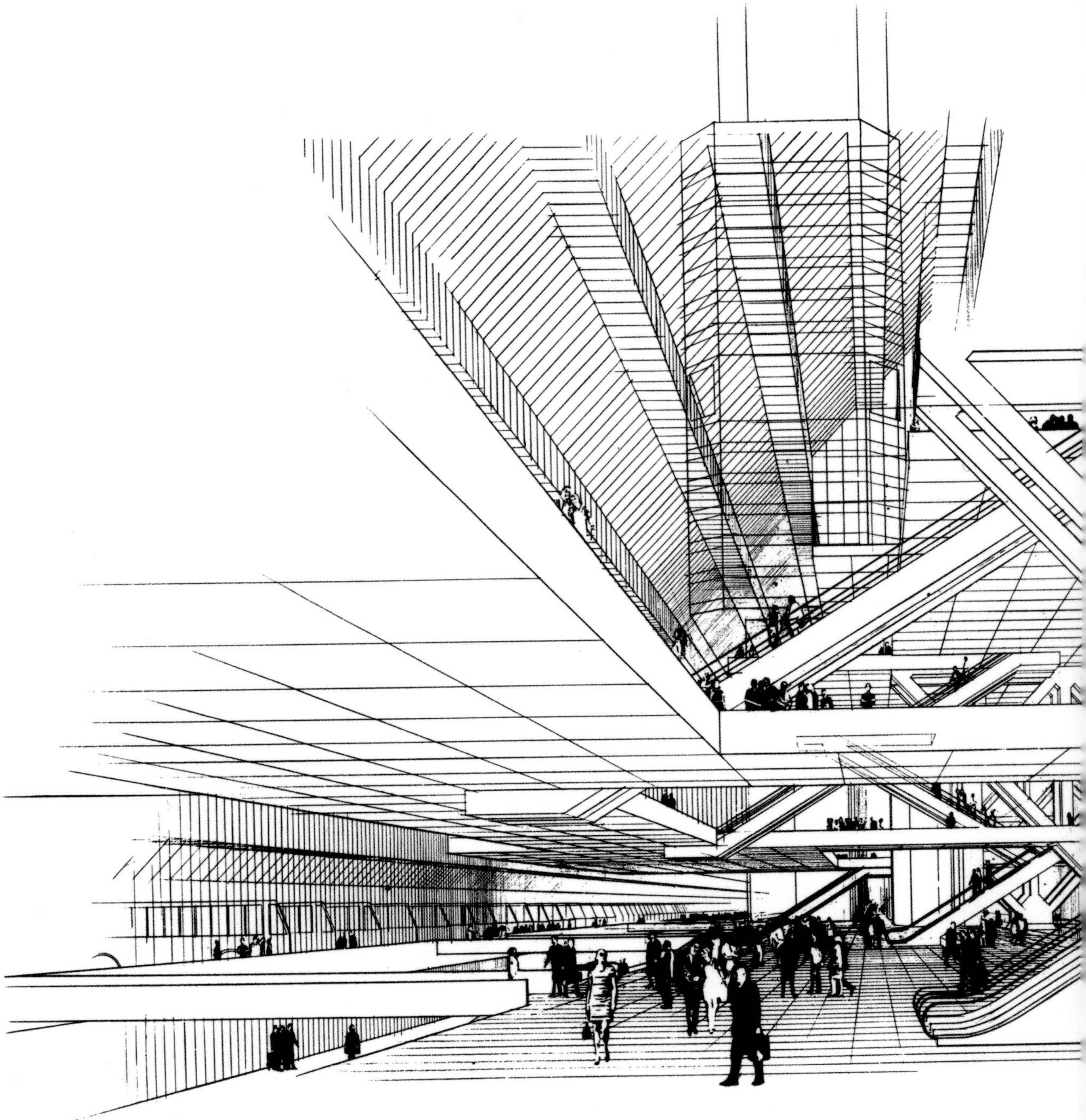

Interior circulation spine

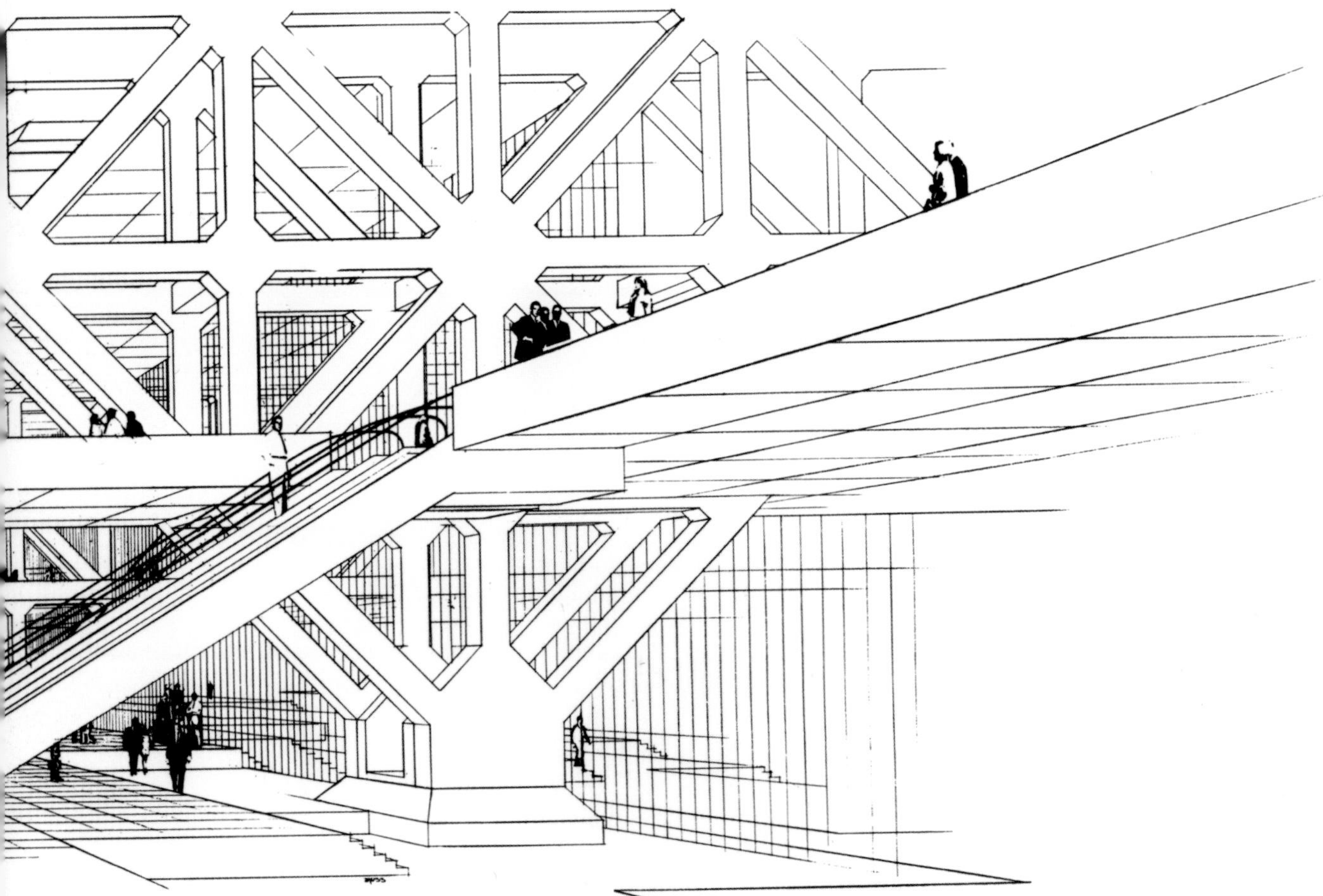

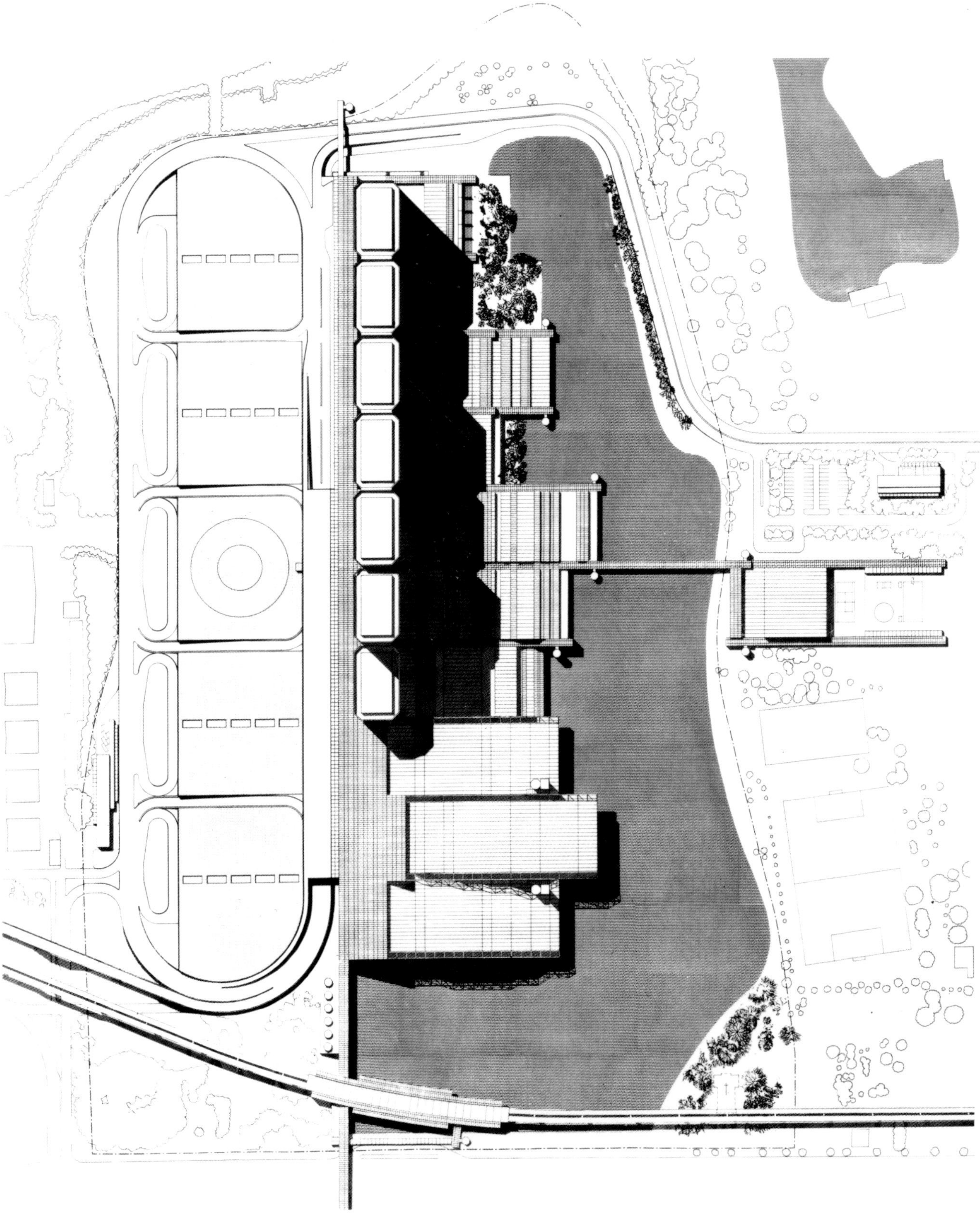

Site plan

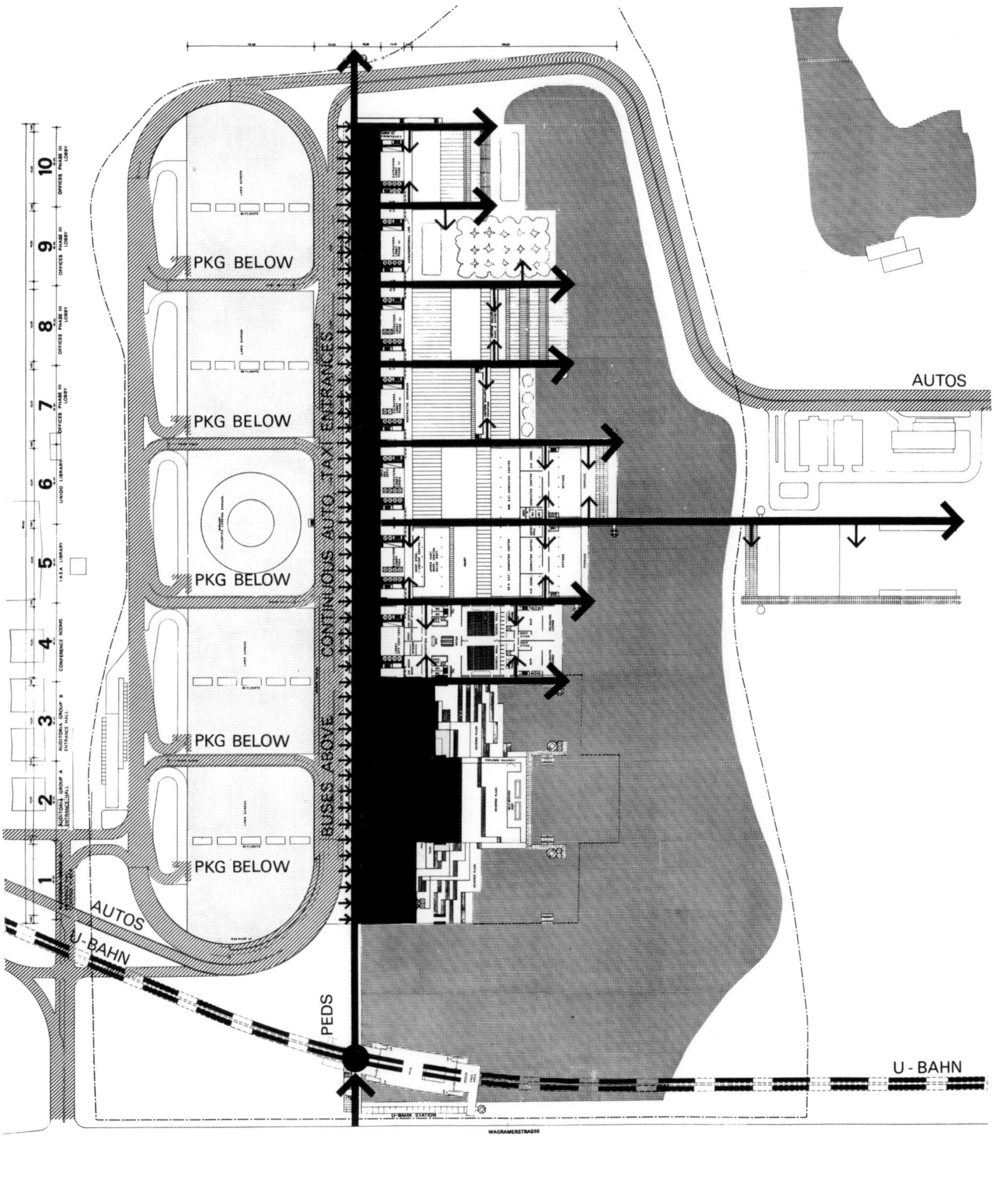

Plan Level +13,50

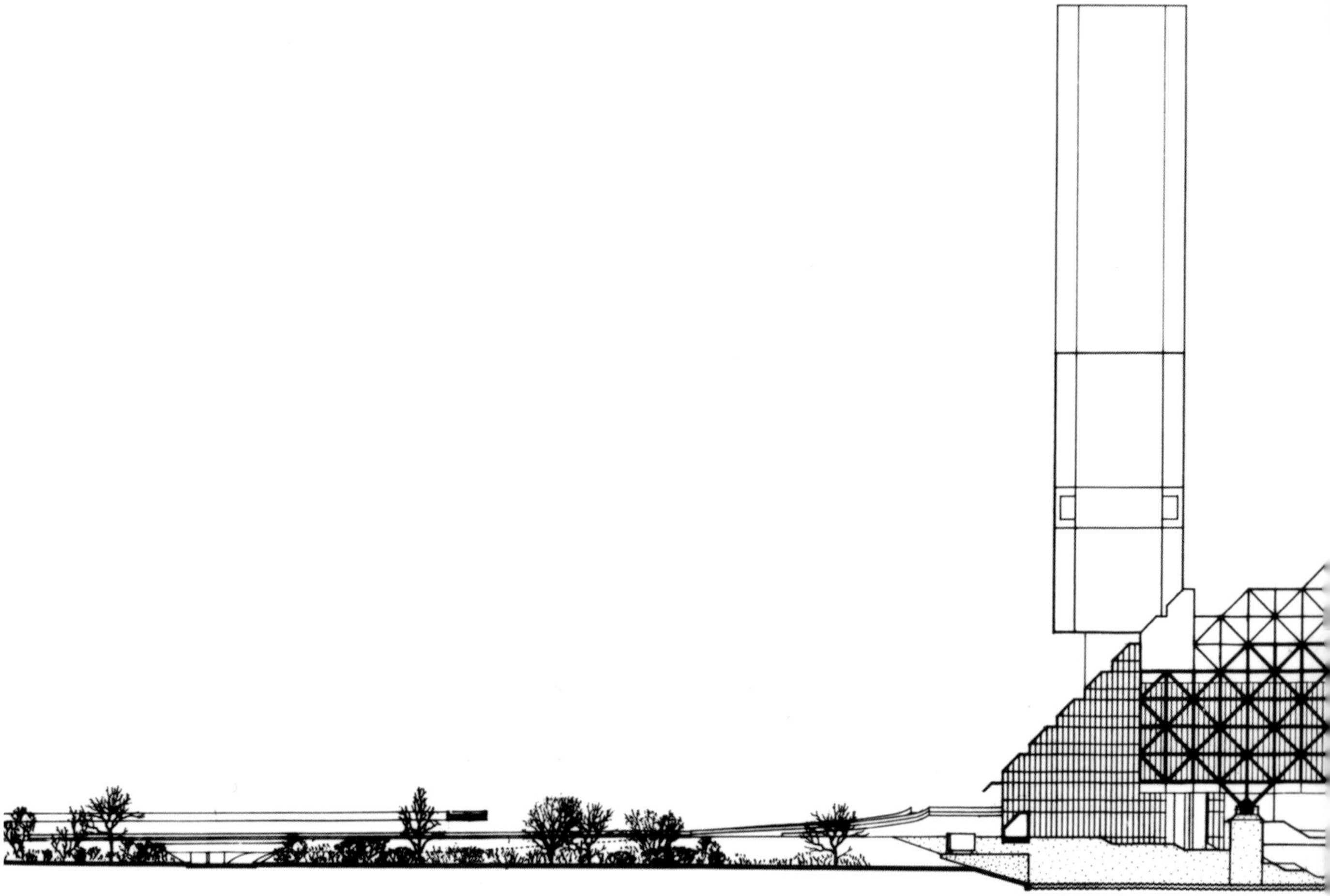

Southeast elevation

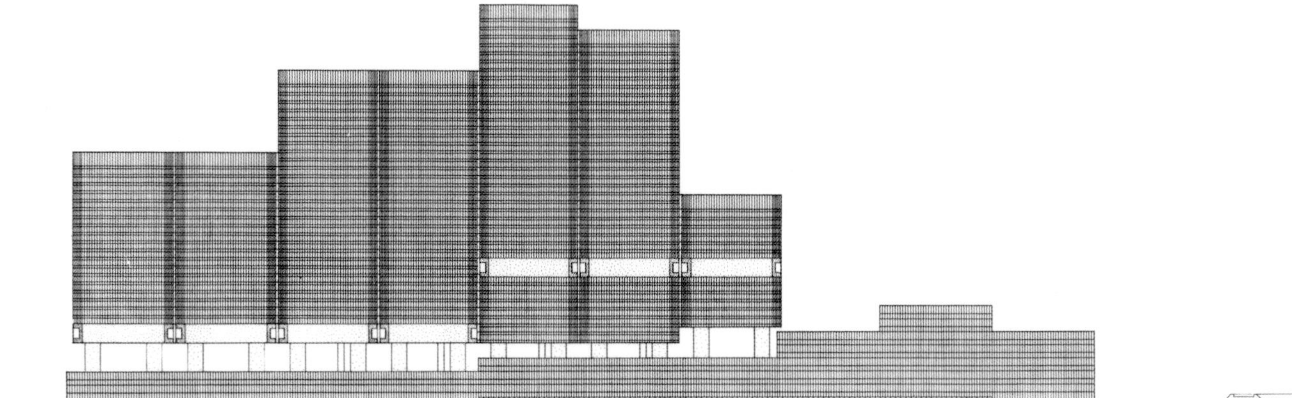

Southwest elevation

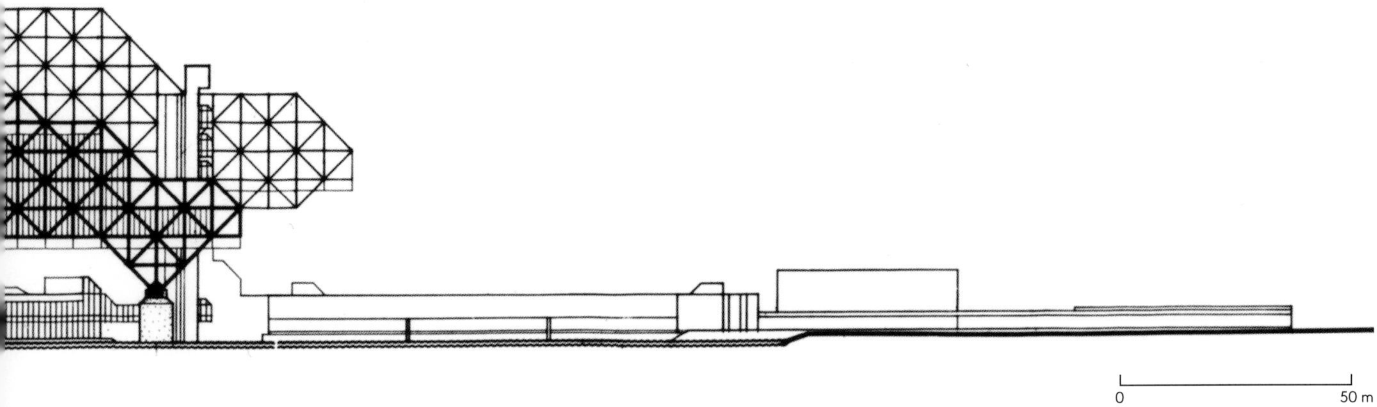

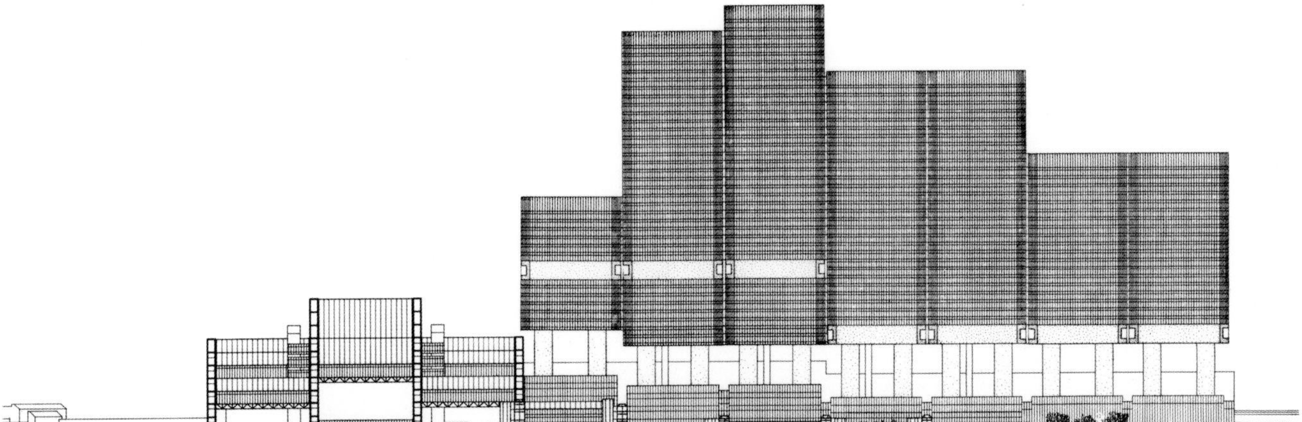

Northeast elevation

Pacific Design Center

1975, 1988, 2014
Los Angeles County & West Hollywood, California, US

I designed the first building of the Pacific Design Center, affectionately referred to as the 'Blue Whale,' in 1971, and it was completed in 1975. The Blue Building was conceived as a single, free-standing structure to house showrooms for the interior design trades. The colored ceramic glass was an innovation, a new way to clad a large building and it gave the Center a powerful and memorable image. Today, the Center is a multi-building complex which also includes offices for the design, entertainment, and arts industries.

After establishing my own office I designed the Green Building, which was finished in 1988, and the Red Building in 2014. All three buildings express a thin, brightly colored envelope enclosing a large volume. Their expressive power lies within this skin.

The Blue Building received an Honor Award and a 25-Year Award from the Southern California Chapter of the American Institute of Architects.

Phase II, the Green Building, originally included showrooms and offices, parking for 1,900 cars, a conference center with auditorium, and a public plaza. The expansion also included a 465-square-meter (5,000-square-foot) exhibition gallery (now an outpost of the Museum of Contemporary Art).

The Red Building completed the Pacific Design Center. In the meantime, this area of Los Angeles County had been incorporated as North Hollywood. The most dynamic of the three structures, the Red Building is composed of two curved, sloping towers atop seven levels of parking. The five-story West Tower slopes inward against the Hollywood Hills to the north. The eight-story East Tower continues the gesture, curving upward and culminating in a high point to the east.

On the eighth floor, between the two towers and over parking levels, is a courtyard, verdant with palm trees. This outdoor space offers views of the Hollywood Hills to the north, and the Green and Blue Buildings and public plaza to the south.

Cesar Pelli

Cesar Pelli

I started the Blue Whale in 1971, and the Red Building completed the project 44 years later. I am not the same designer I was then, but I could follow the same design vision.

ABOVE The glass is most opaque in full sun and lessens as natural light balances with interior illumination.

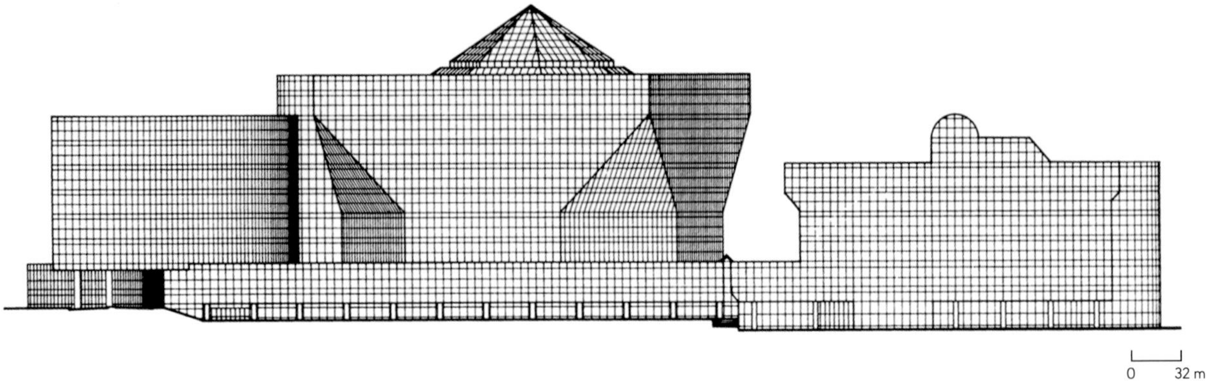

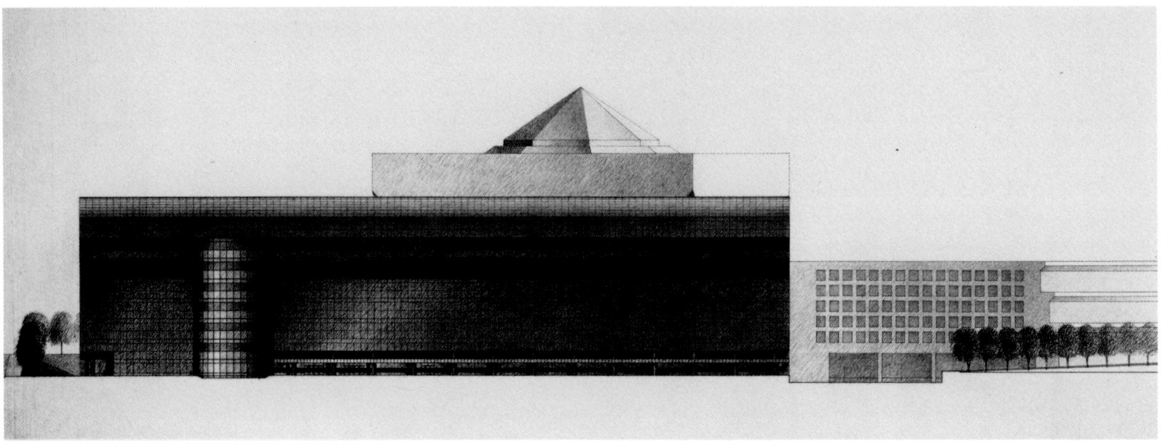

TOP West elevation. BOTTOM South elevation.
OPPOSITE The Green Building as it overlooks the open plaza to the west.

CONCERN II

A landscaped open plaza is at the heart of the Pacific Design Center site as a setting for public and private gatherings.

FOLLOWING PAGES The completed ensemble of the Blue, Green, and Red buildings, which developed over forty years.

PacificDesignCenter

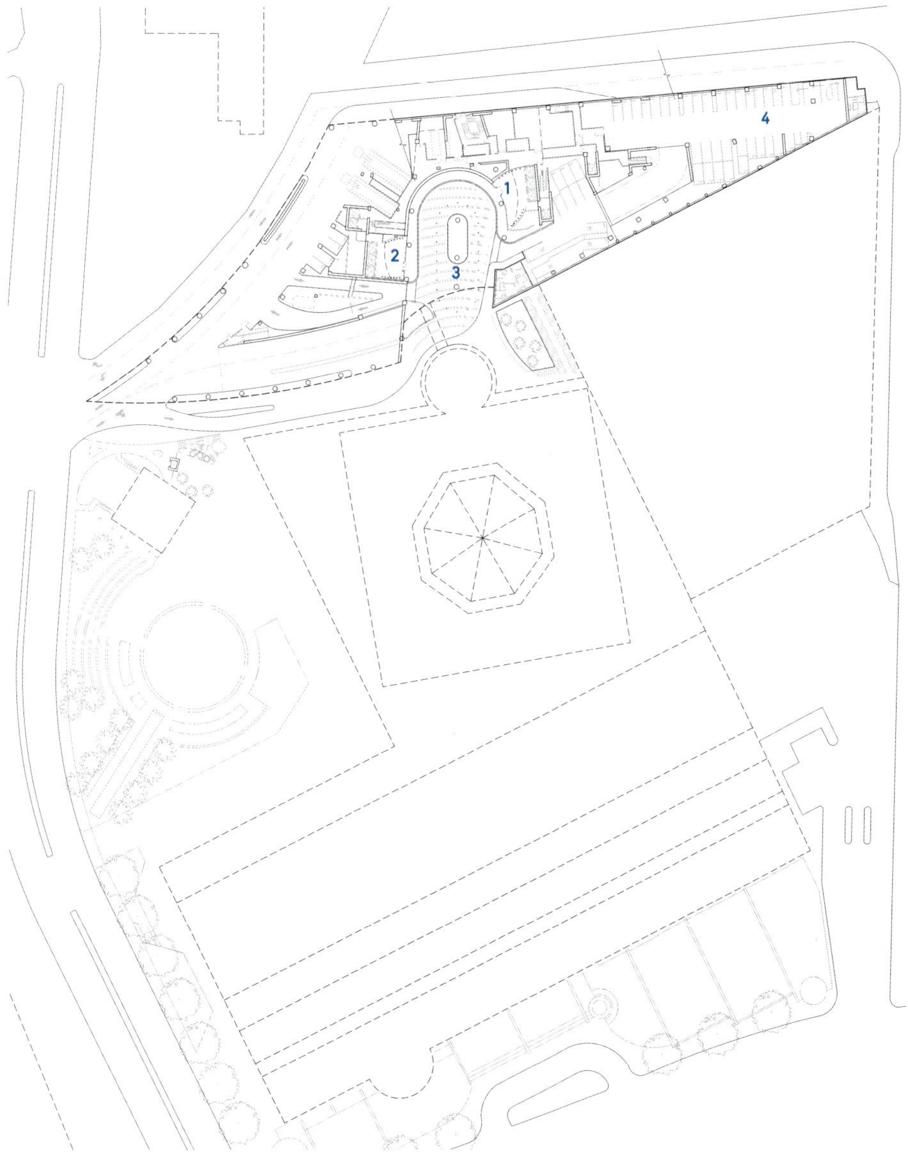

Red building entry plan

1. Lobby East
2. Lobby West
3. Motor Court
4. Parking

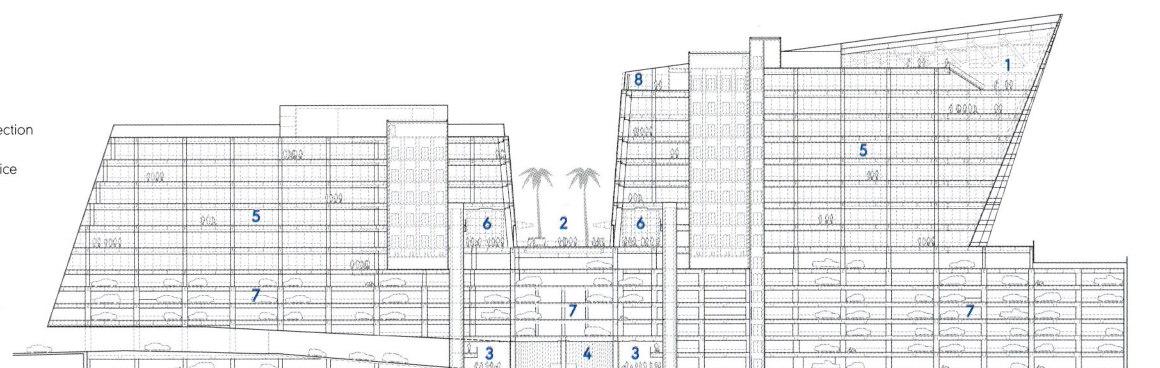

Red building section

1. Executive Office
2. Palm Court
3. Lobby
4. Motor Court
5. Office
6. Sky Lobby
7. Parking
8. Roof Terrace

TOP Aerial view of the completed complex with the Blue Building at the lower end, the Green Building in the middle, and the Red Building near the top of the photo.

Pacific Design Center

MOCA
AT THE PACIFIC DESIGN CENTER
Metro Local

San Bernardino City Hall
5

San Bernardino City Hall

1972

San Bernardino
California, US

I conceived the San Bernardino City Hall project as a spirited presence in the center of a 38-hectare (93 acres) redevelopment district in the heart of downtown. Sited on an urban plaza, the building contains administrative offices and council chambers. Office space is arranged on each floor along a single full-length corridor, with service functions exposed to the sun on the south side and offices in the shade to the north. An exhibition hall is located below the western end of the plaza.

This project is an early example of an exterior wall used as enveloping skin. The building is clad entirely in gray-brown glass, transparent for windows, opaque for spandrels. The small-scale grid of the wall wraps around and under the building form, defining a controlled, sealed volume with a nonstructural skin. This architectural interpretation of the nature of a building is also a form of sculpture.

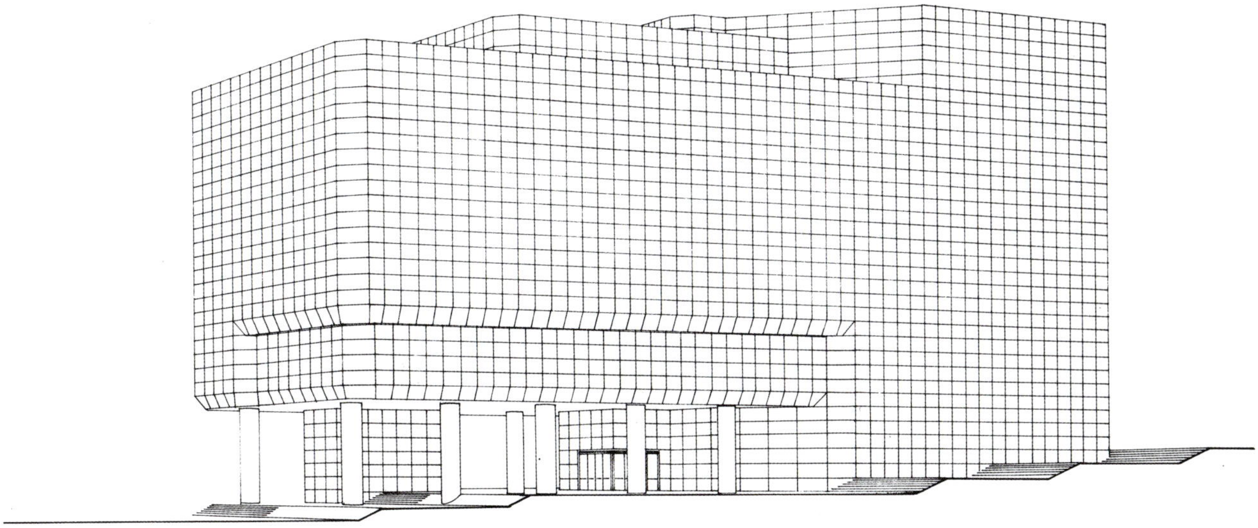

ABOVE Perspective from north. OPPOSITE AND LEFT The taut glass wrapper of the city hall becomes a backdrop for the city and public gatherings.

TOP Model facing south. BOTTOM South elevation.

Exhibit Hall
San Bernardino

US Embassy
1975
Tokyo, Japan

I designed the US Embassy in Tokyo as an elegant building that expresses America's forward thrust while respecting Japanese aesthetic traditions. Its exterior wall is a modular grid which corresponds to the modular plan of the interior office space. The structural grid is made visible at the end of the building and at the ground level, where it forms an entrance portico. The curtain wall is made of finely scored concrete panels finished in a very hard Bon Tile paint which gave the concrete a crisp look and expressed the thinness of the envelope.

The building was designed to meet the requirements of earthquake safety codes of Tokyo and California, and responds to both American and Japanese modern aesthetic pursuits.

The embassy's combination of concrete panels and reflective glass provides a skin of changing textures and reflections.

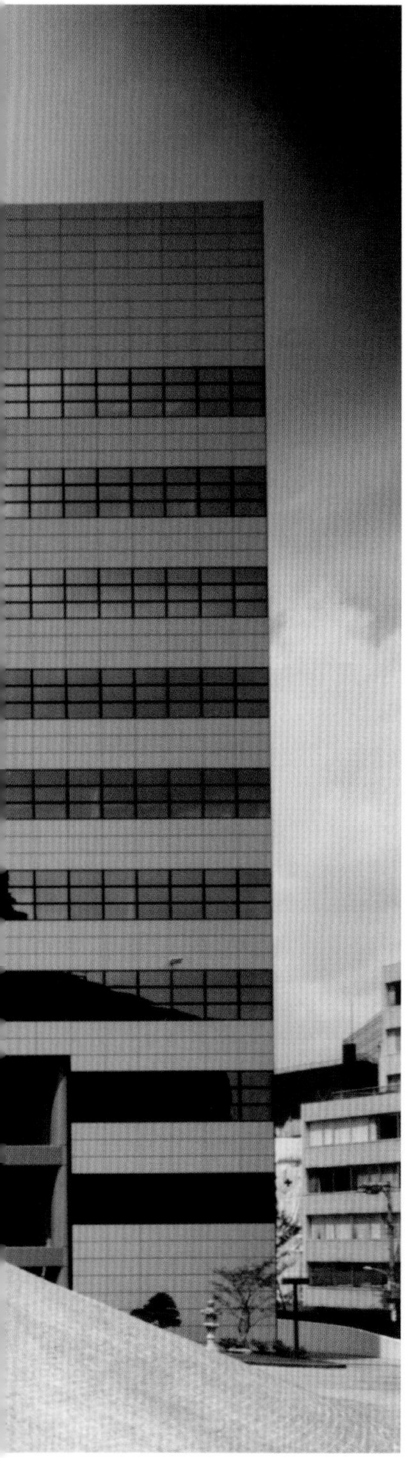

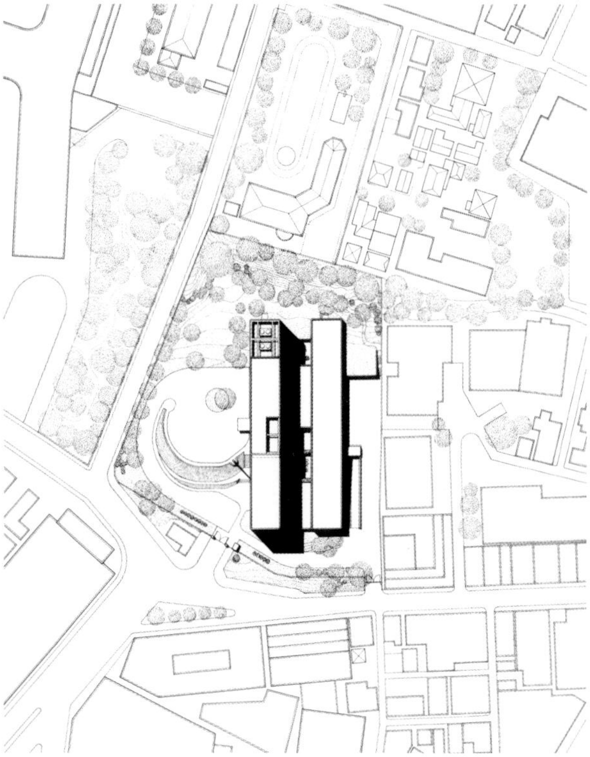

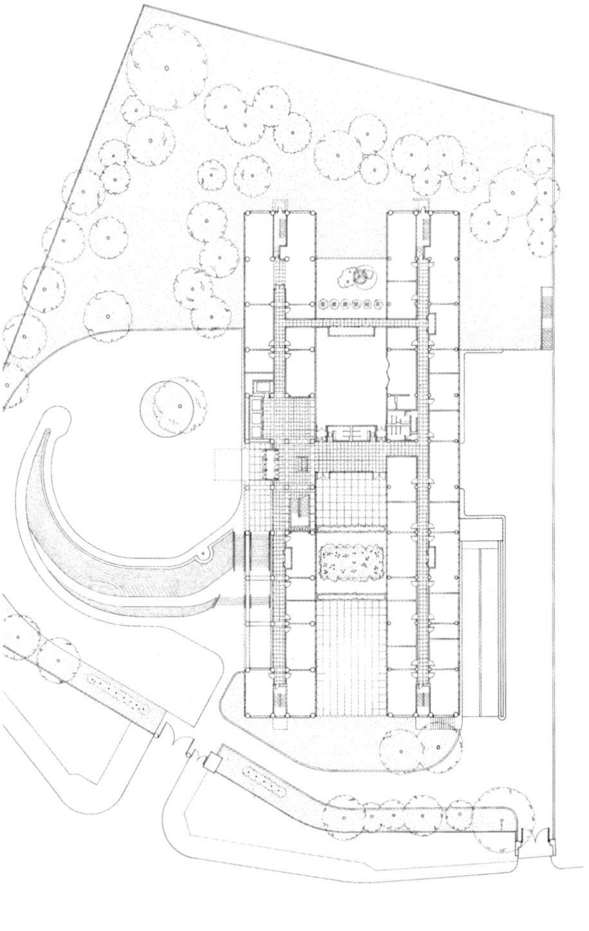

A very thin-skin building wall, like a Shoji screen. I wanted to respect the spirit of architecture in Japan.

Biennale House
1976
Venice Biennale, Italy

This project designed for the Venice Biennale was an abstract, intentionally incomplete, and poetic single-family house design reduced to its elemental parts: a multi-function long gallery, and single-function rooms, with coated glass walls defining the exterior spaces.

I conceived the Biennale House as a building in a process of flux or transformation, offering the possibility of a series of choices about how one lives and about a house's relationship to its site. Just as the building has an essential indeterminacy to its structure, the glass walls with their gradations of color and mirroring use transparency and reflectivity to reveal a new reality in the landscape through continuous changes in the visual field.

In this project I explored the artistic relationship of pure architectural forms in the landscape; I had no functional purpose in mind, only aesthetic delight.

Rainbow Center Winter Garden

1977

Niagara Falls, New York, US

I conceived The Rainbow Center Winter Garden as the main public space in the city of Niagara Falls, which it remained for 34 years. It was a large public space completely enclosed in a symphony of steel and glass.

It was landscaped with a ground cover of vines and shrubs, palms, broadleaf evergreen trees reaching 12 meters (40 feet) in height, and cascading pools. Its demise was lamented by many in the city. And indeed, by me.

I grew up in a culture where there were many open spaces, plazas, social spaces. But in Anglo-Saxon countries they didn't really exist. That's why these early designs are all enclosed spaces, protected from the weather.

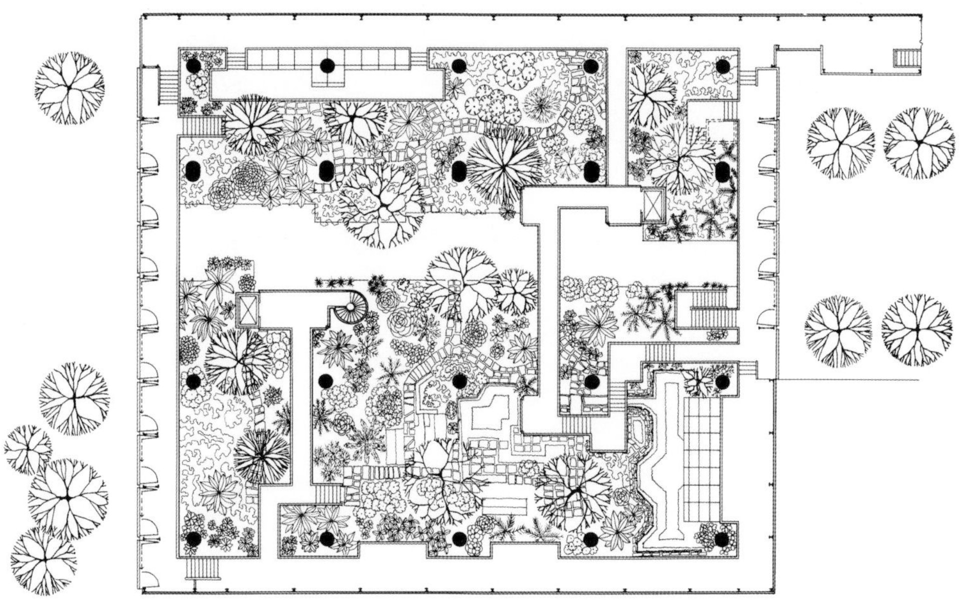

TOP Section looking east. BOTTOM Plan.

ABOVE AND OPPOSITE Interior steel structure of warm red provides a vibrant contrast with the green foliage.

Herring Hall

1984
Rice University, Houston, Texas, US

This design of the building for the Jesse H. Jones Graduate School of Management at Rice University responded to the building's role in shaping a green open space and its position on campus paths. The building forms the third wall of a green quadrangle on the central campus axis. Composed of shifted, parallel blocks skewered by arcades and corridors, Herring Hall respects the organization, typology, and narrow proportions of earlier Rice University buildings.

Herring Hall also extends the architectural vocabulary of the early Rice projects, which used expressive walls, arches, and arcades, with brick patterning, limestone, and terra cotta details. Instead of load-bearing masonry, Herring Hall could support only lightweight steel and brick veneer construction. In earlier buildings, carved stone entrance portals were layered to express mass. Entrances in Herring Hall are layered in a way consistent with thin-wall construction, by cutting and folding the brick skin.

In 1986, Herring Hall received an Honor Award from the American Institute of Architects as well as awards from the Brick Institute of America, and the American Institute of Architects Connecticut.

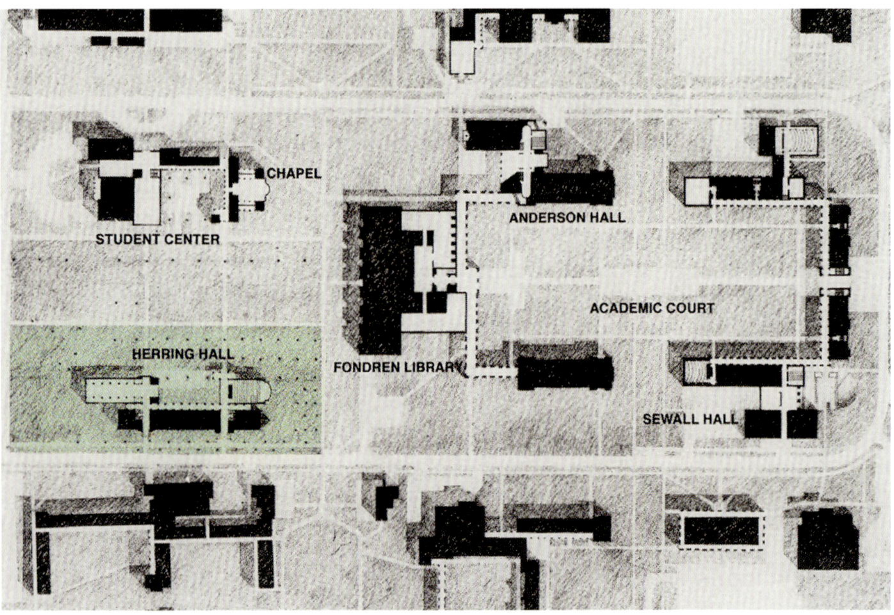
CHAPEL
STUDENT CENTER
ANDERSON HALL
ACADEMIC COURT
HERRING HALL
FONDREN LIBRARY
SEWALL HALL

The thin veneer of the exterior walls allows for shifts in scale expressed through the brick patterns.

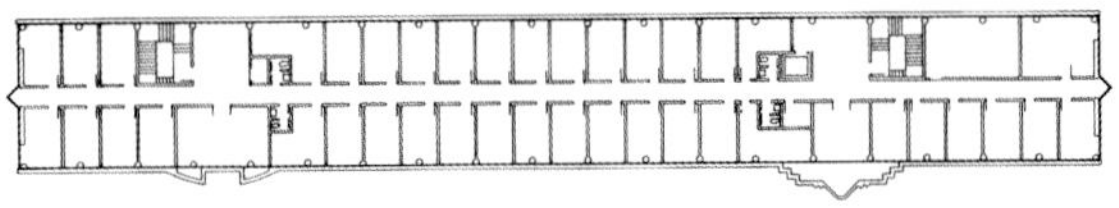

Third-floor plan

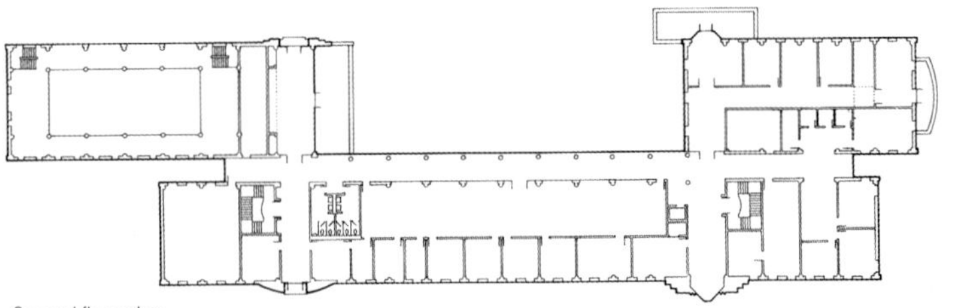

Second-floor plan

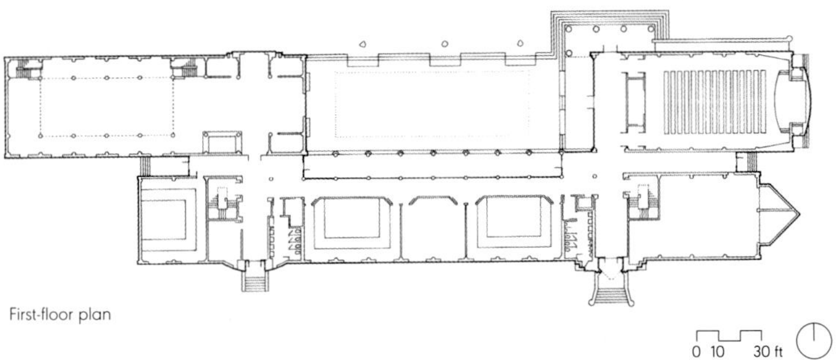

First-floor plan

At Rice, they wanted something to fit into the existing context. I don't believe in the postmodern focus on style. I believe one could fit into another environment, and I expressed the brick as veneer, and expressed the columns half with metal, half with brick. The brick diaper pattern expresses the thinness of the wall.

HERRING HALL

55

Reflections of an Apprentice
by John J. Casbarian

In April 1969, minutes after the appointed time, a list of Preceptorship assignments was posted on a bulletin board in the School of Architecture's building, Anderson Hall, on the Rice University campus, where a number of fourth year students were anxiously waiting to see if they had made the cut. At that time, the fledgling Preceptorship program, now a hallmark of the undergraduate program at Rice, was not mandatory nor open to all students so only half the class of 20 was assigned a Preceptorship—a paid one-year internship at a leading architectural office in the US and abroad. I was relieved to see my name on the list and elated that I was assigned to Gruen Associates in Los Angles where a young architect, Cesar Pelli, had recently been named Partner in charge of design.

On my first day at Gruen on a Monday in late June 1969, there was an unusual amount of activity as a group of young architects was scrambling to put the finishing touches on a competition entry for a United Nations Office and Conference Center in Vienna. A very large and shiny silver model of faceted high-rise building forms was being photographed, even as the box for its crating and shipping was being readied. I had never before seen anything like this and being around this group of talented and enthusiastic architects, directed by Cesar, was my first introduction to an exciting way of practice.
I was struck immediately by Cesar's accessibility in the office, his uplifting spirit of optimism, his passion, and his intense engagement with the group of young architects he had assembled upon his arrival at Gruen from DMJM. Architects like Arthur Golding and Lance Bird and, in the following year, Fred Clarke made invaluable contributions encouraged by Cesar's openness and generosity. While clearly the leader, Cesar nurtured the group effort, a lesson that I learned early and applied to my own practice a number of years later.

I remember the weekly meetings, almost like academic pin-ups, where the project team would present large-scale drawings for Cesar to critique. More indelible in my memory were the very large elevations that Cesar would render with Prismacolor pencils, depicting shadows and subtle color changes transforming the two-dimensional elevations before our eyes into vibrant three-dimensional forms. While the early projects appeared to be explorations in skin and form, Cesar always considered the urban context and how the building engaged in the social activity of the community. This was certainly the case on two projects I worked on: the San Bernardino City Hall, and more importantly the Commons Mall, in Columbus, Indiana, with its innovation of programmed space for civic and recreational activities within a retail center.

The 18-month experience was the most formative and influential in my architectural career and I owe a great debt to Cesar for the foundation this provided in both my professional and teaching careers.

ONE
WAY

OPPOSITE Cesar with the sculptor Jean Tinguely in front of the artist's *Chaos No. 1* in the Commons Mall, in Columbus.

Museum of Modern Art Expansion and Tower

1984

New York, New York, US

For its 50th anniversary, the Museum of Modern Art (MoMA) embarked on a major expansion consisting of the renovation of existing spaces, the addition of a new wing, and a 56-story residential tower directly above the new galleries. The project more than doubled MoMA's gallery space. The Museum Tower was included as a revenue-producing element to offset MoMA's operating expenses.

The four-story, glass-enclosed garden hall overlooked the refurbished sculpture garden and enclosed a sequence of escalators with views to the garden. Riding up or down on them was a delight.

The 53rd Street façade, designed by Philip Goodwin and Edward Durell Stone in the 1930s, was rebuilt. A symbol of MoMA, the façade continued to mark the entrance and maintained its historic relationship with the rest of the block.

The MoMA was an exploration of a multi-colored glass curtain wall with 11 shades of color of ceramic glass. Its elevations are suited to the mid-Manhattan urban context in color, pattern, and scale.

I was selected to design this project when I had just assumed the deanship of the School of Architecture at Yale University, with plans to dedicate the rest of my life to teaching. The opportunity was extraordinary and to design this project I had to open my office in New Haven, near the Yale School of Architecture, where my practice is still based. It was the unexpected beginning of a new career and a long and successful practice.

In 1984, the MoMA Expansion and Renovation received a Restoration and Expansion Award from the Building Owners and Managers Association of Greater New York, Inc. In 1985, it was recognized with an Award from the Urban Land Institute, and in 1988, it received an Excellence in Design Award from the New York State Society of Architects.

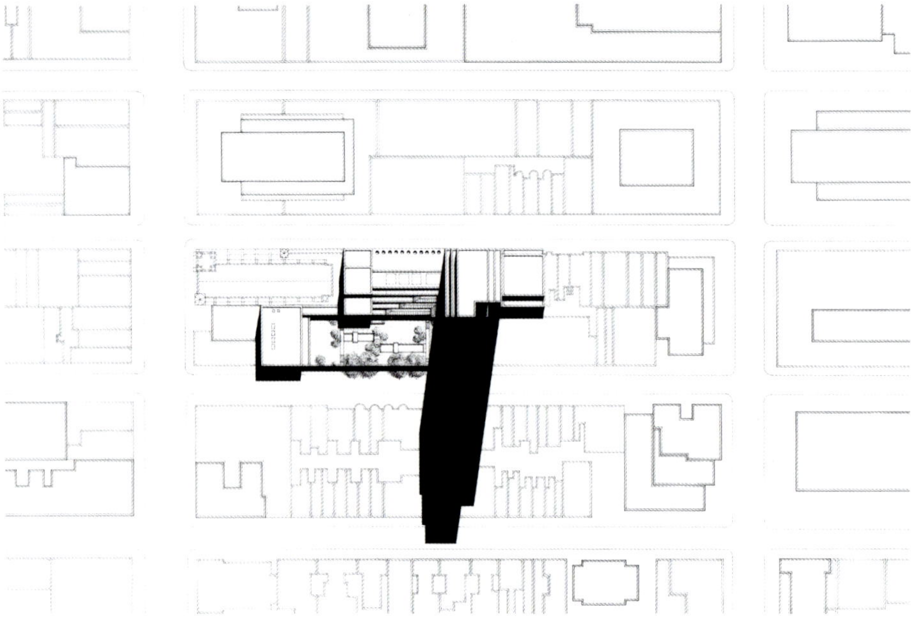

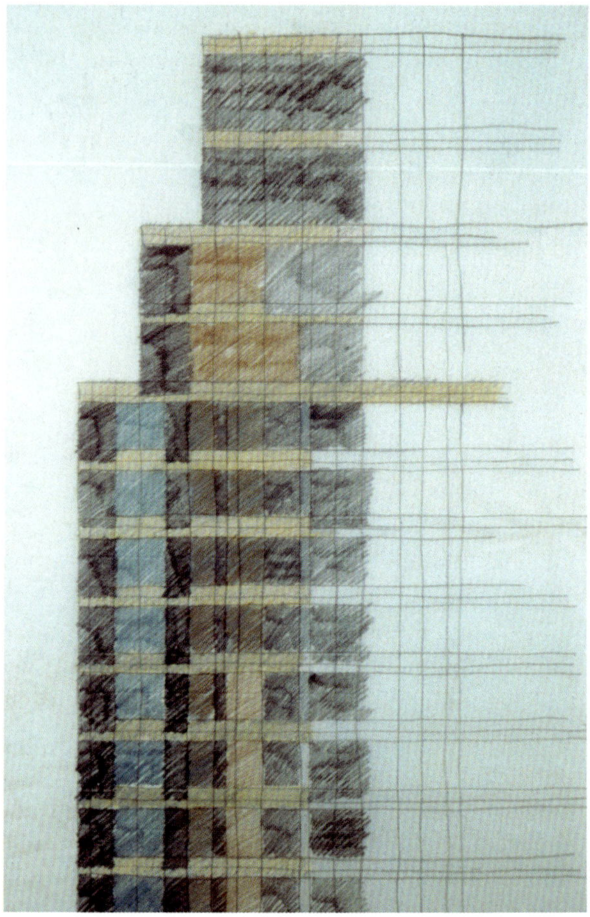

Pelli experimented with different colors and patterns for the MoMA project's façades.

OPTION 3: WIDE NON-CONTINUOUS BAND OF WINDOWS IN TRANSFER FLOORS
BROWN CONTINUES INTO FIRST FLOOR OF APTS

Ground-floor plan

1 Museum Public Lobby
2 Garden Hall
3 Elevator Lobby
4 Temporary Exhibition
5 Tower Lobby
6 Coatroom
7 Staff Reception
8 Membership Sales
9 Bookstore
10 Cafeteria
11 Public Restaurant
12 Group Reception
13 Museum Service
14 Tower Service

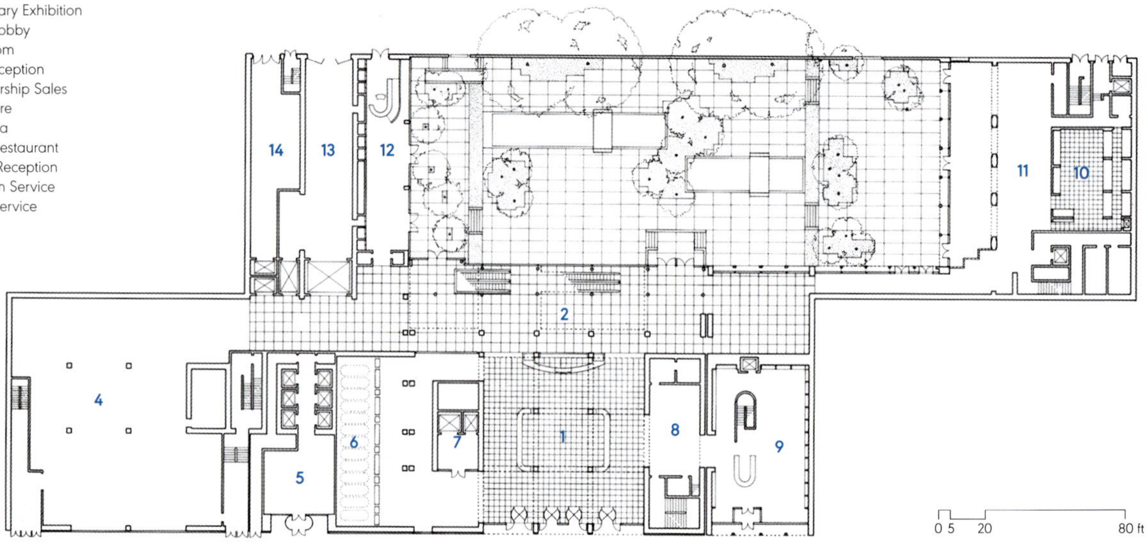

Second-floor plan

1 Elevator Lobby
2 Garden Hall
3 Permanent Painting and Sculpture Garden
4 Food Preparation
5 Members Restaurant
6 Photography Gallery

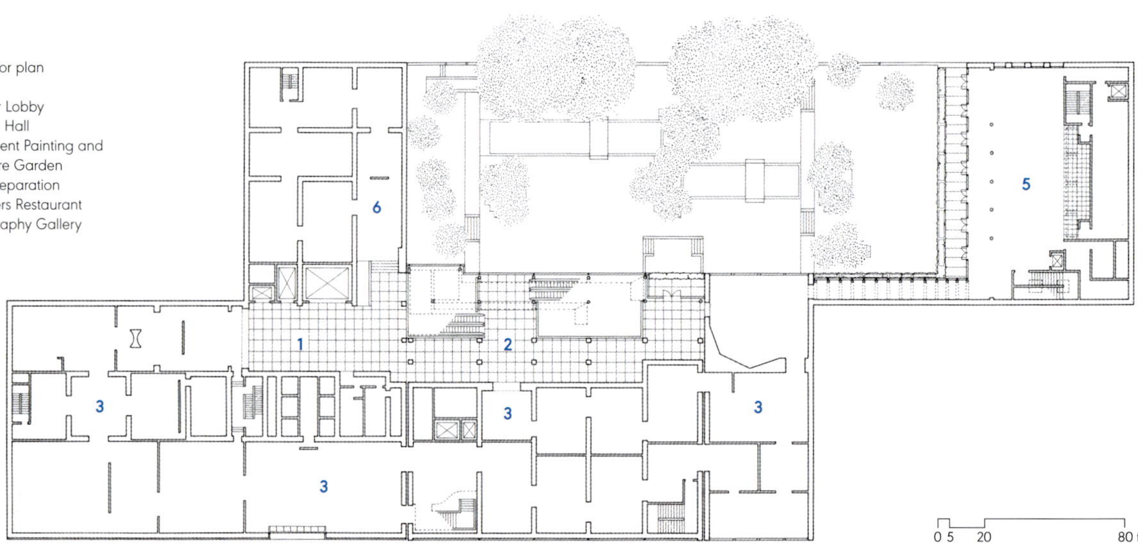

TOP Ground-floor plan. BOTTOM Second-floor plan.
OPPOSITE TOP Section looking west. BOTTOM Section looking north.

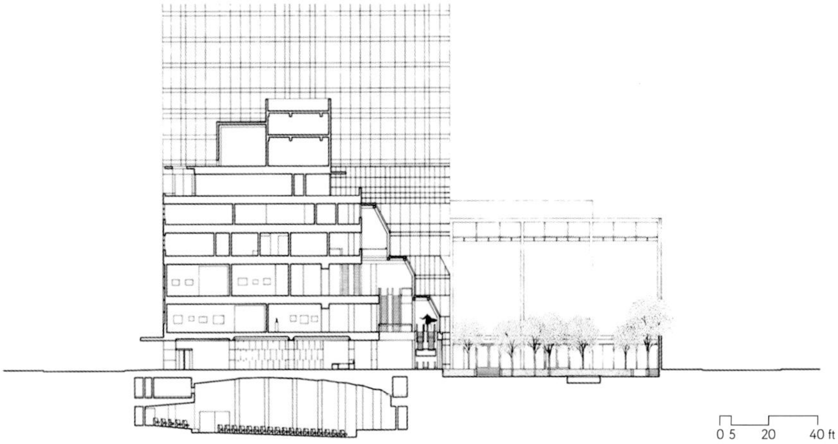
0 5 20 40 ft

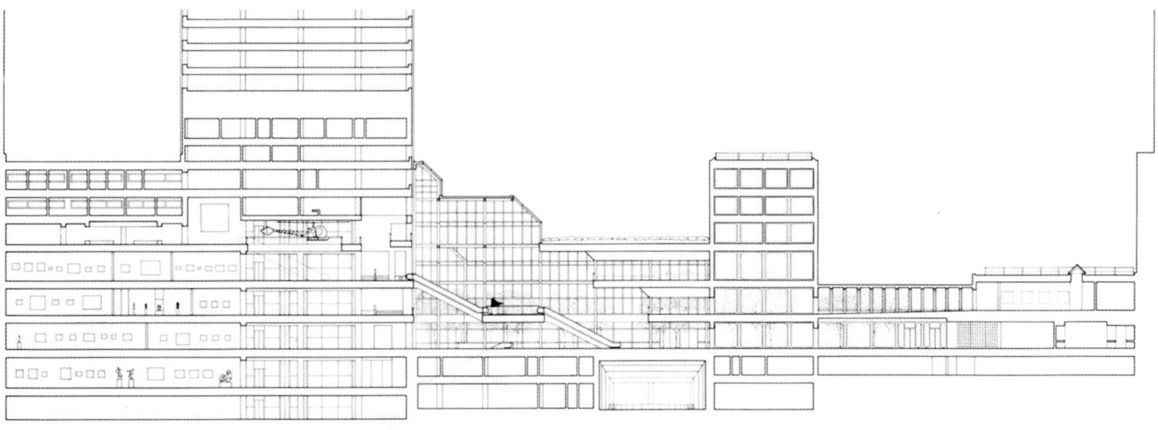
0 5 20 80 ft

The MoMA project was critical in my career—it led to me opening my own office. When I came to New Haven I thought I was just going to be an academic architect. This project changed my life, completely.

The Roy and Niuta Titus Theaters

I designed this building with a great deal of love. On the façade of the tower, I started with bright colors. But there were some museum board members who were scared that people might think we were trying to do art. They were worried about criticism; they said the colors were too bright. We ended up with a very New York color scheme.

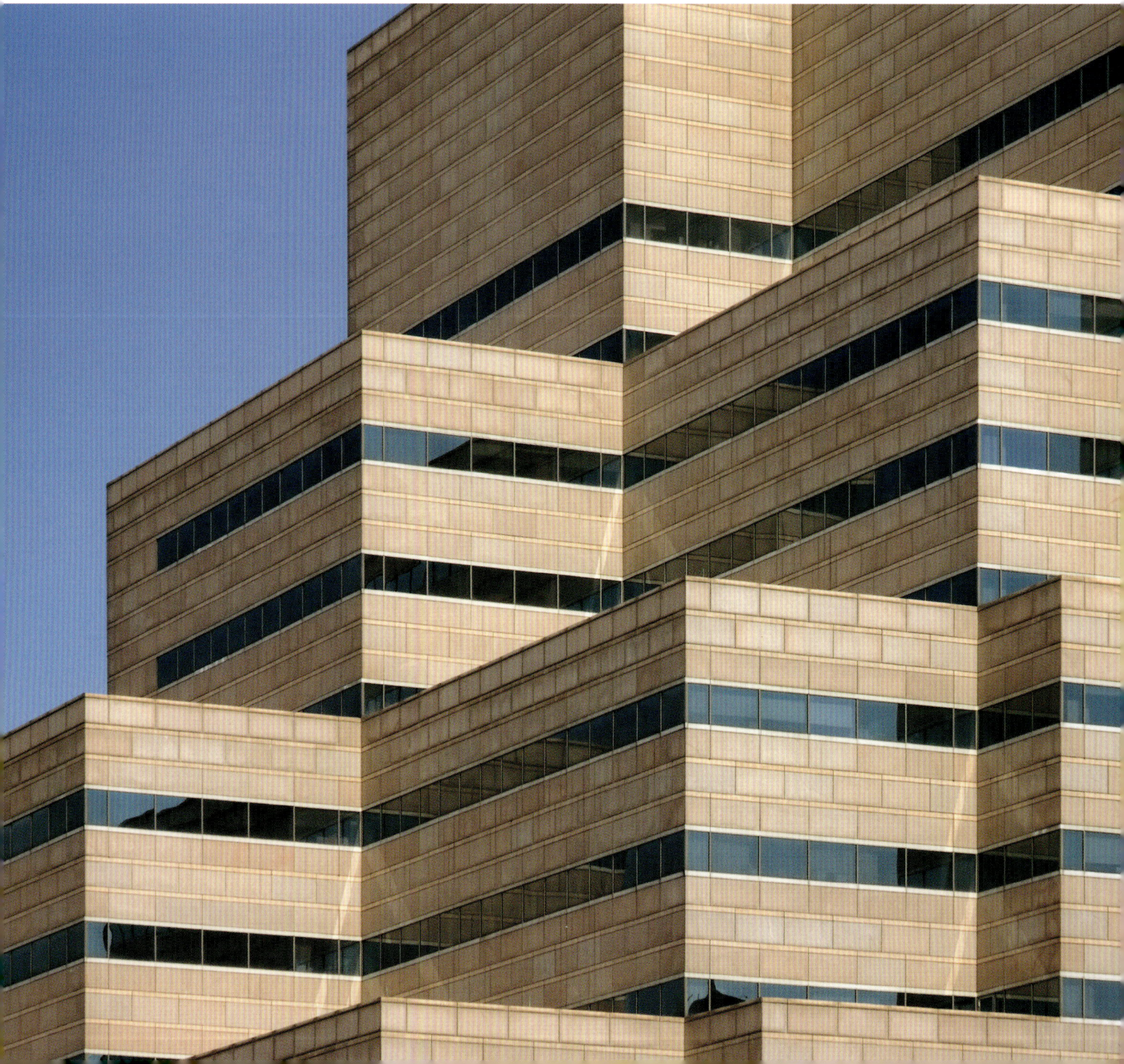

Crile Clinic Building
1984
Cleveland, Ohio, US

The signature building of the Cleveland Clinic, the Crile Building houses the outpatient services department. Within these 14 stories are doctors' offices for nearly every medical specialty. The Crile Building was the first completed under the Cleveland Clinic Green campus master plan, which I also designed.

The building is friendly and inviting but it also has a strong presence. Its façade is an exploration of a frontal, symmetrical, and expressive taut wall as the terminus of the center green. This building was the first major commission I obtained after MoMA and it assured the viability of my office.

The 0.8-hectare (2 acres) green is a central gathering place and a unifying core for the Cleveland Clinic. It is a much-used and enjoyed space within the site.

In 1986, the Crile Building received an Honor Award from the American Institute of Architects.

Pelli's design process often involves extensive studies in model form, a technique he learned working for Eero Saarinen.

This project is about the dialogue between the building and the mall; Diana Balmori designed the mall. I wanted people to be easily oriented in the building. All of the interior public spaces, clearly expressed on the west elevation, view the mall, making wayfinding easy within the building.

World Financial Center

1988

New York, New York, US

I was selected to design the World Financial Center, now Brookfield Place, in a competition with seven other architects. My firm was very new and with little experience on projects of this size and complexity. The success of this project opened the doors for my firm to be selected to design others of similar size and complexity.

The World Financial Center was a very early project in Battery Park City, now a vibrant neighborhood in Manhattan. The 6-hectare (14 acres) complex consists of four office towers, ranging in height from 34 to 51 stories, and the Winter Garden, a glass-roofed public hall. The towers are very modern, but they have forms sympathetic to the traditional towers of Downtown Manhattan.

The World Financial Center has received numerous awards. In 1991, the American Institute of Architects cited the World Financial Center and Winter Garden as one of the 10 best works of the decade. And in 1993, the AIA/ACSA Council on Architectural Research, the International Union of Architects, and the DuPont Company named the Winter Garden a Merit Finalist in the Benedictus Awards competition.

The docks along the west side of Manhattan were removed and fill was used to create a new waterfront, part of which became the site for the World Financial Center.

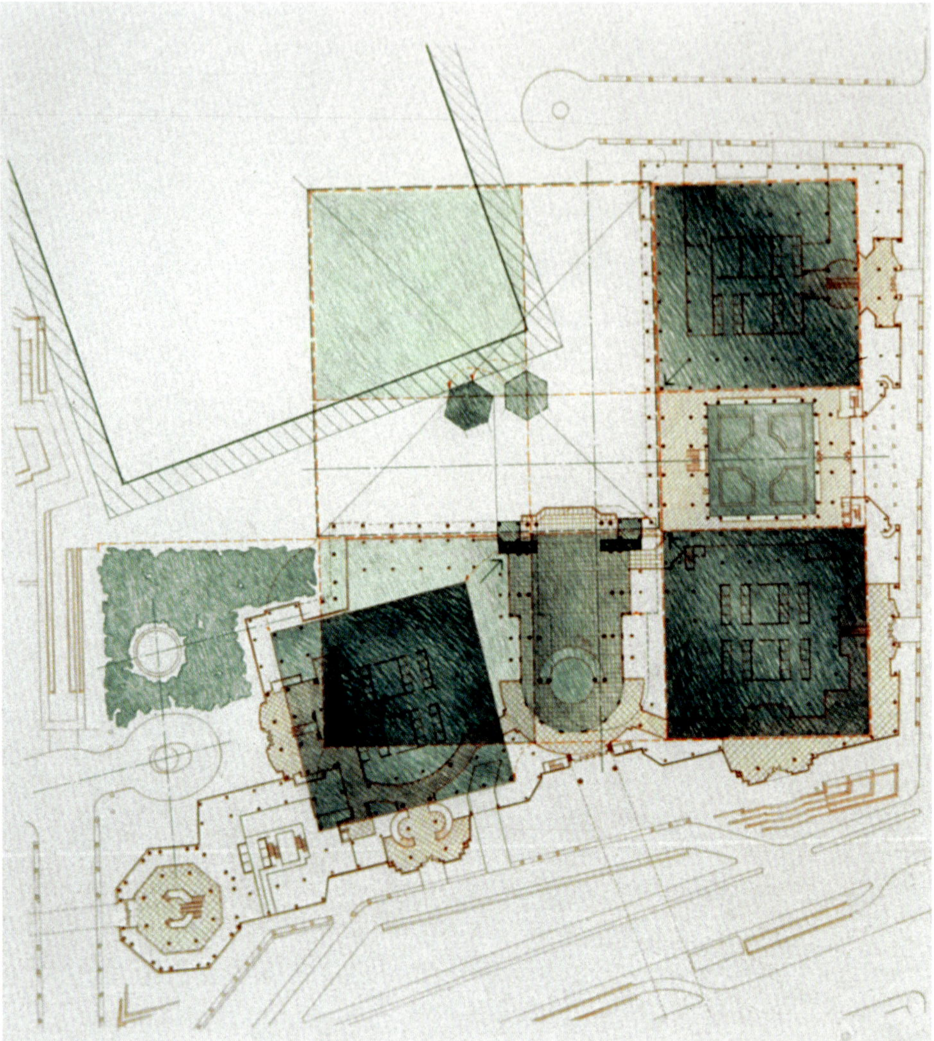

This project was critical for our firm. It established us as architects who could handle very large, complex programs and create a successful place. We were invited at the last minute to compete for it. We had proposed a tower in a competition in Los Angeles that peeled back, with an interior public space. Olympia & York was intrigued by that design, and added us to the World Financial Center competition.

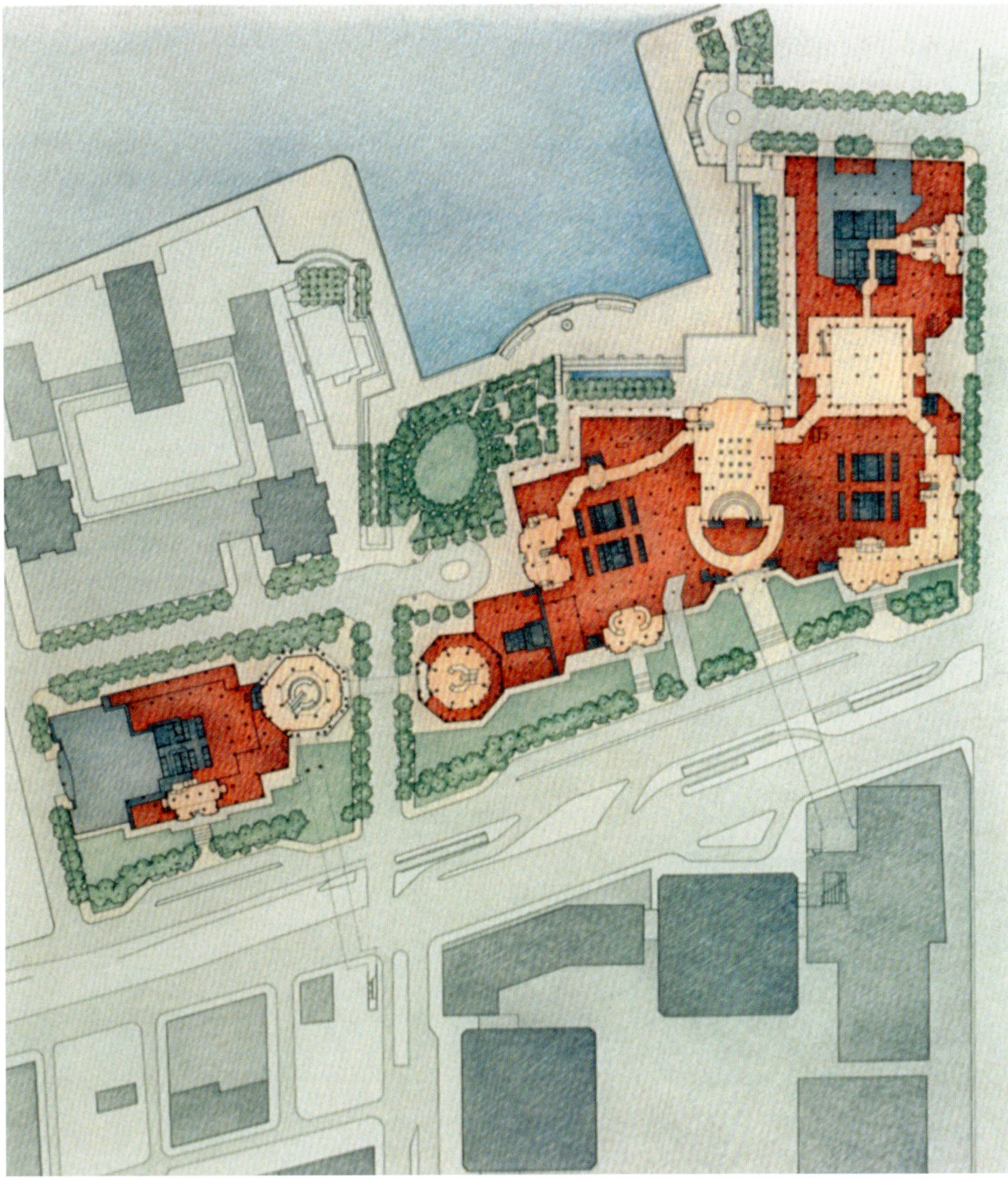

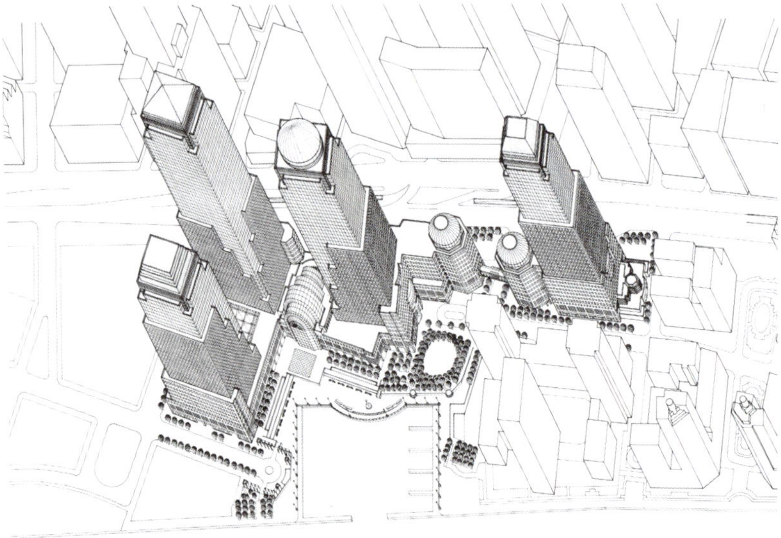

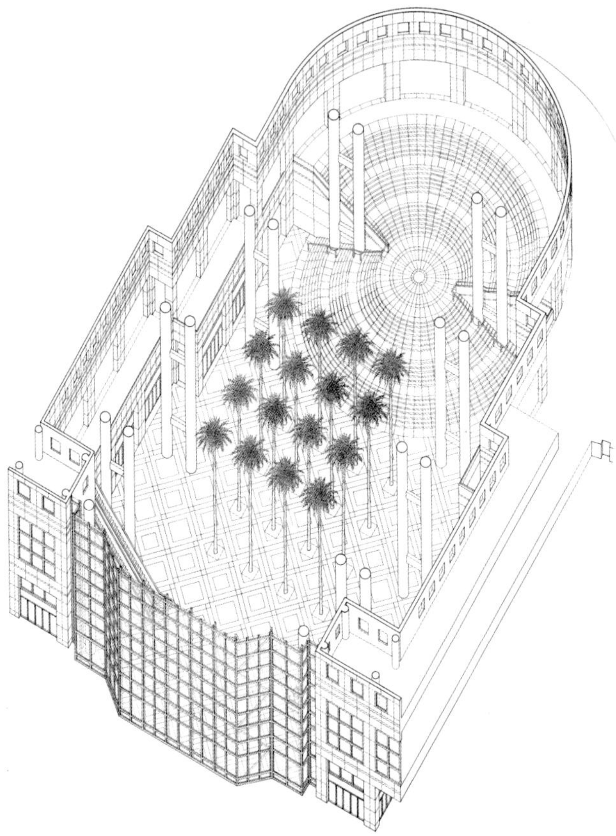

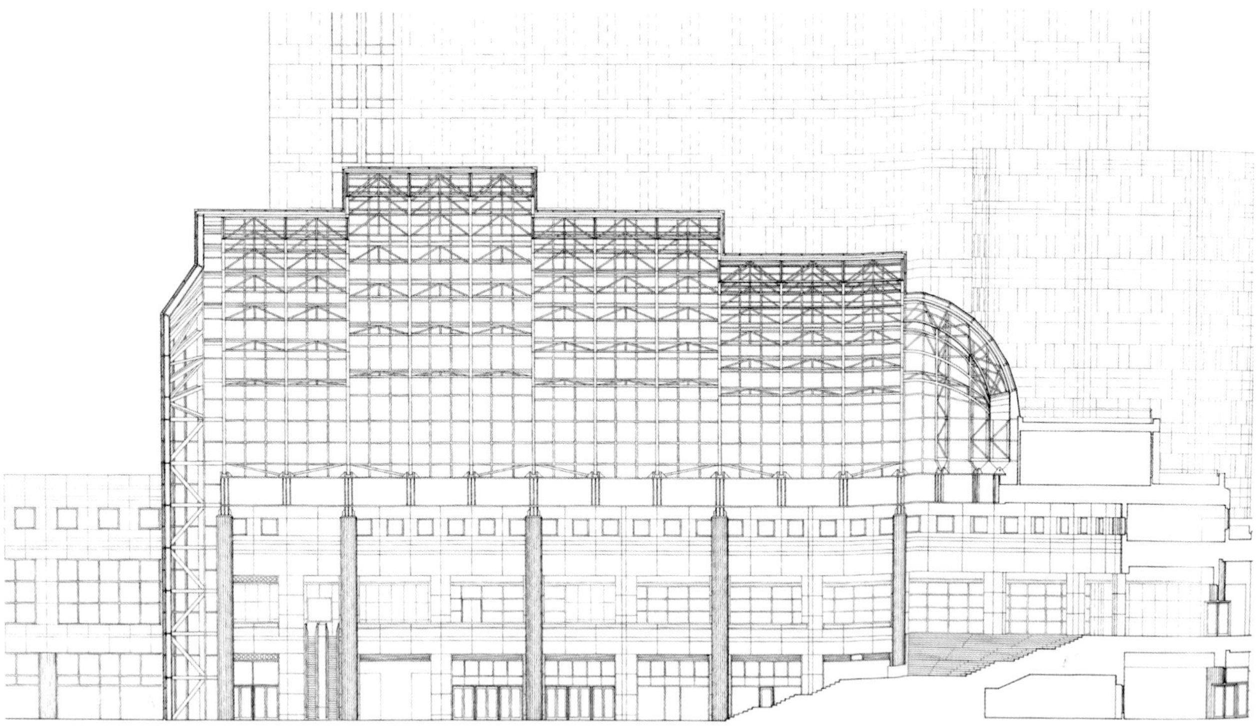

TOP Winter Garden axonometric.

We had to span over the commuter trains below, which called for a glazed corridor. We proposed the Winter Garden to be a huge public room—something that was not in the building's program. I thought this might be the first thing the client eliminated in the design.

I am a great admirer of the work of Joseph Paxton, designer of London's Crystal Palace in the 1850s. The Winter Garden is very Paxtonian.

View from the World Financial Center complex toward the west and New York Harbor, with art installation by Siah Armajani along the railing overlooking the water.

Wells Fargo Center

1989

Minneapolis, Minnesota, US

Wells Fargo Center is a true American skyscraper. I designed it to capture the spirit of the city in its architecture. Originally known as the Norwest Tower, this 57-story building was commissioned to replace the Northwestern Bank Building, which was destroyed by fire in 1982.

Steps at the top of the tower give the building a distinctive silhouette and steps at the base relate it to pedestrian scale. There are two main entrances: one leading to a large lobby and one that opens onto a five-story rotunda. A central skylight and plentiful windows transform the rotunda into a luminous, glowing space. We took great care to reuse elements from the old bank building, including chandeliers in the rotunda and elevator lobbies, cast rails on the second floor balconies, sculptured bronze plaques on the main floor, and commemorative medallions in the rotunda.

The building's skin is primarily ocher-colored Minnesota stone. The skybridge across Marquette Avenue, designed in collaboration with artist Siah Armajani, is filled with color and light.

Wells Fargo Center received the 1989 Urban Land Institute Award for Excellence for Outstanding Large-Scale Office Building; a 1989 Award from the Minnesota Chapter of the National Association of Industrial and Office Parks; 1990 Award of Excellence from American Institute of Architects Connecticut; and the 1994 Office Building of the Year Award from the Building Owners and Managers Association.

Since its completion, the Wells Fargo Center has earned two designations for energy efficiency. In 2010, the building received a Gold EB rating under the LEED system for existing buildings. The Center has also earned the Energy Star label every year since 1999. With an Energy Star score of 93, Wells Fargo Center is 49 percent more energy efficient than the average office building in the US.

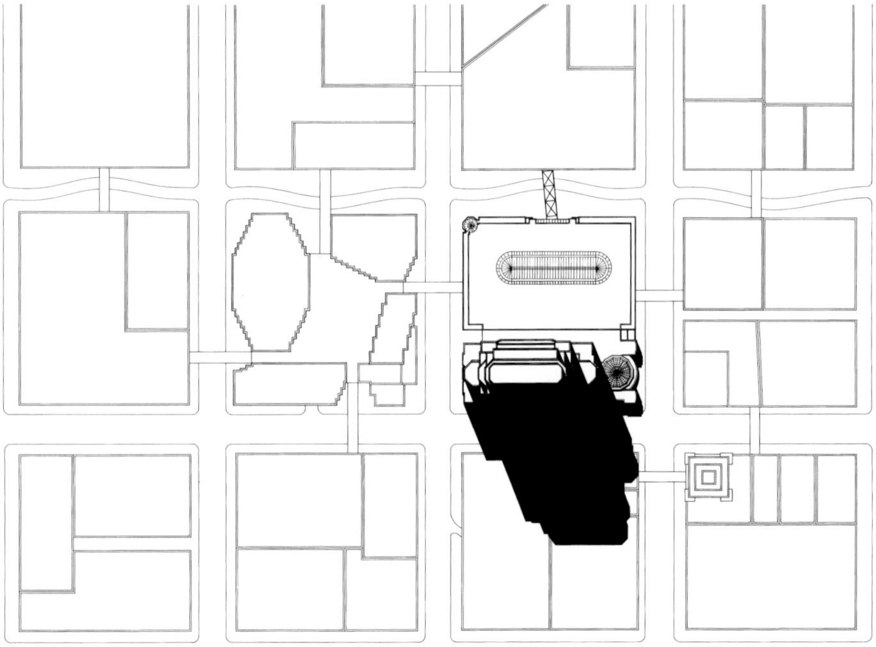

This was the first project we did for Gerald Hines. He had a sliver of a square block, and he wanted to talk to me about it, but his time was always pressed. So he interviewed me on a plane ride from New York to Chicago. He got off, and I turned around and came right back.

Working on Wells Fargo Center was wonderful because of the orange-colored Minnesota stone. It is the color of the city; it is part of the place. Those connections are subliminal, but very important.

Colored glass offers a warm and inviting space in the building's pedestrian bridge over South Marquette Avenue.

Elements from the destroyed old Northwestern Bank Building (which the new tower replaced), such as chandeliers and railings, are used in the main lobby.

ESSEX
HOUSE

Carnegie Hall Tower

1991

New York,
New York, US

Carnegie Hall Tower, a 60-story office tower, added 2,325 square meters (25,000 square feet) of support space to Carnegie Hall. The client wanted to make this tower into an integral part of the hall. I designed it as a vertical extension of the original building. Its exterior cladding is principally composed of brick, in colors selected and carefully composed to make it one with the music hall, and a beautiful tower in its own right.

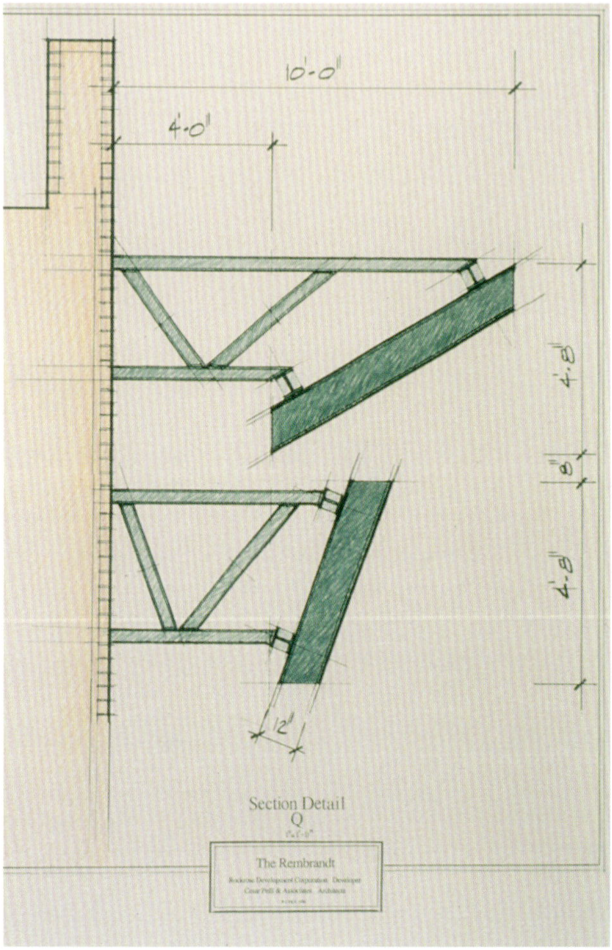

The structure is all concrete, a material that became more advanced at the time, so it could compete with steel. The exterior colors relate to the concert hall next door. The sculptural band at the top reminds us of a cornice, in a contemporary way, relating to the older hall without copying it.

West Elevation

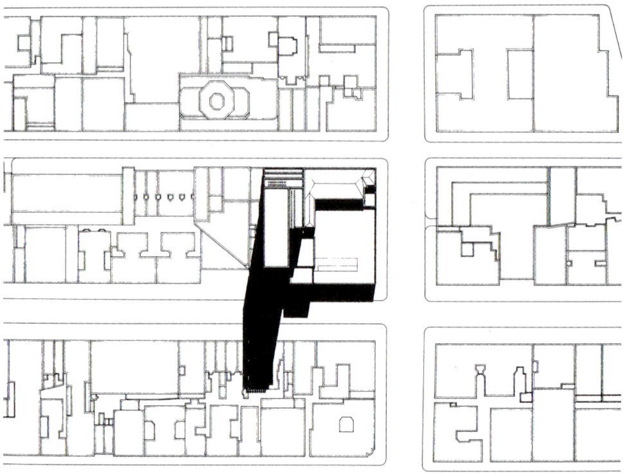

HSBC
citigroup

One Canada Square Tower and Docklands Light Railway Station

1986–1991

Canary Wharf, London, England

One Canada Square is the centerpiece of Canary Wharf, a very large private development by Olympia & York—the same developer for whom I designed the World Financial Center. This 48-story tower is a simple square prism crowned by a roof in pyramid form. I conceived it as a clear and strong volume to create a landmark readily identifiable from all directions. Clad in linen-finish stainless steel panels, it is a high-technology wall. The tower has a traditional scale and softly reflects London's often misty climate.

The lobby of One Canada Square connects to the Dockland Light Railway (DLR) station, the gateway to Canary Wharf, connecting it to the City of London. The DLR was established in conjunction with the redevelopment of the formerly industrial east London area, which includes the business district of Canary Wharf. Six platforms serve three rail lines.

With a vaulted roof of glass and steel, the station is a smaller, modern reinterpretation of London's great 19th-century vaulted railroad stations.

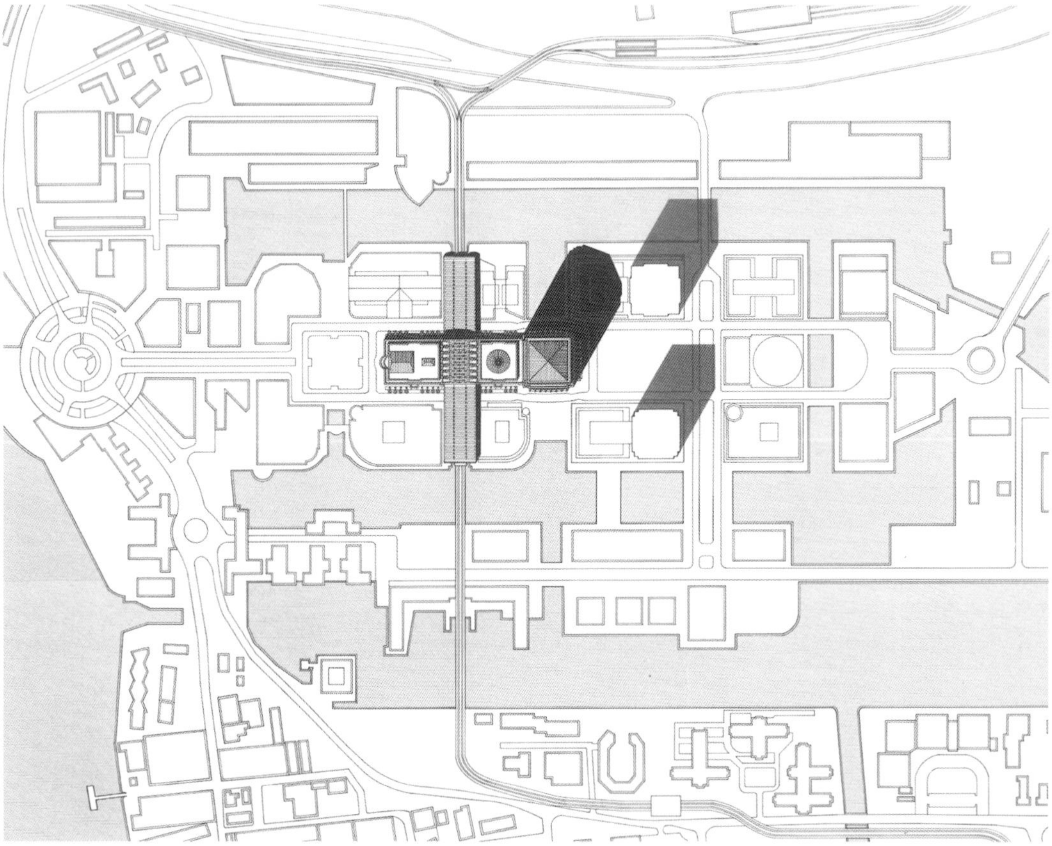

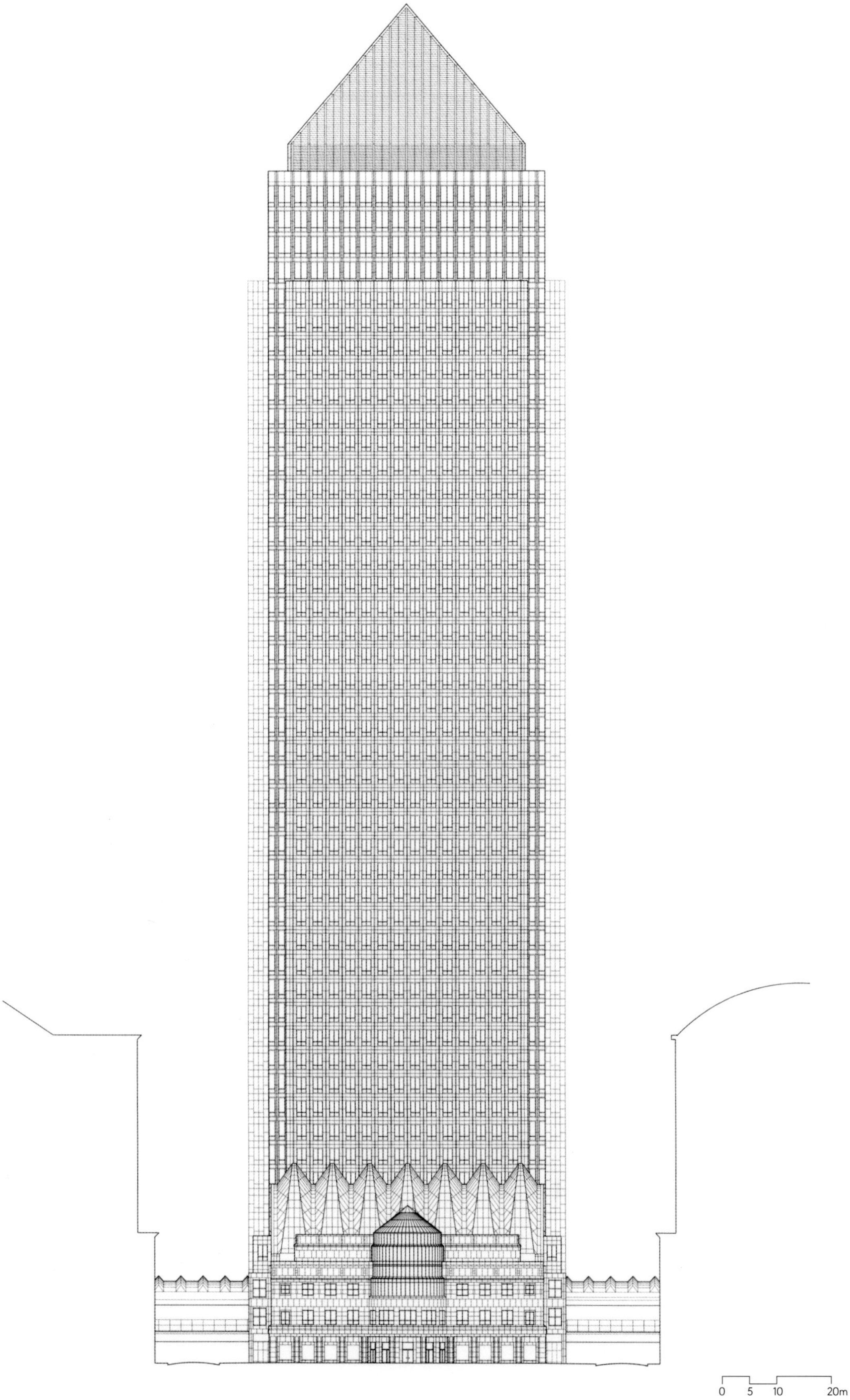

West elevation

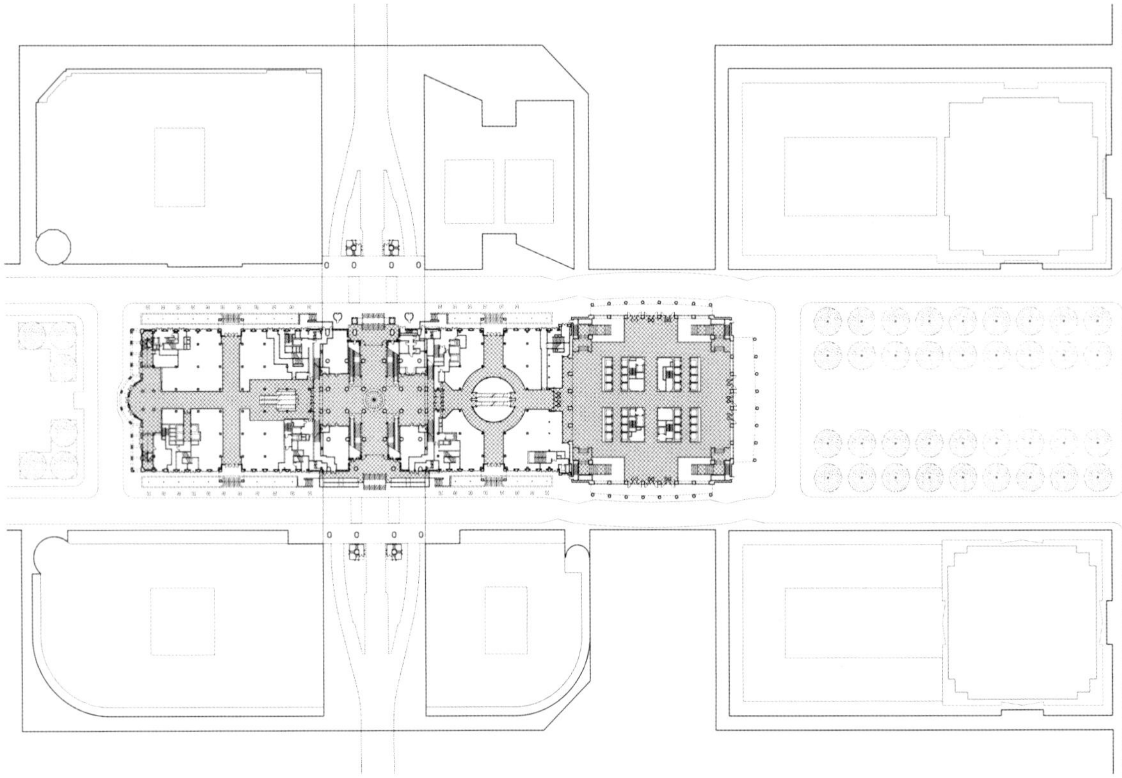

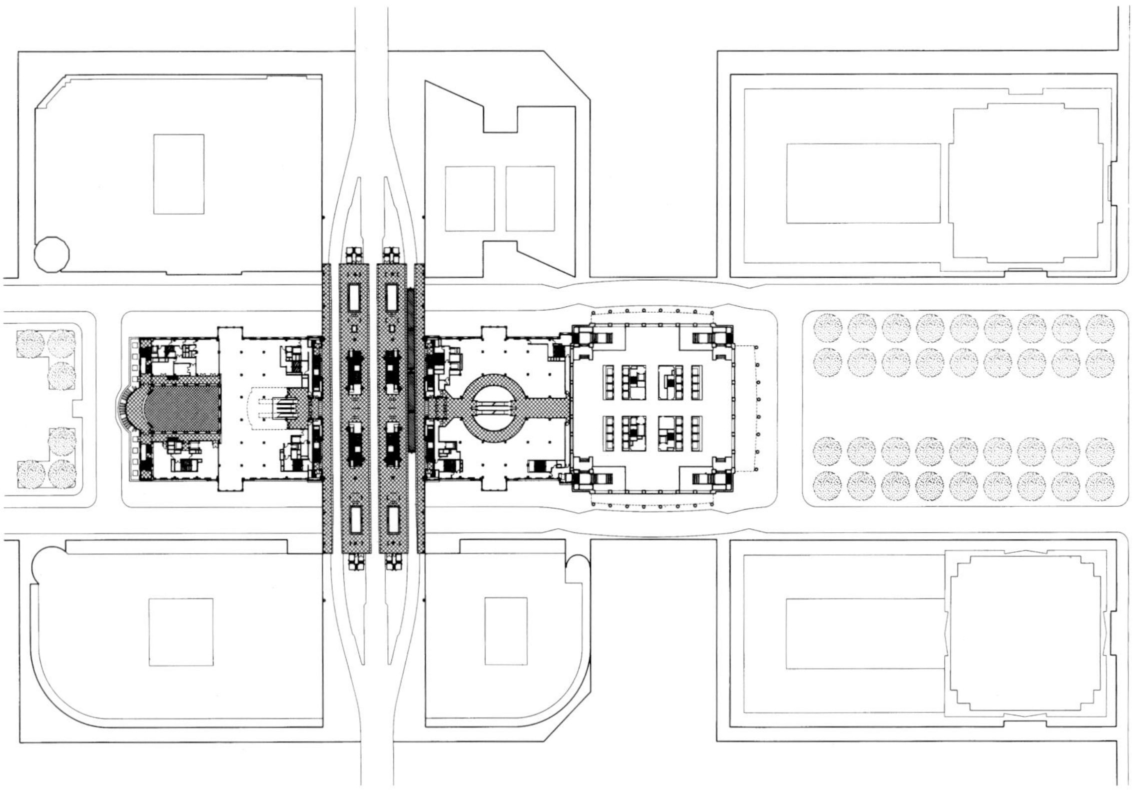

TOP Ground-floor plan. BOTTOM Train platform level.
OPPOSITE MIDDLE South-north section through station. BOTTOM Train platform level.

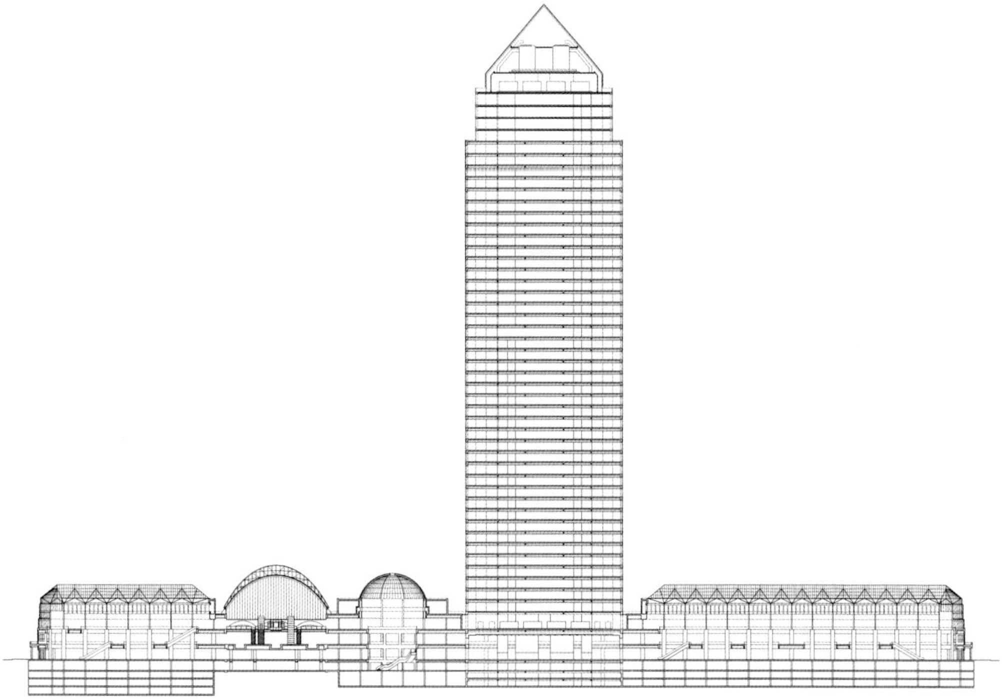

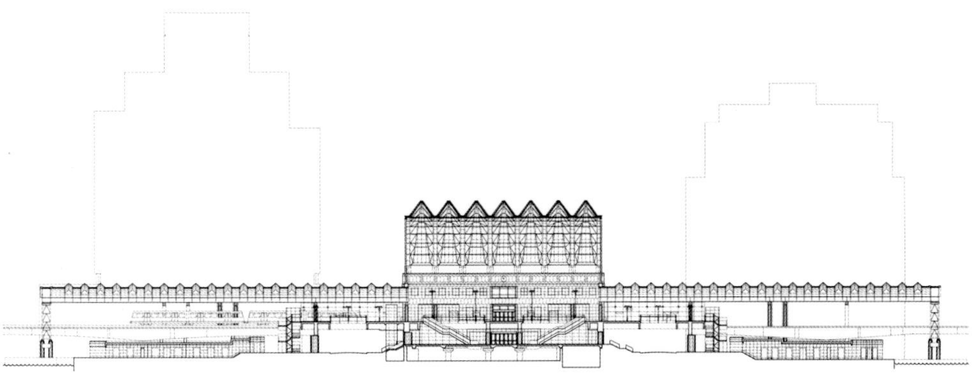

0 5 10 20m

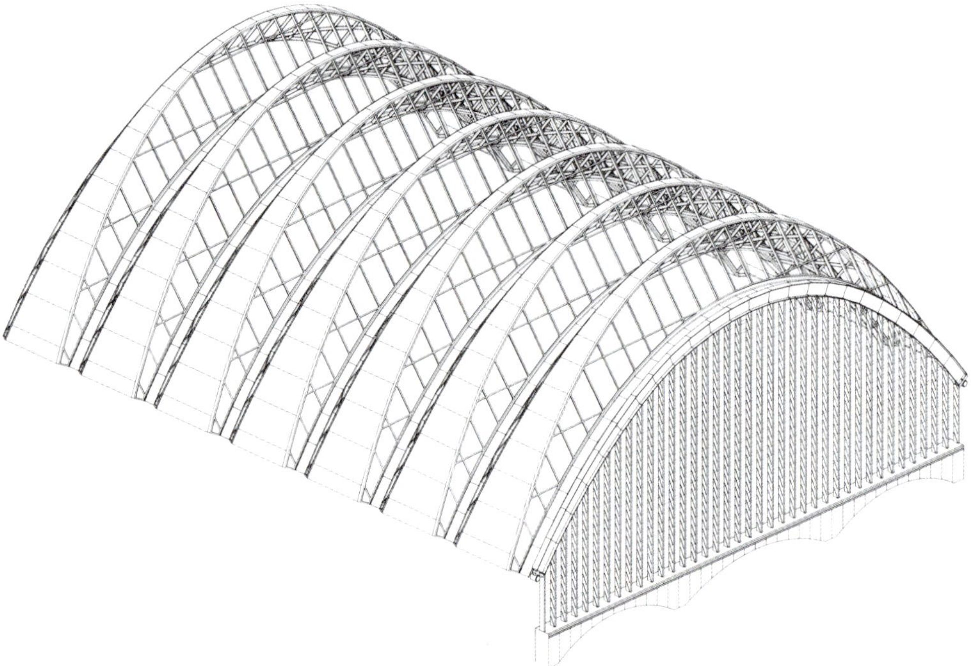

The pleated glass roof of the station recalls Victorian-era London train sheds.

HSBC

Plaza Tower

1991
Costa Mesa, California, US

Clad in stainless steel, Plaza Tower rises 21 stories above South Coast Plaza Town Center. I curved the main façade to make the stainless steel wall gleam, bringing to life the best qualities of this elegant material.

In 1991, Plaza Tower received an Honor Award from the Orange County Chapter of the American Institute of Architects, as well as a Design for Excellence/Certificate of Merit from Southern California Edison. In 1992, the project was acknowledged with an Award of Merit from the Illuminating Engineering Society of North America.

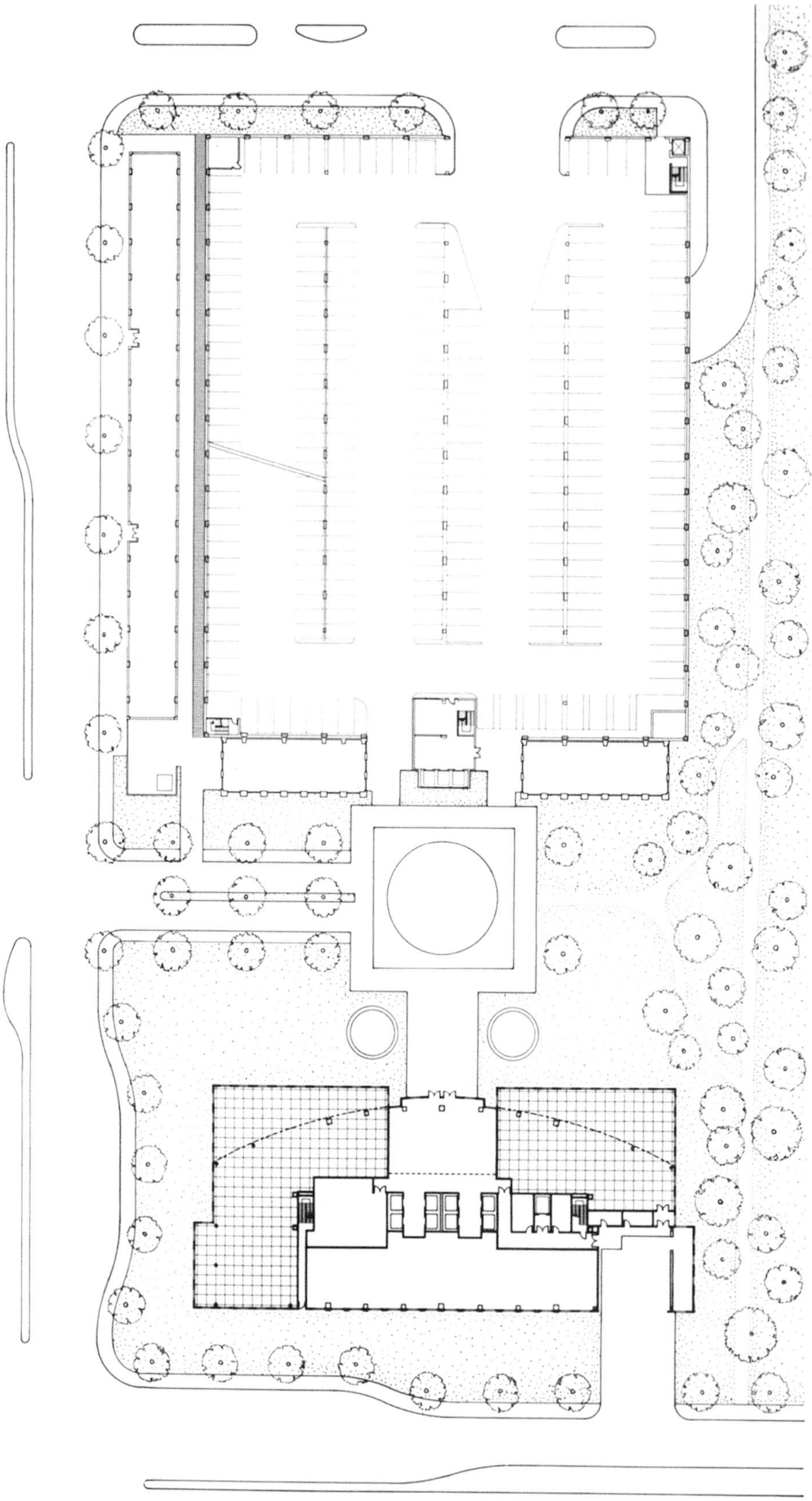

We first used stainless steel with a linen finish at Canary Wharf; here the bending of the wall is particularly beautiful, and that is what makes the steel glow. It is very alive.

Private Residence

1993
Western US

The design of this house was my response to its powerful and beautiful setting. The house feels like an integral and essential part of the landscape.

The two-level main house follows an organizing central spine-corridor, with public functions to one side and private areas on the other. The house is on a 39-hectare (96 acres) wooded site alongside a creek, oriented to capture views of the Grand Teton mountain range. The guest house is near a corner of the site by a stream surrounded by cottonwoods and evergreen trees.

The two houses were constructed using post and beam. Douglas-fir beams are joined by mortise and tenons to 55 hand-shaven Engelman spruce logs used as columns. Large windows face west to views of the creek and mountains.

In 1993, this project received an Honor Award from the American Wood Council's Wood Design Award Program.

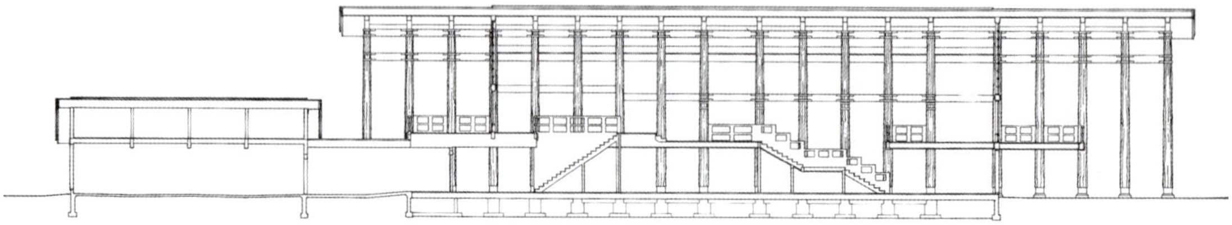

TOP Structural section looking east. MIDDLE West elevation.
BOTTOM House's west elevation overlooks a creek and mountain views.

How to attach wood members was what I learned here mostly, and how to mix one wood with another. The columns' bark had been lost over time, leaving a natural finish.

CARNEGIE HALL

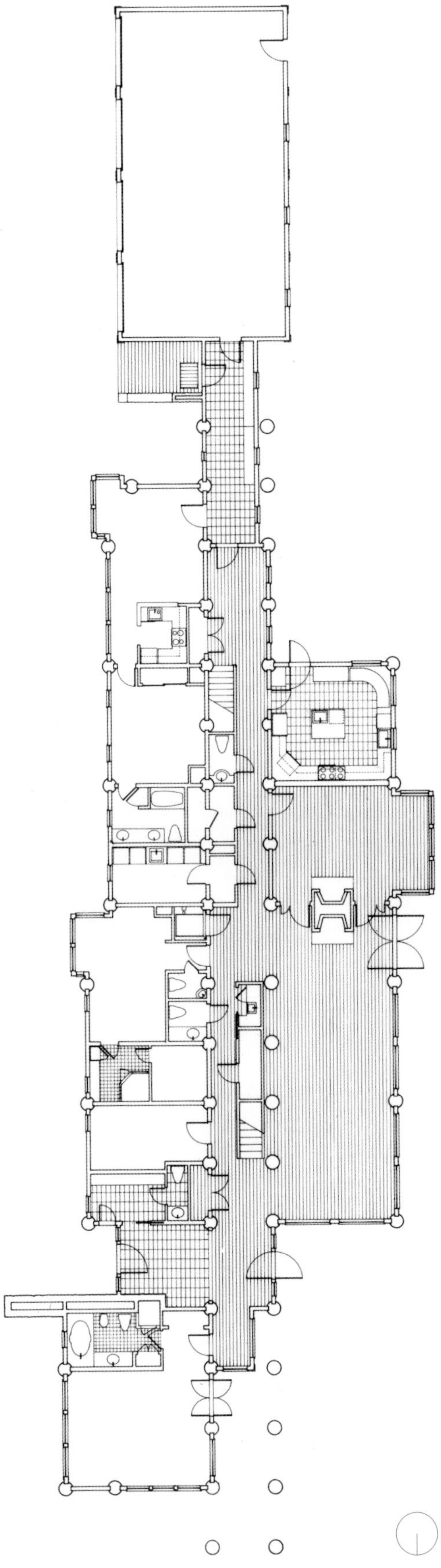

This is a spine scheme, just like COMSAT. You are moving down the spine, with elements off it.

TOP North elevation of finished guesthouse, and model studies.
OPPOSITE Guesthouse from the east.

Aronoff Center for the Arts

1995
Cincinnati, Ohio, US

We were selected to design the Aronoff Center for the Arts in a competition. The Center has three theaters, with a capacity of 2,700 seats, 440 seats, and 150 seats.

The two larger halls and lobbies are on an interior public pathway which connects two small plazas. Performance spaces and their lobbies have a civic scale and are contained between monumental masonry walls of brick and stone. These wall-like forms contain vertical elements such as elevators, fire stairs, and ducts, freeing the main space for public use.

A metal-frame grid with stone and glass infill panels encloses areas that have a small urban scale and character. The use of the masonry, brick and stone, and metal-frame building elements with infill panels, responds to Cincinnati's building traditions.

In 1997, the Aronoff Center for the Arts received an Honor Award from the American Institute of Architects Connecticut. In 1996, the project received a Design Award from the American Institute of Architects Cincinnati and an Honor Award from the US Institute for Theatre Technology.

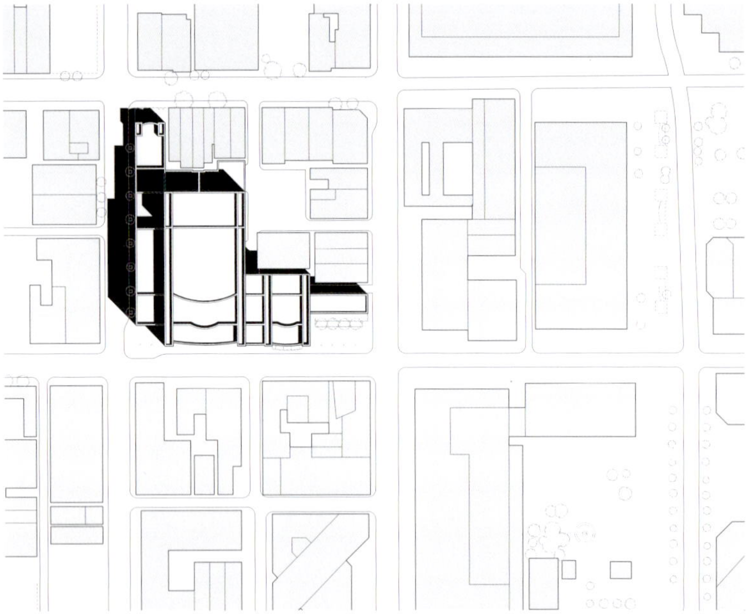

Front elevation of Aronoff Center's Procter & Gamble Hall, at left in site plan above, addresses its urban condition with masonry mass. OPPOSITE Ground-floor plan.

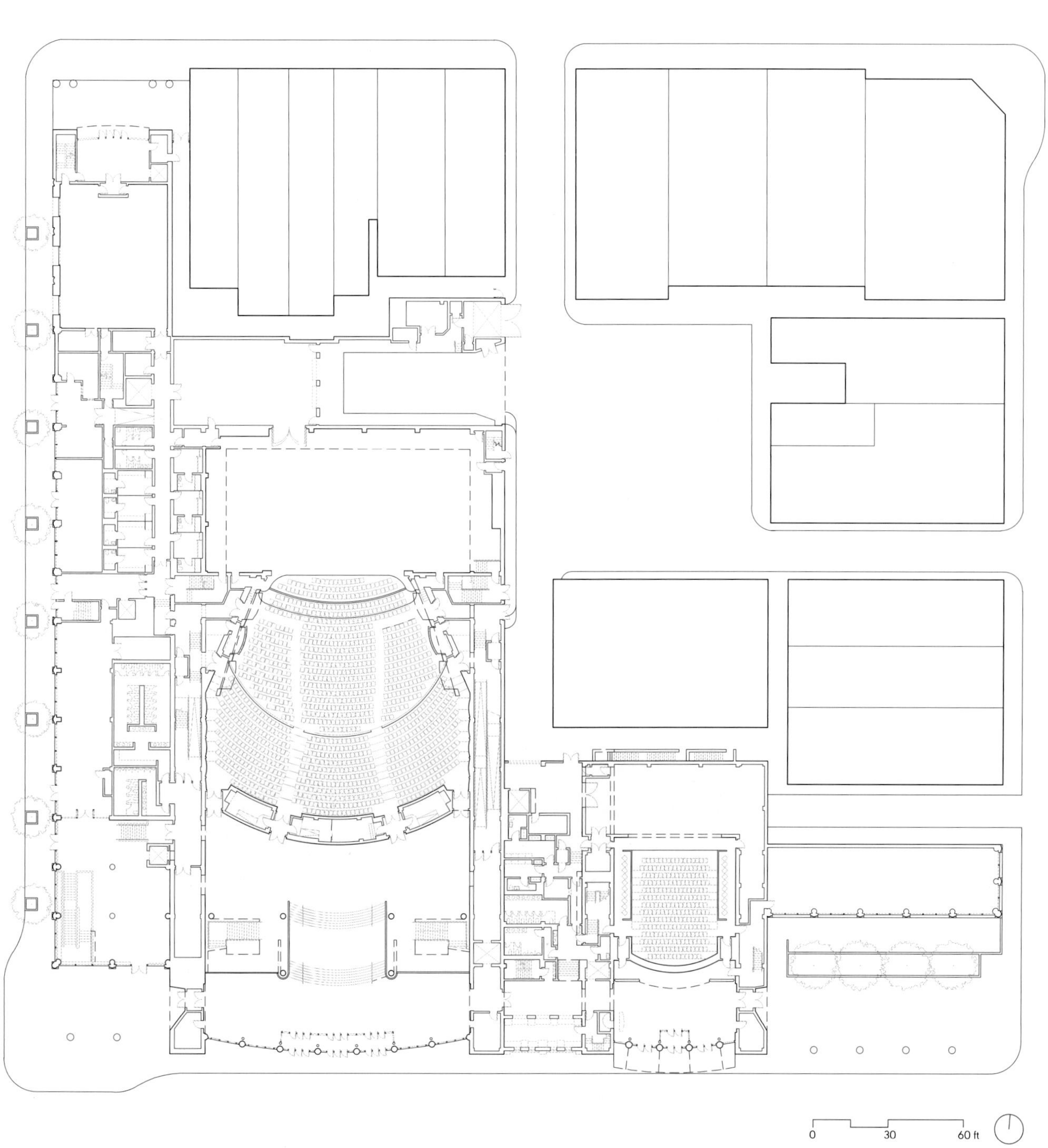
0
30
60 ft

ARONOFF CENTER
PROCTER

ARONOFF CENTER
& GAMBLE HALL

I wanted these theaters to be very civic buildings with a lot of mass. We used the thick walls for circulation and structure, leaving spaces in the center free for audience members and artists.

ABOVE Interior of the Jarson-Kaplan Theater. OPPOSITE The theater as it faces Walnut Street.

EASTERN
OFFICE
SUPPLY
ARONOFF CENTER
ARONOFF CENTER
ARONOFF CENTER
ARONOFF CENTER
KAPLAN THEATER

ABOVE AND OPPOSITE The dynamic, multi-storied lobby of Procter & Gamble Hall.

Details sparkle in the lobby and within the performance space of Procter & Gamble Hall.

NTT Headquarters
1995
Tokyo, Japan

The NTT Headquarters is a 30-story tower which includes corporate offices and a six-level, below-grade telecommunications center. Connected to the tower is a Special Purposes Building.

My design responded to the purpose and location of the building, as the headquarters for one of the largest and most advanced high-technology companies in the world. The site is in a new and rapidly growing area of Shinjuku Center.

Several restrictions informed the design, including a 127-meter (417 feet) height limit and a requirement that 20 percent of the site be dedicated to public open space. Other challenges included an elevated highway to the south of the site, two microwave corridors, and accommodating transmission equipment and an emergency helipad on the roof.

A fan-shaped block of offices is oriented toward the interior garden and the long views. Support facilities occupy the remainder of the allowable triangular envelope. These functions are expressed in the exterior and give form to the tower. The garden, designed by Balmori Associates, is used for recreation, exhibitions, and performances. The building and the garden have deep roots in Japanese traditions.

In 1997, the NTT Headquarters received an Honor Award from the American Institute of Architects Connecticut.

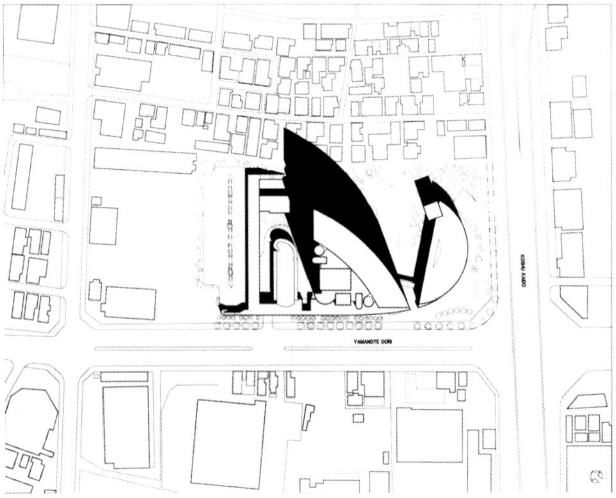

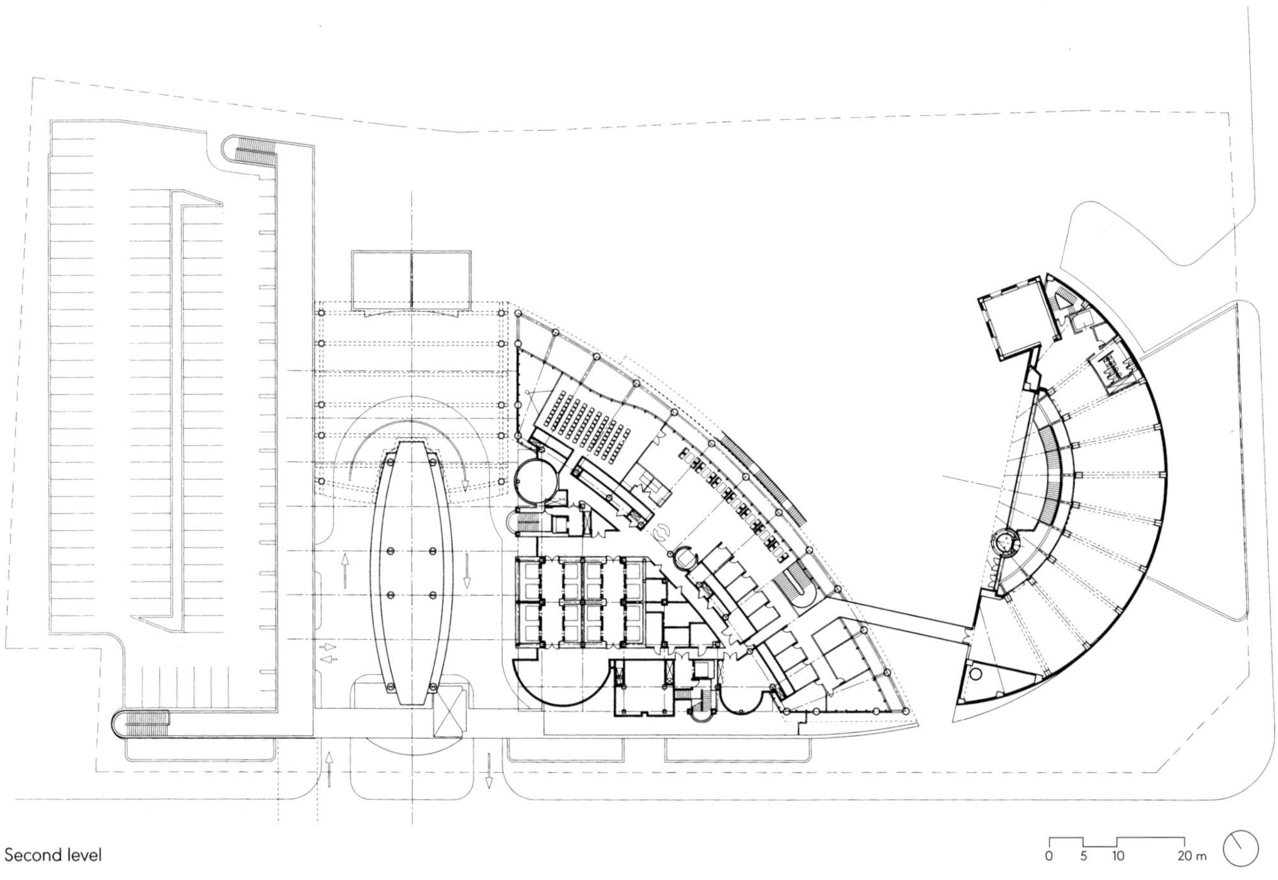

Second level

徐行

Open staircase contrasts a range of materials from steel to marble to wood inlay.

Celebrating Pelli

By Berto González Montaner

"Amazing, great! It's been a lot of fun!"

That's how my most recent interview with Cesar Pelli in Buenos Aires ended. It lasted for about two hours and he was ready for more, as has been the case in the many other interviews that I've done with him over the past 20 years.

The first interview was held when he visited Buenos Aires for the inauguration of Edificio República, back in 1996. He explained to me in detail how the building is located (masterfully, I would say) and how it relates to its surroundings, paying due respect to the city's traditional longitudinal balconies. He also described the depth of its cladding and its articulation, which resembles the uncut stone of traditional Beaux-Arts architecture, which is so typical of Buenos Aires. The Petronas Towers in Kuala Lumpur were also built during that time. Despite being a foreign architect, born in the Tucumán province of Argentina, Pelli clearly understood the "genius loci." He designed those wonderful towers so that they visibly belong to that city and, furthermore, he ensured that they enhance the city landscape and make it more beautiful.

Years later, Pelli-designed towers sprung up in Buenos Aires. The first was for Bank Boston, in the Catalinas Norte neighborhood, by the harbor. Its shape resembles the sails of a boat or old harbor silos from the time before the redevelopment of Puerto Madero. Later he designed the YPF Tower in that neighborhood, with a six-story winter garden in the upper third of the building that houses tall, living trees as a symbol of clean energy. At present, he is completing the Macro Tower in one of the last vacant lots in Catalinas, with a building whose enclosure is almost a continuous single line.

The three towers are clearly in a different league from other buildings in the city. Their careful design, the quality of detailing, and changes in brightness and color during the day, make them look like beautiful living organisms. These are distinguished buildings that fit harmoniously in the urban environment, and are conscious of the role that they play within the neighborhood. The ground floors honor what Pelli loves so much about Buenos Aires: strolling its sidewalks and stopping by a storefront or shop window, or having a coffee at one of the many cafés that public spaces in Buenos Aires have to offer.

His work is grounded in humanity and a deep sensibility. As Pelli points out, his architecture is indebted to his student years in Tucumán: to professors such as Eduardo Sacriste, Horacio Caminos, and Jorge Vivanco; to the school that during the 1940s competed with Harvard for academic excellence; and, dare I say, to his family. His brother Carlos was a wonderful filmmaker; Diana Balmori, to whom he was married, an exceptional landscape architect; and both his brother Víctor Saúl and his niece Bela are architects and professors committed to achieving affordable architecture for low-income households.

Edificio República
1997
Buenos Aires, Argentina

Edificio República was my first design in Buenos Aires and also the first in Argentina since I came to the US in 1952.

Located on a narrow triangular site, the Edificio República marks the northern end of the row of blocks between Madero and Bouchard, the edge of the city. It adapts itself to the triangular block with a broad convex curve towards the river. The gently curved form opens the interior views towards Puerto Madero and the river. The building is highly contemporary and it also fits well within the city and its architectural traditions.

The garden's sculptured shape is based on the triangular site as well as the tower form, offering a counterpoint to its curved façade. Landscape designer Balmori Associates focused the open space as a public garden, which is raised above street level to avoid noise and pollution.

I tried to design a building that would be most appropriate for Buenos Aires, reflecting on the traditions and character of the city, on its special place at the urban edge, and at the same time I wanted it to be an edifice of our times—the most contemporary and up-to-date building I could design. This is a building for Buenos Aires as a great world city.

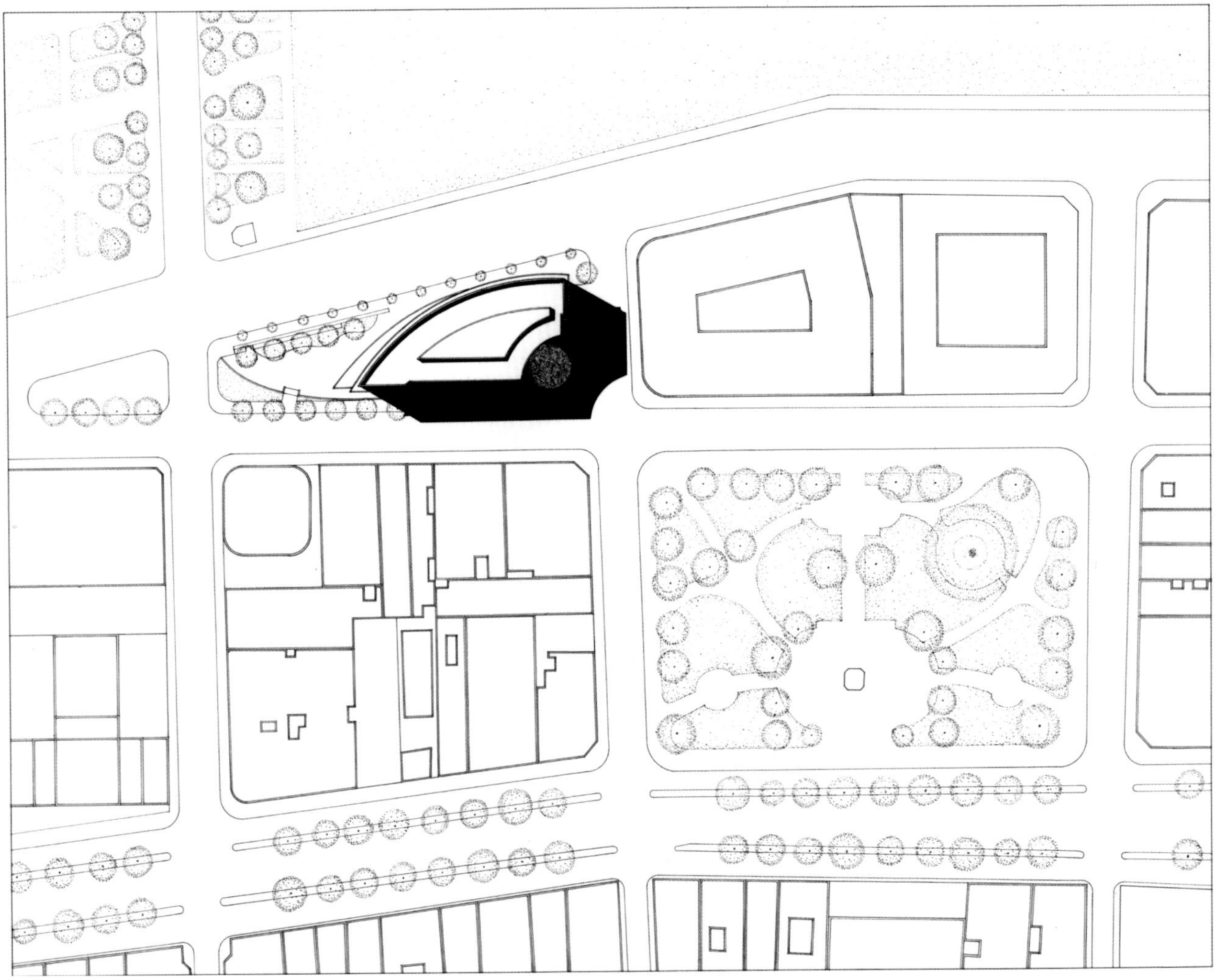

Edif. República
Plaza Roma

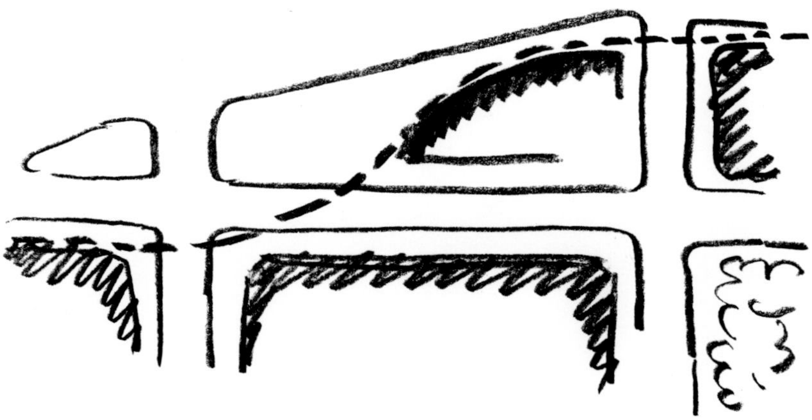

Fachada de Ciudad

1 Elevator lobby
2 Conference room
3 Open office space
4 Office
5 Corridor

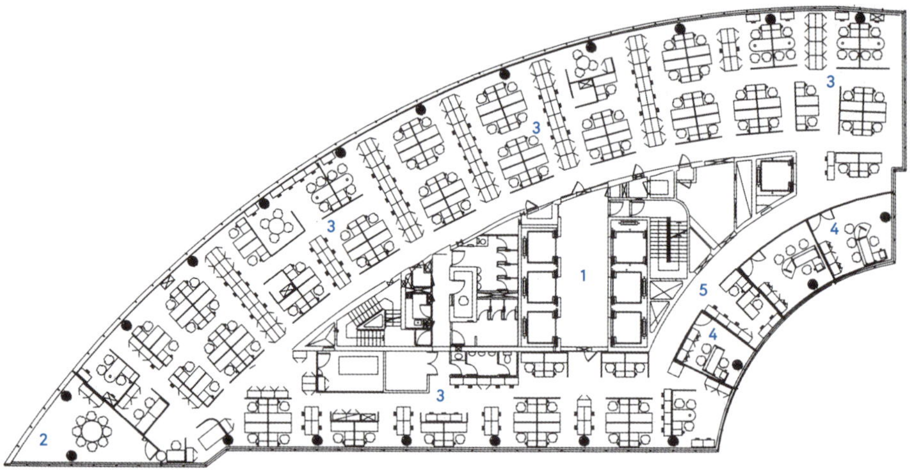

Petronas Towers
1997
Kuala Lumpur, Malaysia

The Petronas Towers, a project I won in a major international competition, are a modern response to Malaysia's culture, history, and climate, and symbols of its economic growth and its hopes for the future. Until 2004, they were the world's tallest buildings.

The main, but unplanned accomplishment of the Petronas Towers, was to demonstrate that great, very tall skyscrapers can be built outside the US. Today most skyscrapers are built in Asia and are as ambitious as any structures elsewhere in the world. Indeed, the Petronas Towers changed the paradigm.

To create a uniquely Malaysian building, we drew from Islamic culture, Kuala Lumpur's climate and light, and traditional Malaysian crafts and design. The plan of the towers is generated from two overlapping squares, a pattern basic to Islamic design with eight partially cylindrical lobes that compose a 16-point star. Between the two towers is a strong, figural void—the center of the composition. The towers are not only symmetrical but strongly figurative, creating another figurative space between them.

This space is the key element in the composition. Each tower has its own vertical axis, but the axis of the total composition is in the center of the void. According to the philosopher Lao Tse, the reality of a hollow object is in the void and not in the walls that define it.

The power of the void is increased and made more explicit by the pedestrian bridge that connects the two towers on the 41st and 42nd floors, the sky lobby floors. The bridge with its supporting structure creates a portal to the sky, a 170-meter-high (558 feet) portal—a door to the infinite.

The Petronas Towers received the Aga Khan Award for Architecture in 2004, which is given every three years to projects that set new standards of excellence in architecture, planning practices, historic preservation, and landscape architecture.

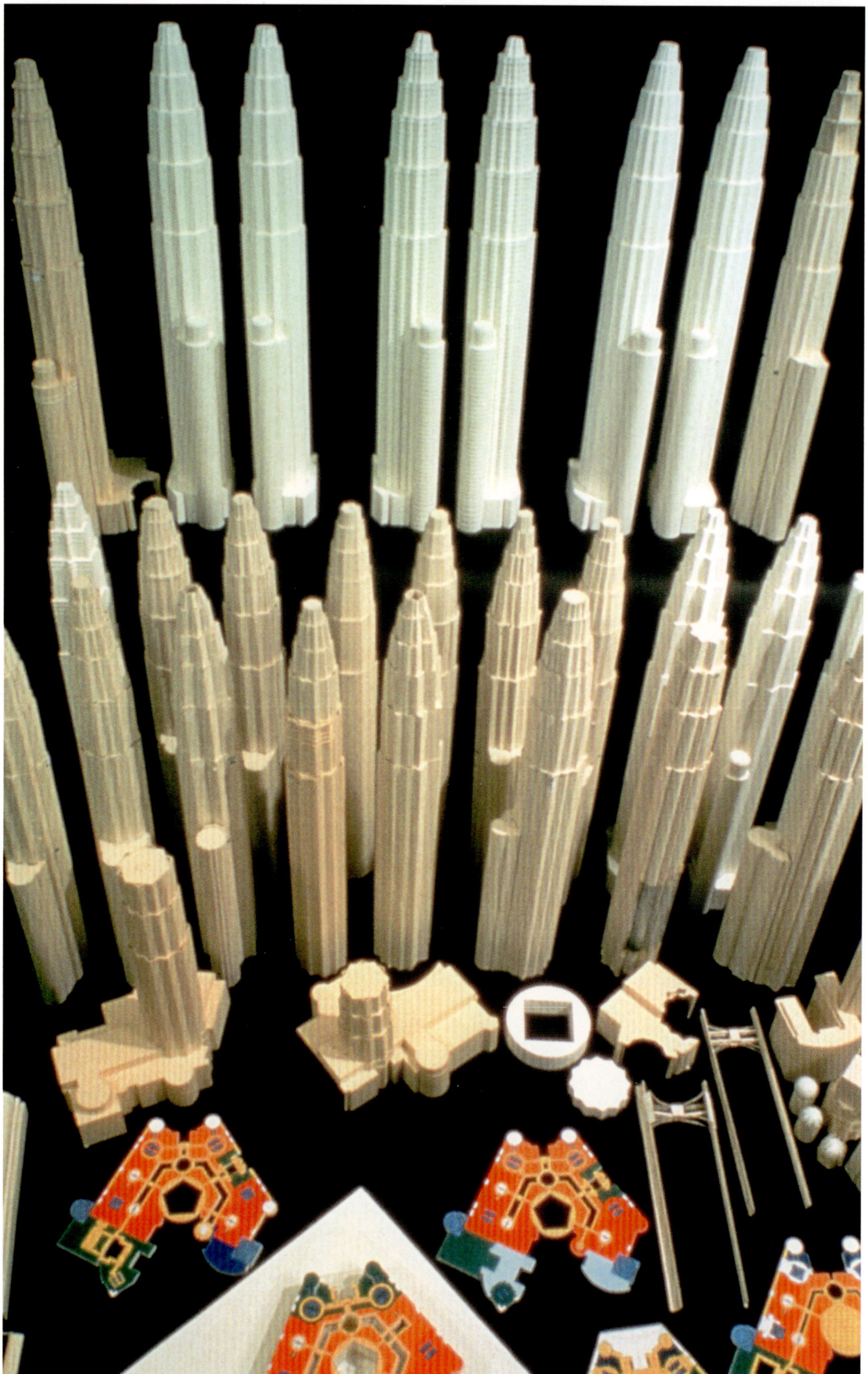

The shape, setbacks, and taper of the towers were extensively studied through models.

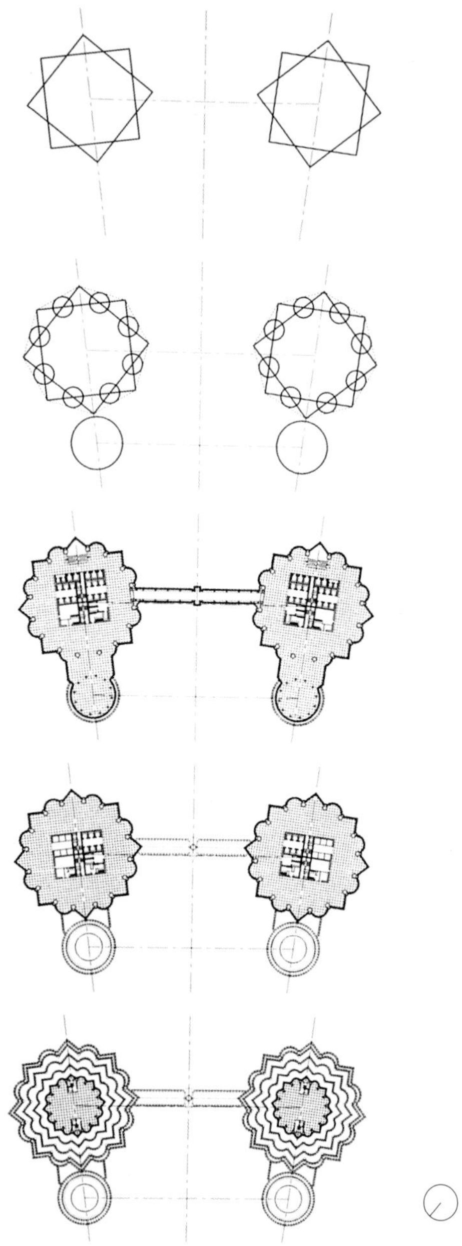

The client indicated to each of us in the competition that they wanted the architecture of the building to be Malaysian. We asked them what that meant, and they said they had no idea. So we endeavored to understand and capture the spirit of Malaysia in the building's design.

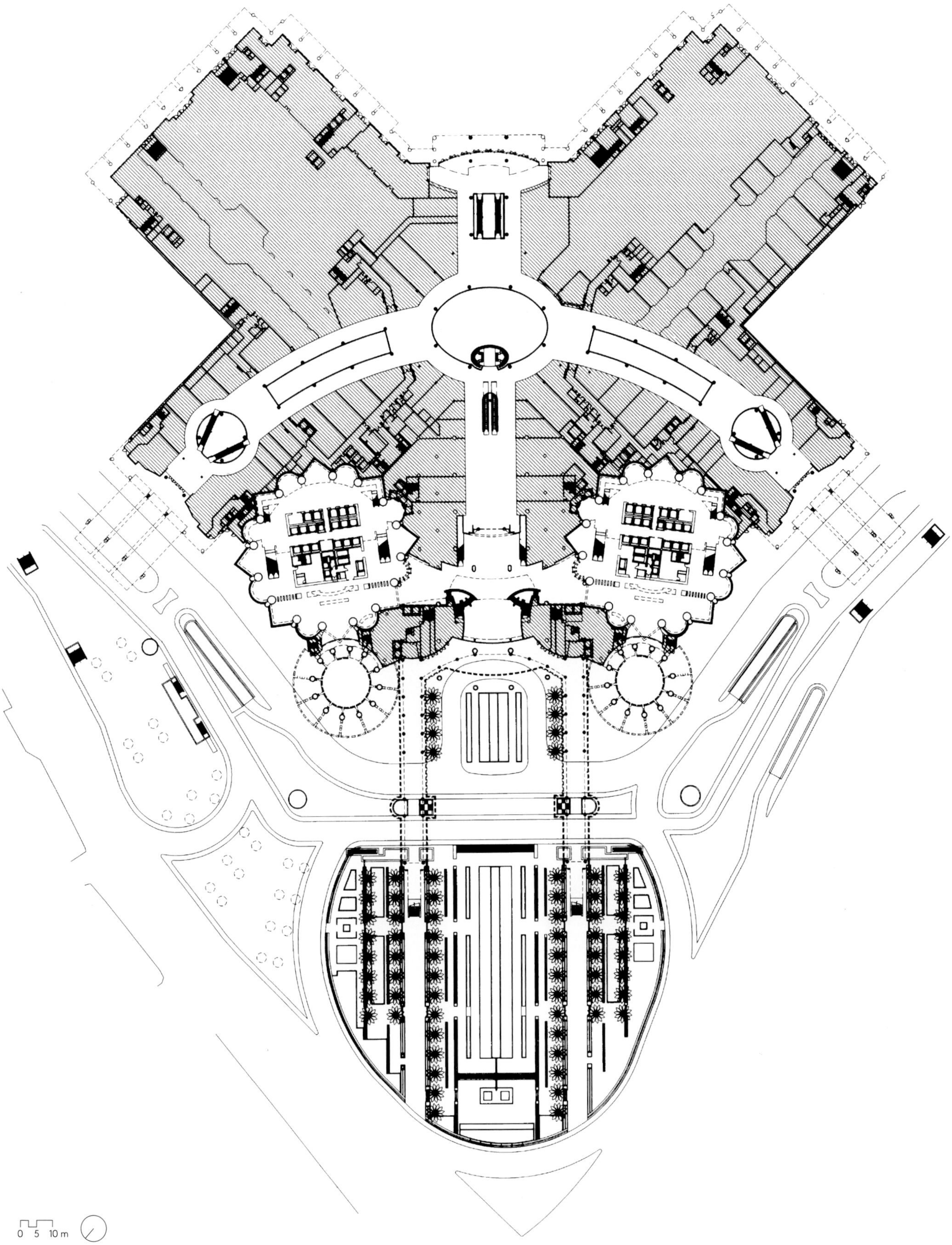
0 5 10 m

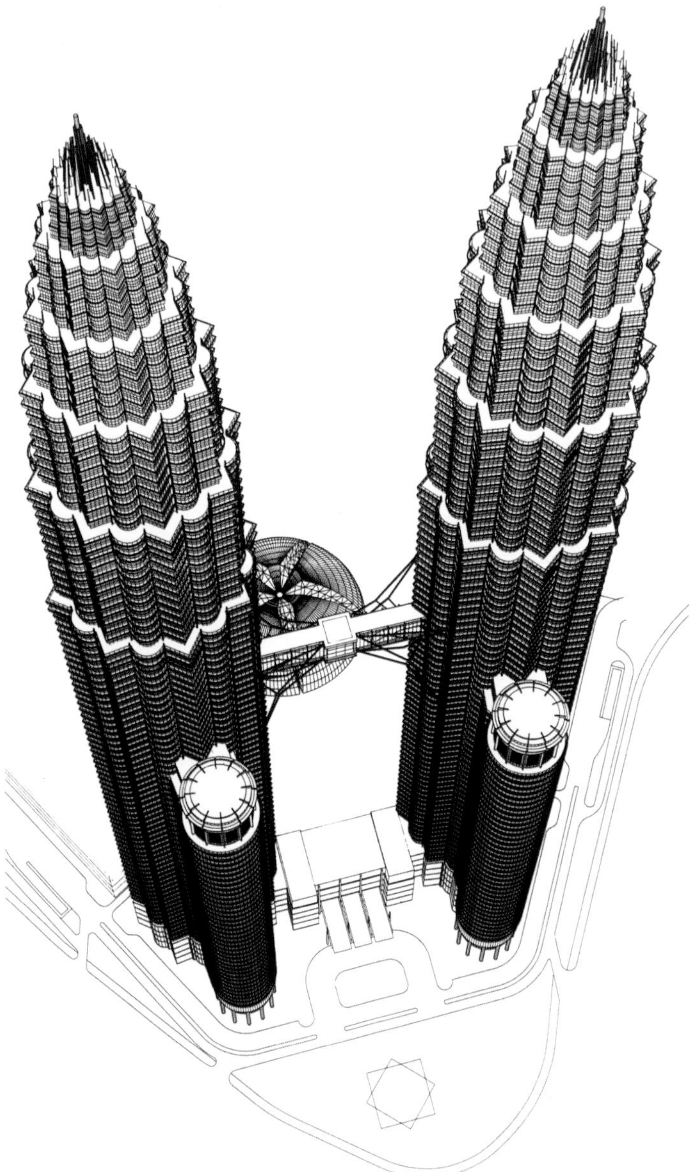

The bridge between the two gives the towers majesty and mystery. It is a portal to the infinite.

The towers, with concrete structures, were bid to separate construction companies to encourage competition.

North Terminal Reagan National Airport

1997

Washington, D.C., US

The North Terminal of Reagan National Airport in Washington, D.C., created a new gateway to the nation's capital—a welcoming and functional public place.

The main space of the new terminal is a long concourse made of steel and glass, formed from two rows of square bays topped by shallow domes. I based the design on a 13.5-meter-by-13.5-meter (45 feet by 45 feet) repetitive structural steel bay which establishes scale, flexibility, and architectural proportions. These spatial, modular units are on a recognizable human scale. Each bay is covered by a dome with a central glass oculus. The dome is an ancient symbol of shelter and serves to establish a connection with the civic architecture of Washington, D.C.

The concourse is the 'main street' of the terminal. It is an uplifting space opened to the airfield on one side and is lined with shops, cafés, restaurants, and airport services on the other. Some thirty site-specific artworks are integrated into the architecture of the concourse.

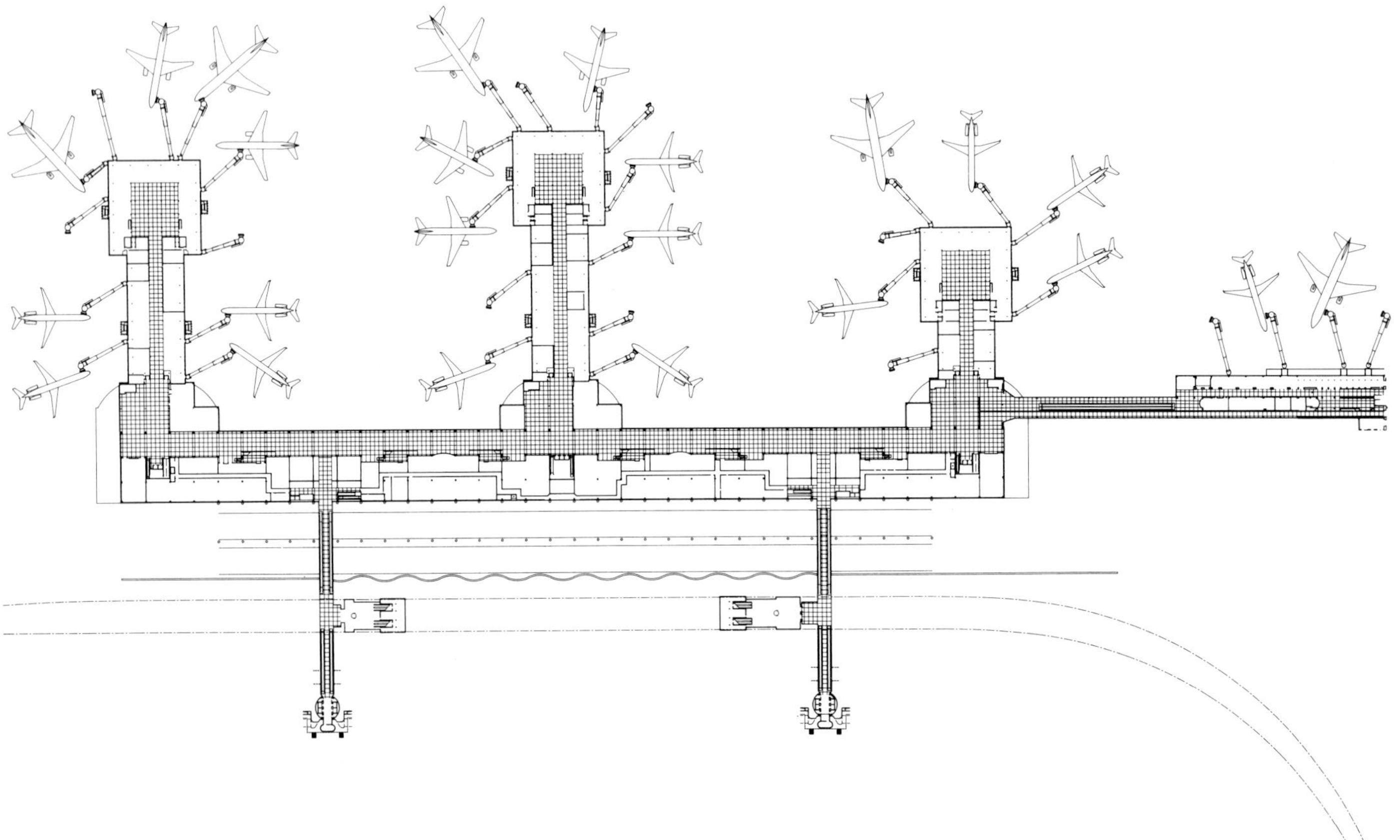

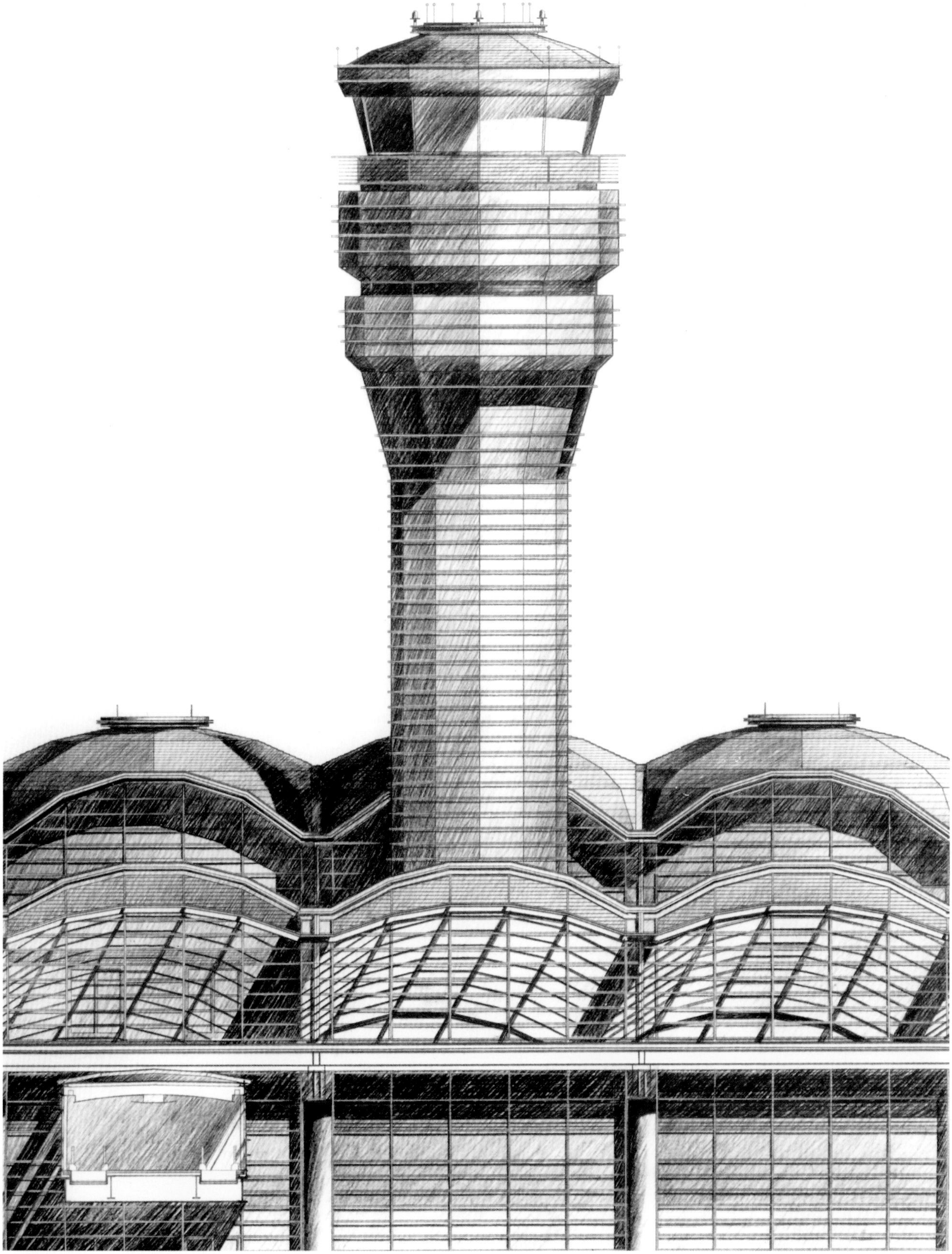

TOP SPAN East elevation. MIDDLE SPAN West elevation. BOTTOM LEFT North Terminal from the east as it overlooks the runway. BOTTOM RIGHT Shade-filled terraces reside on the north and south ends of the terminal.

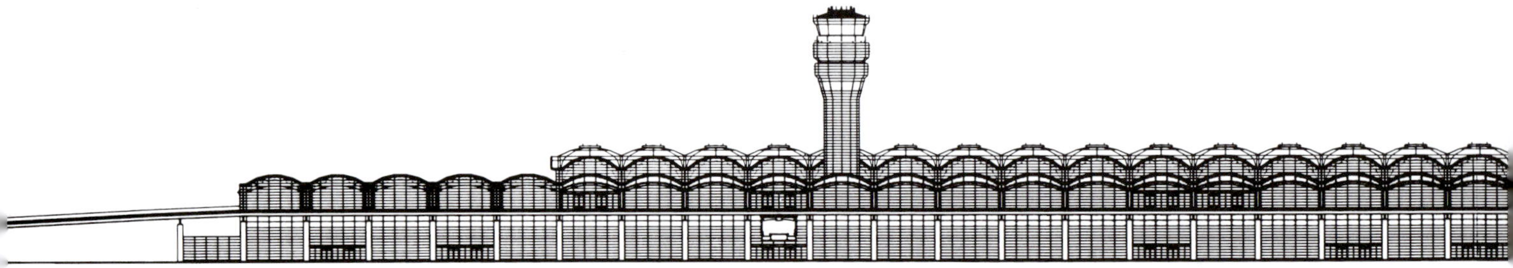

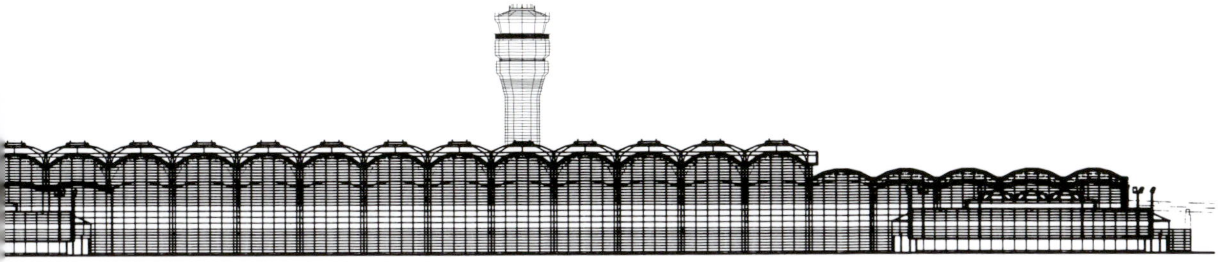

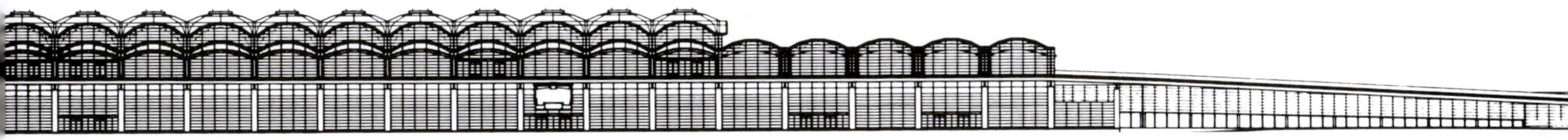

NORTH TERMINAL, REAGAN NATIONAL AIRPORT

B
American

B

Gates 1-34
Parking
Metro/Parking
Elevator/Escalator
Pet Relief Area
Chapel
Restrooms
Escalator to
Ticketing/Check-In
DIRECTORY
DIRECTORY
BAYER

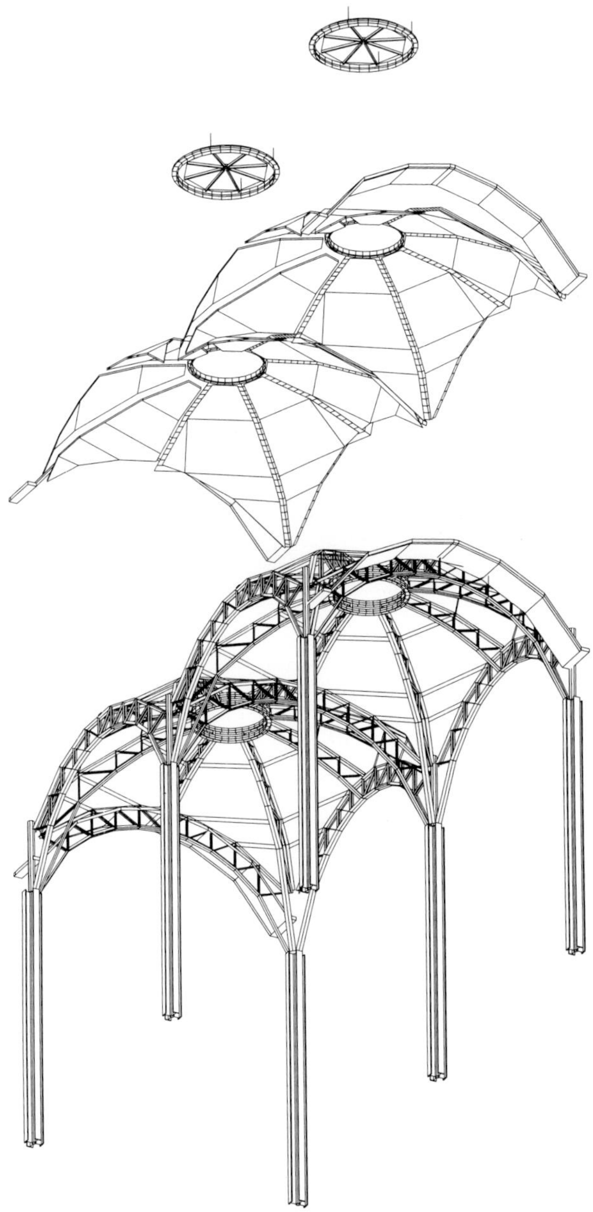

The architecture of Labrouste was in the back of my mind, while the spatial organization pairs with Eero Saarinen's Dulles Airport.

We were requested to do a competition design, and they loved the interior with the repeating domes, which is very economical construction with short spans. The domes also make it very Jeffersonian, and that clicked and made it a winner.

Aluminum, steel, and wood trellis by Kent Bloomer on the south end of the terminal's upper level.

Glass art by Jennifer Bartlett is found in the east wall's frieze.
OPPOSITE Al Held's colorful frieze incorporated into the terminal's east wall.

To All Gates
To All Gates

LEFT At far left in photo, the balustrade panel by artist Cary Smith titled *Views or Mirrors.* TOP Concourse medallion *Hooloomooloo* by Frank Stella.

TOP *Medallion Flight* by Michele Oka Doner. BOTTOM *Untitled* by Joyce Kozloff. RIGHT *Lips* by Joyce Scott.

FROM LEFT TO RIGHT *Lips* by Joyce Scott; *Astral* by Richard Anuszkiewicz; *Untitled* by Joyce Kozloff; Sol Lewitt's *Black & White Bands within a Circle.*

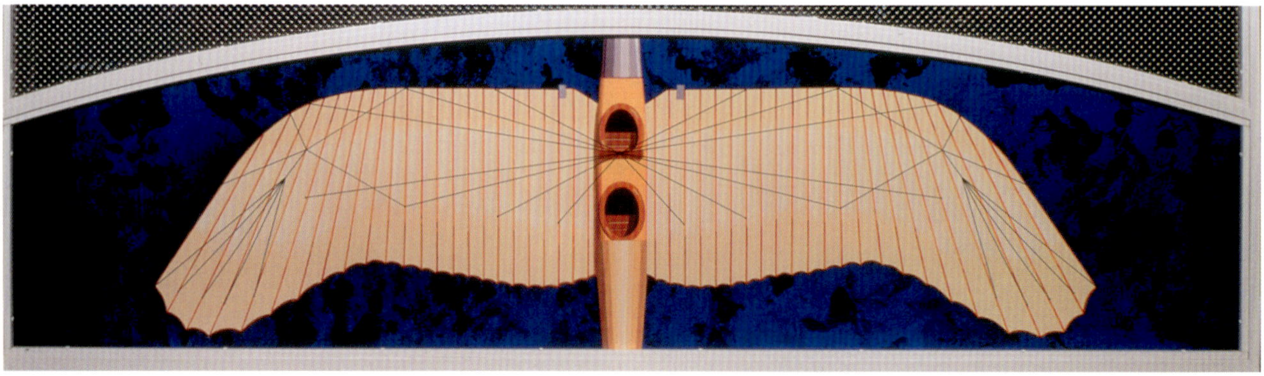

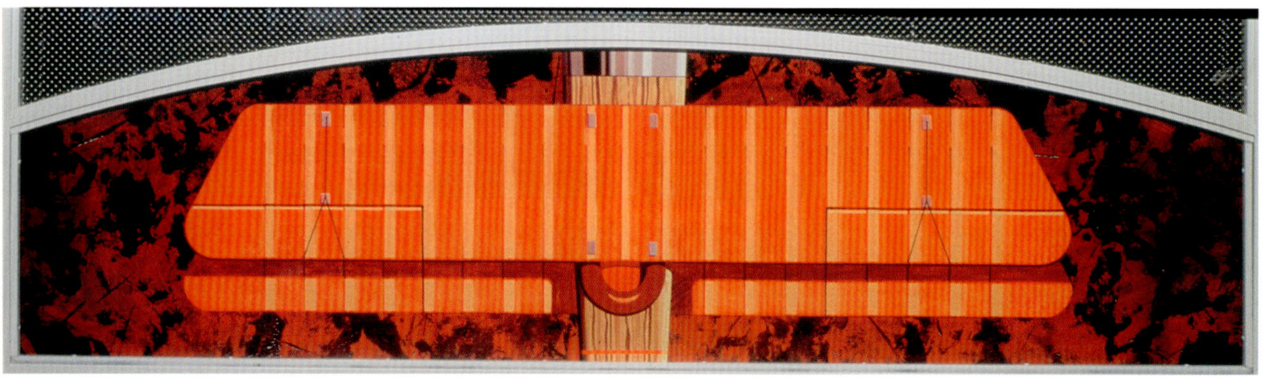

ABOVE Balustrade panels with *Wings* by Robert Cottingham.
OPPOSITE TOP *Untitled* by Wayne Edson. BOTTOM *Untitled* by Robert Reed.

36
N840AY

American

REPERTOR

South Coast Repertory
2002
Costa Mesa, California, US

This renovation and expansion added a new performance space to the home of the famous Orange County theater company, while giving the existing building a bright and welcoming new foyer and façade.

The new front façade is a curving expanse of glass which creates inviting entrances for the original 500-seat Segerstrom Stage and the new 320-seat Julianne Argyros Stage.

The South Coast Repertory theater is a key component of an arts campus around Town Center Drive. The campus unifies a group of performing arts centers—which includes the Renée and Henry Segerstrom Concert Hall, Samueli Theater, and other venues of the Orange County Performing Arts Center—around a plaza. The master plan for the arts district included the eventual construction of a major art museum.

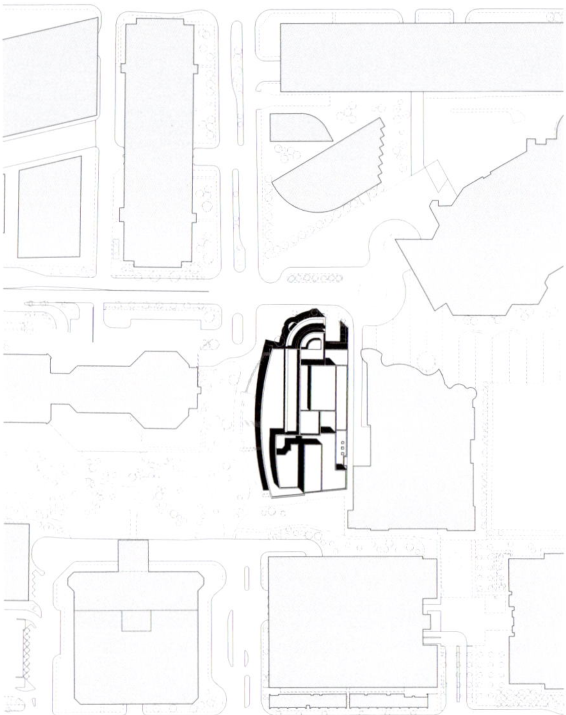

Ground-floor plan

1 Lobby terrace
2 Lobby
3 Box office
4 Concessions
5 Courtyard theater
6 Stage
7 Rehearsal room
8 Thrust Theater
9 Scene dock
10 Dressing rooms
11 Offices
12 Loading bay

0 25 50 ft

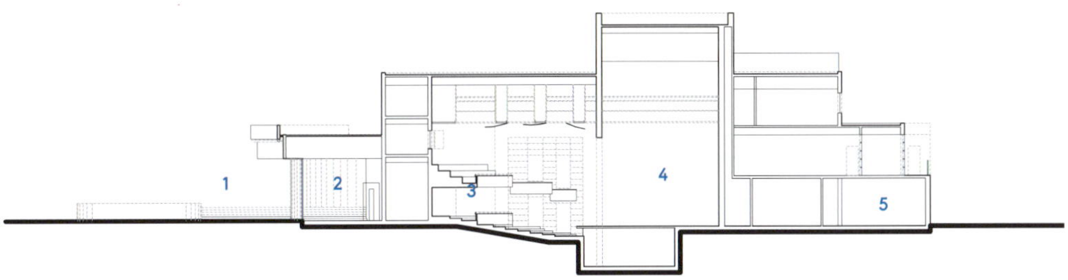

Section looking north

1 Lobby terrace
2 Lobby
3 Courtyard Theater
4 Stage
5 Scene dock

0 20 40 ft

TOP Gently curving and terraced lobby along west façade of building.

JPMorgan Chase Building
2002
San Francisco, California, US

Located in San Francisco's Financial District, 560 Mission Street is the West Coast headquarters of JPMorgan Chase.
The nearby Hallidie Building, the first glass curtain wall building in the western US, inspired Fred Clarke and me. The tower rises in a series of setbacks, responding to its dense urban surroundings. The building is clad in glass and aluminum painted dark green. The tapestry of lines becomes sparser as the tower rises, but the texture is restored in the final setback, culminating in a dense crown. The completed tower is urbane and very elegant.

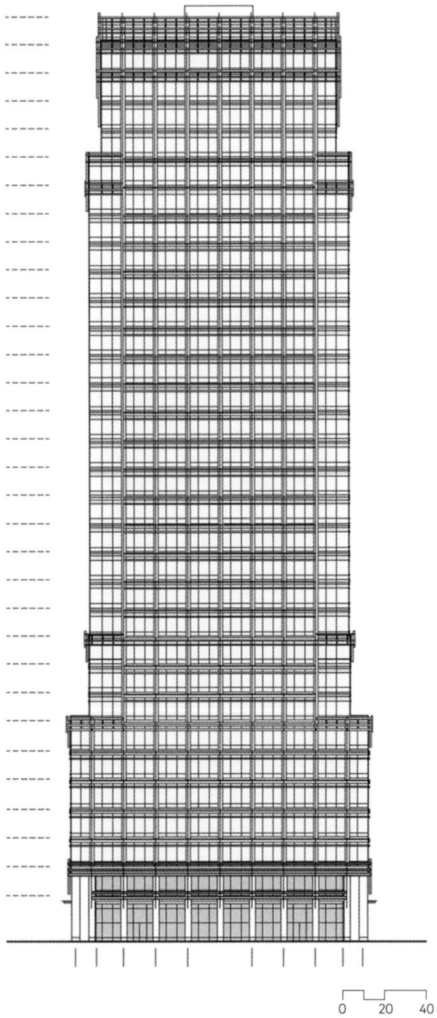

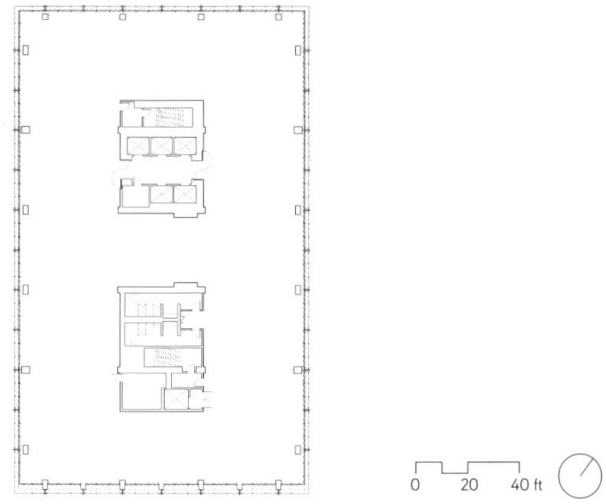

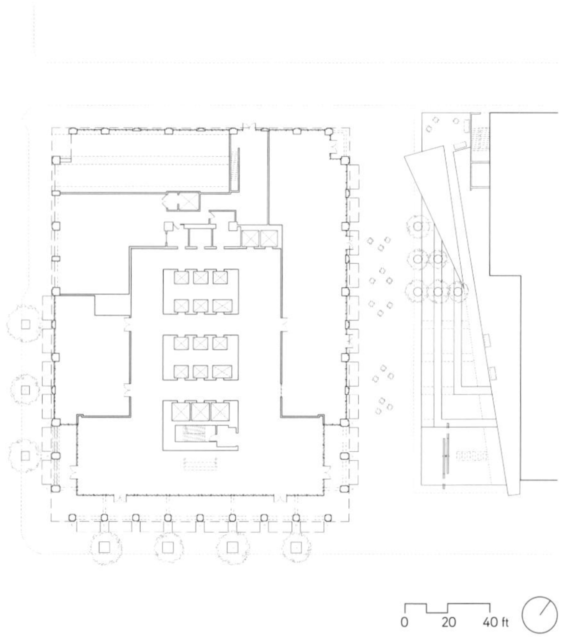

The exterior is a beautiful, very dark green, playing off the Hallidie Building landmark nearby, not copying it, but influenced by it.

JPMorgan

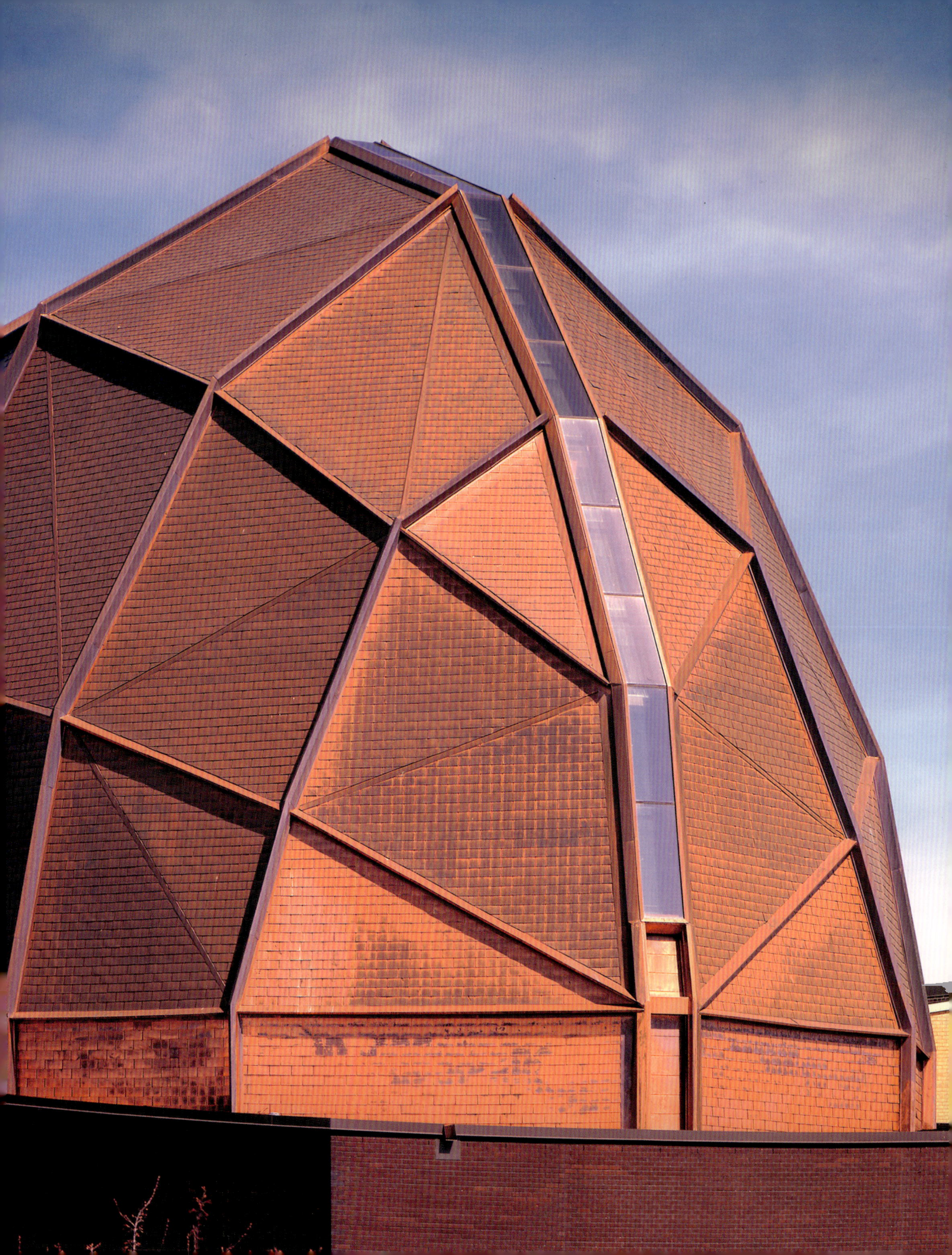

Weber Music Hall
2002
Duluth, Minnesota, US

Weber Music Hall fronts the entrance to the University of Minnesota Duluth, facing Lake Superior, as well as the performing arts courtyard, Ordean Court. The building contains a 325-seat performance hall.

A faceted, copper-shingled dome, delineated by a skylight, makes this building a jewel on the campus. Illuminated by night, the skylight calls the community to a performance. During the day, the skylight fills the room with daylight.

The dome and the performance space below house a large acoustic volume which we designed especially for large orchestral performances. The performance space supports an orchestra of up to 70 musicians and a chorus of 60. It is a small hall but its acoustics are excellent—as good as those of any large concert hall.

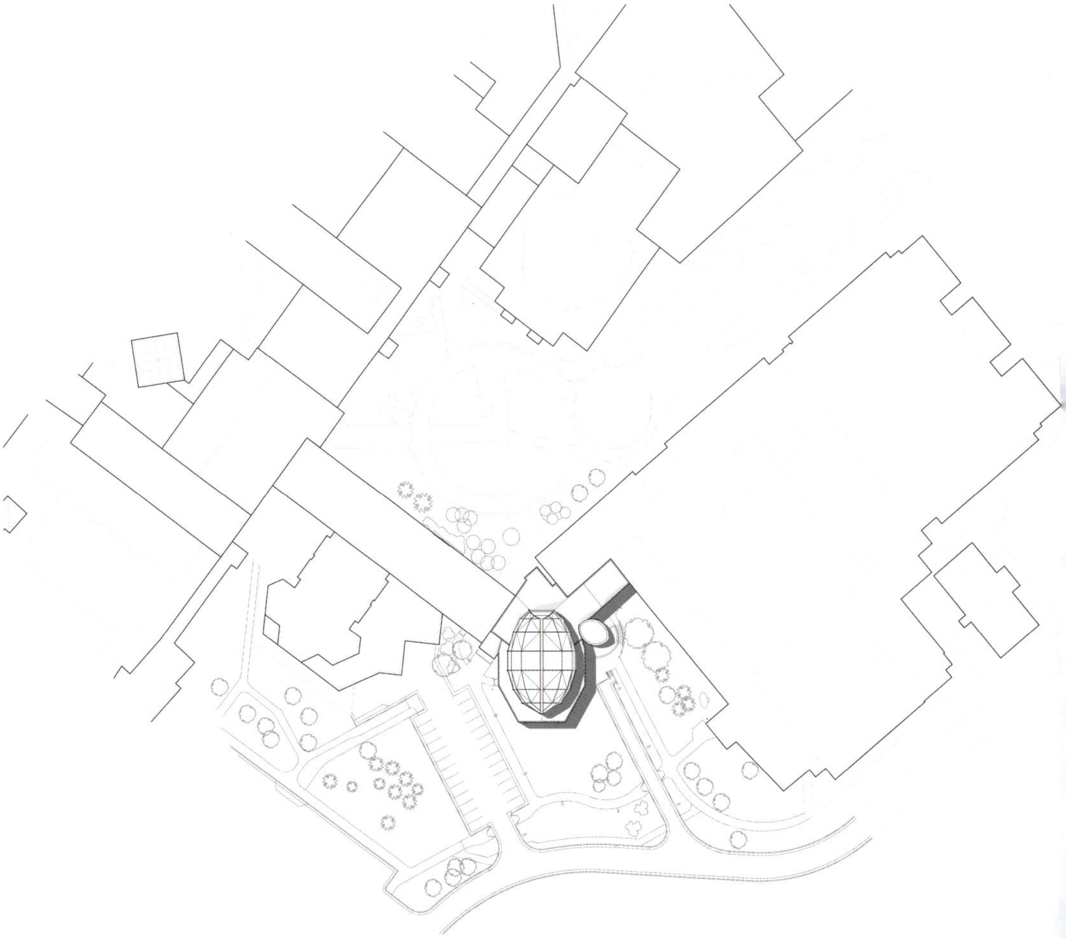

The dome is the reverberation volume, and it is clad in copper—now a very dark brown copper, but it will turn bright green eventually.

WEBER MUSIC

ABOVE Stairway offers an out-of-the-way place for respite.
OPPOSITE Performance space with domed roof.

Schuster Performing Arts Center
2003 Dayton, Ohio, US

The Schuster Performing Arts Center occupies an entire block at the very heart of Dayton. The complex, located opposite the Victoria Theatre and the Loft Theatre, is the centerpiece of Dayton's arts district.

The Schuster Center was a really engaging project for us: first, because we enjoy the very public and artistic nature of working on a performing arts center, and second, because this project was meant to give life to downtown Dayton and to fulfill an important social purpose. The nature of this project led us to conceive a lobby that would be lively much of the time, and function as a great public room: a place for people to gather at all times of the day. This has become the Kettering Wintergarden, a magical place, open to the city. We installed two groupings of palm trees in this windowed room. They inhabit the place and makes us feel like we have company, even when we are alone there.

The heart of the project is Mead Hall, a unique and marvelous room. We were able to design it as a vertical space—a rare or non-existent opportunity in recently executed theaters. The ceiling soars upwards in elliptical rings organized as telescoping cones that direct the eye to its apex, where we see the image of the heavens as they were over Dayton the night the Wright Brothers (natives of Dayton) flew an airplane for the very first time. The image has been formed by more than 2,000 fiber-optic points, representing stars in several magnitudes, arranged to recreate the night sky of that groundbreaking flight early on December 17, 1903.

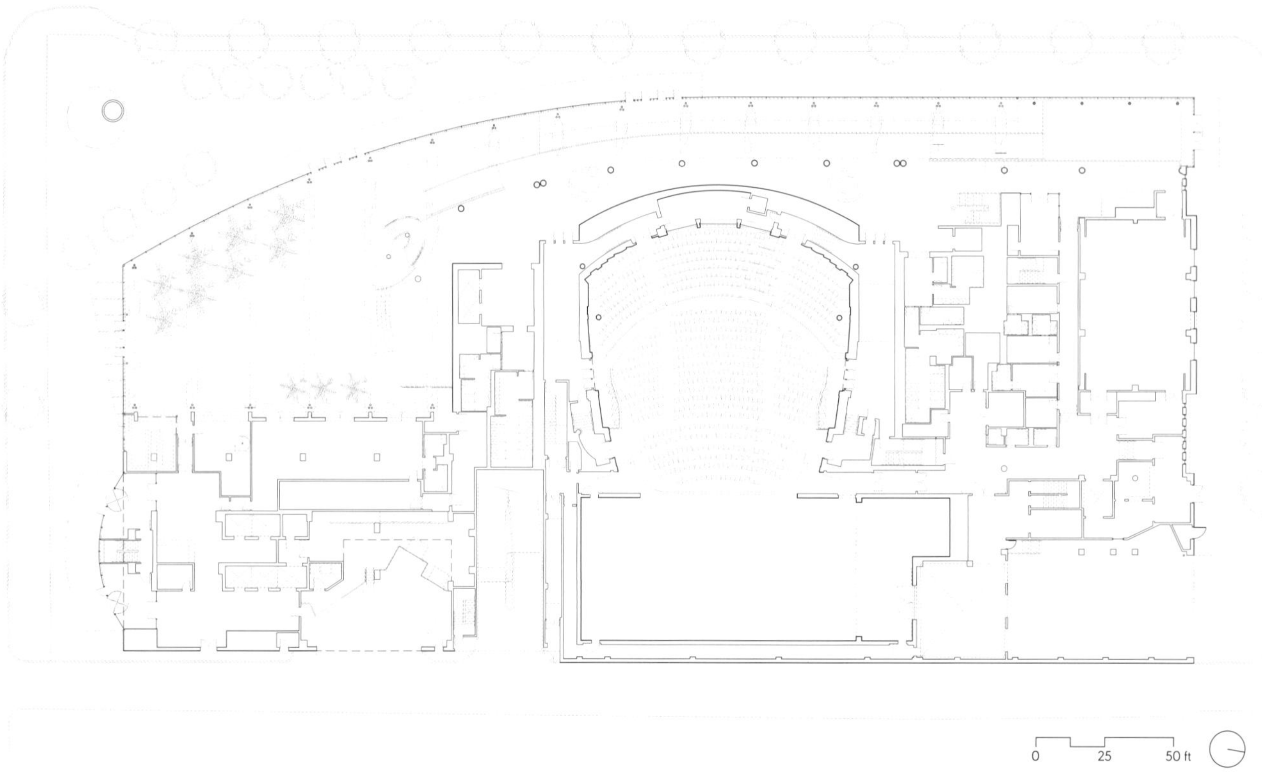
0
25
50 ft

0
20
40 ft

This was an effort to bring people back in to downtown Dayton, to give it life. The lobby of the theater is transformed into a public winter garden, so it can be used all the time, outside of performances.

Abandoibarra Master Plan
2003
Bilbao, Spain

Now a major cultural center best known for the Guggenheim Museum, Abandoibarra is the former industrial center of Bilbao. When the city's port was relocated, there was an opportunity to reconnect Abandoibarra and the River Nervión to the rest of the city. This master plan—won in an international competition by a collaboration of Cesar Pelli and Associates, Aguinaga y Asociados, and Balmori Associates—provides a framework for the district's reinvention as a cultural and business center and tourist destination. The plan weaves the new development into the old city, while increasing the overall amount of green open space. Two-thirds of the master plan area is dedicated to parks and open spaces, making Abandoibarra the most pedestrian-friendly and greenest area of Bilbao.

The large, 6-meter (20-foot) drop from the street to the river was corrected by creating a smooth, sloping path that comfortably accommodates pedestrians.

The plan includes buildings with a variety of functions. New buildings were required to match the height of the buildings on the Ensanche, the heart of Bilbao. Almost all buildings in the Abandoibarra master plan have now been built and the development is considered a great success by the City of Bilbao authorities.

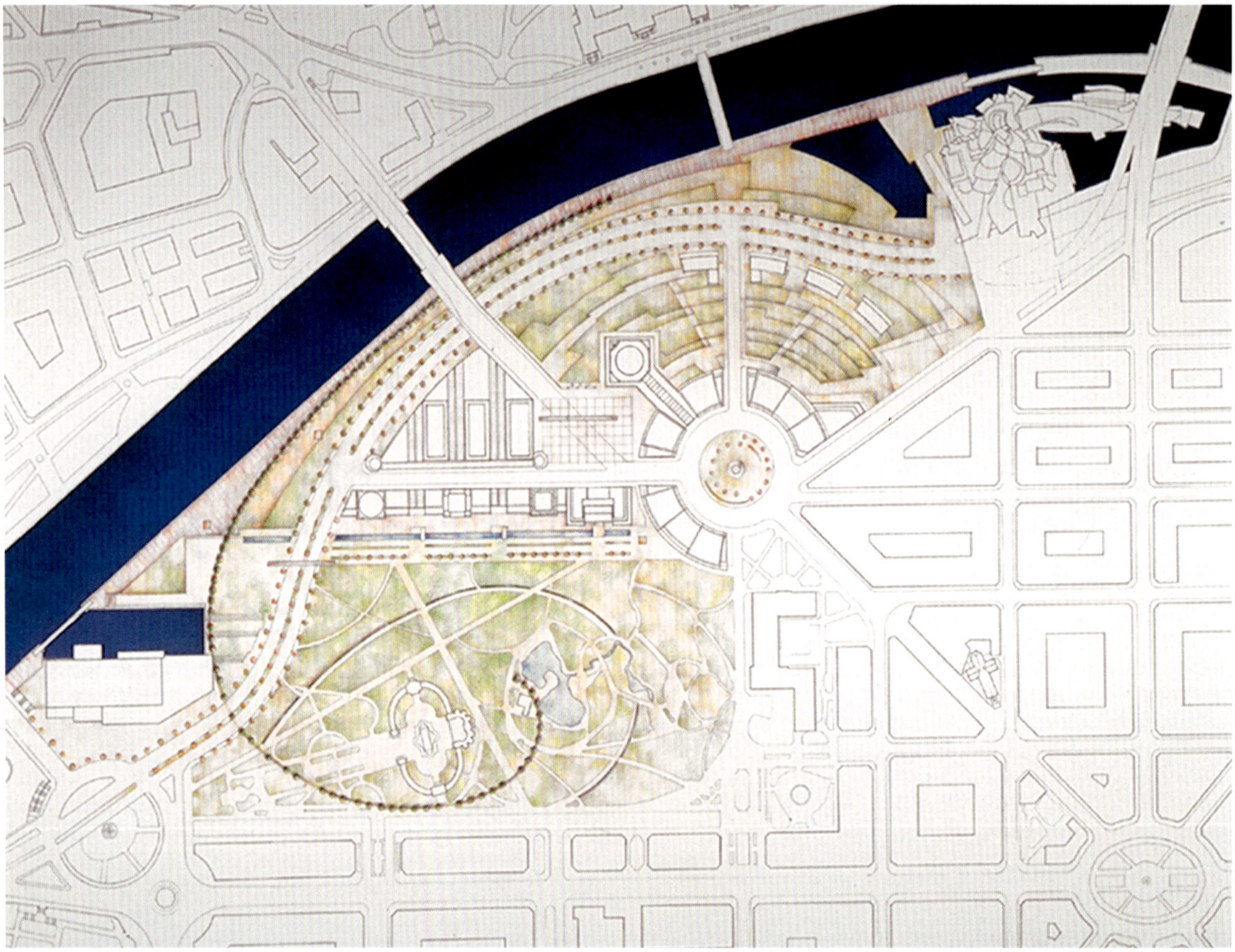

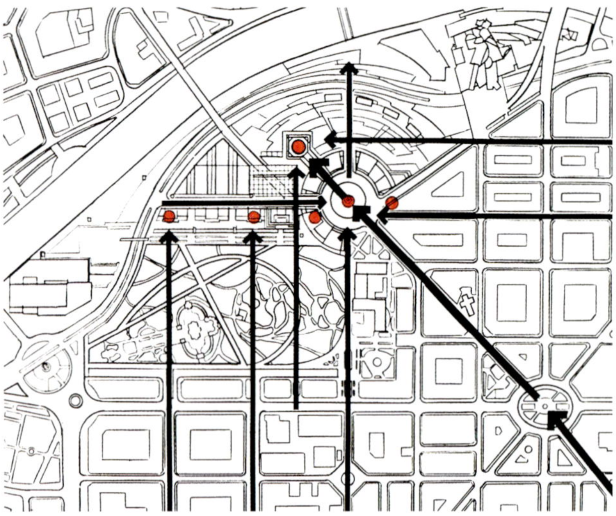

TOP Landscape site plan. BOTTOM LEFT AND RIGHT Plan nodes.

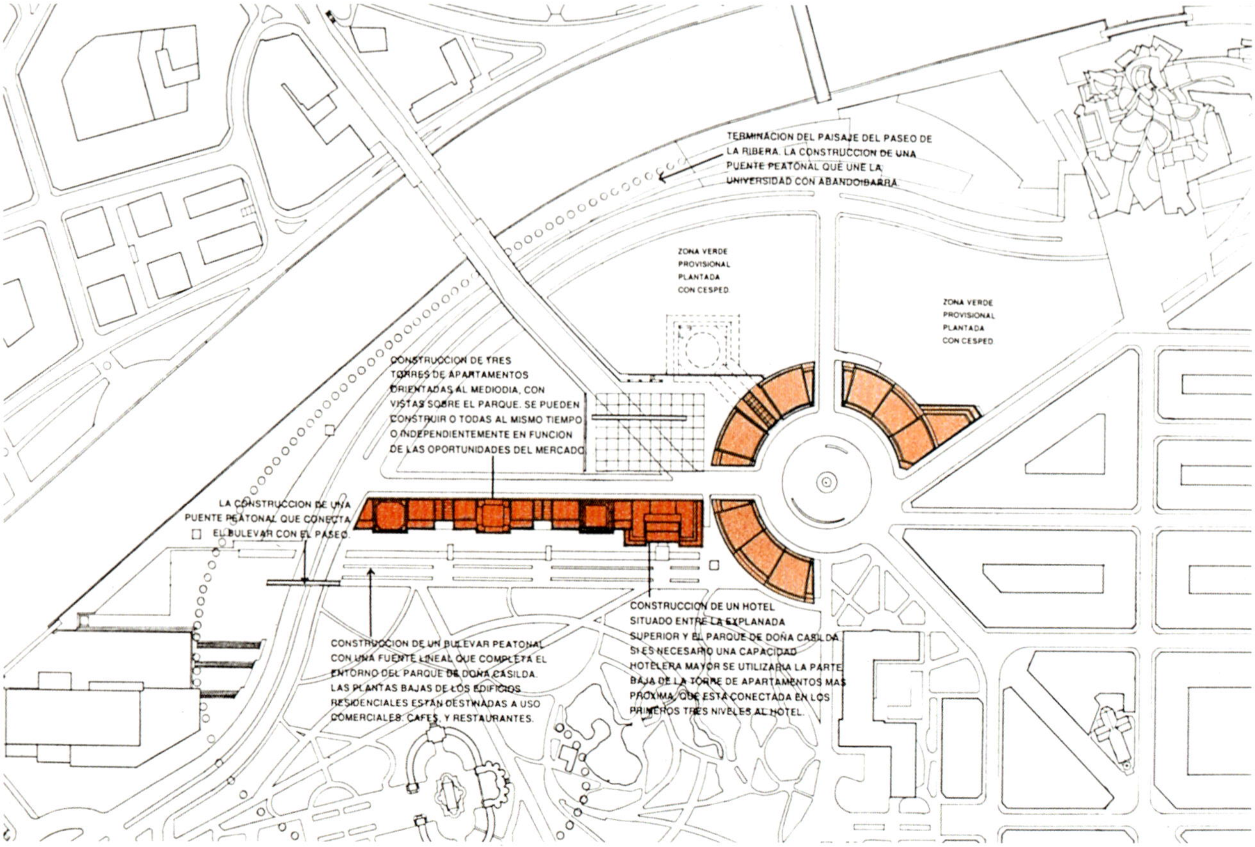
TERMINACION DEL PAISAJE DEL PASEO DE LA RIBERA. LA CONSTRUCCION DE UNA PUENTE PEATONAL QUE UNE LA UNIVERSIDAD CON ABANDOIBARRA.
ZONA VERDE PROVISIONAL PLANTADA CON CESPED.
ZONA VERDE PROVISIONAL PLANTADA CON CESPED.
CONSTRUCCION DE TRES TORRES DE APARTAMENTOS ORIENTADAS AL MEDIODIA, CON VISTAS SOBRE EL PARQUE. SE PUEDEN CONSTRUIR O TODAS AL MISMO TIEMPO O INDEPENDIENTEMENTE EN FUNCION DE LAS OPORTUNIDADES DEL MERCADO.
LA CONSTRUCCION DE UNA PUENTE PEATONAL QUE CONECTA EL BULEVAR CON EL PASEO.
CONSTRUCCION DE UN HOTEL SITUADO ENTRE LA EXPLANADA SUPERIOR Y EL PARQUE DE DOÑA CASILDA. SI ES NECESARIO UNA CAPACIDAD HOTELERA MAYOR SE UTILIZARIA LA PARTE BAJA DE LA TORRE DE APARTAMENTOS MAS PROXIMA, QUE ESTA CONECTADA EN LOS PRIMEROS TRES NIVELES AL HOTEL.
CONSTRUCCION DE UN BULEVAR PEATONAL CON UNA FUENTE LINEAL QUE COMPLETA EL ENTORNO DEL PARQUE DE DOÑA CASILDA. LAS PLANTAS BAJAS DE LOS EDIFICIOS RESIDENCIALES ESTAN DESTINADAS A USO COMERCIALES, CAFES, Y RESTAURANTES.

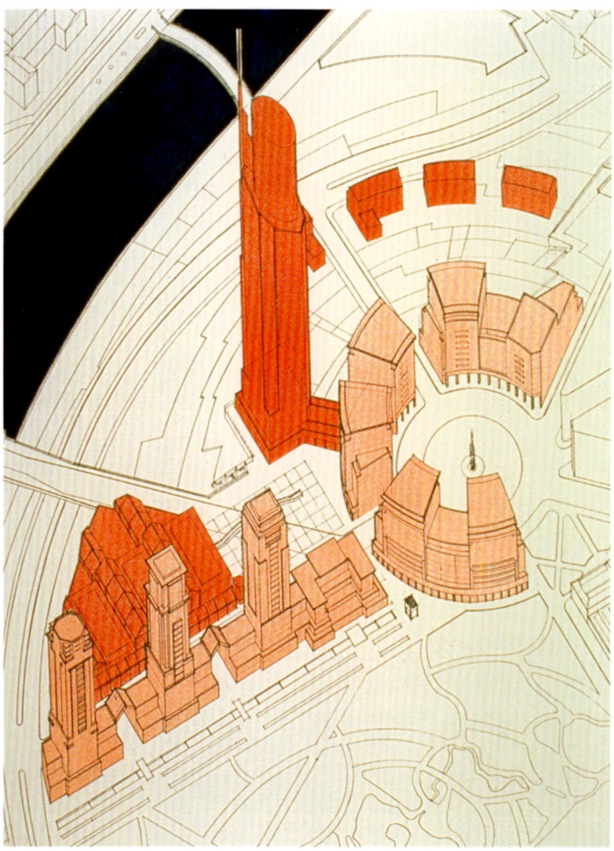

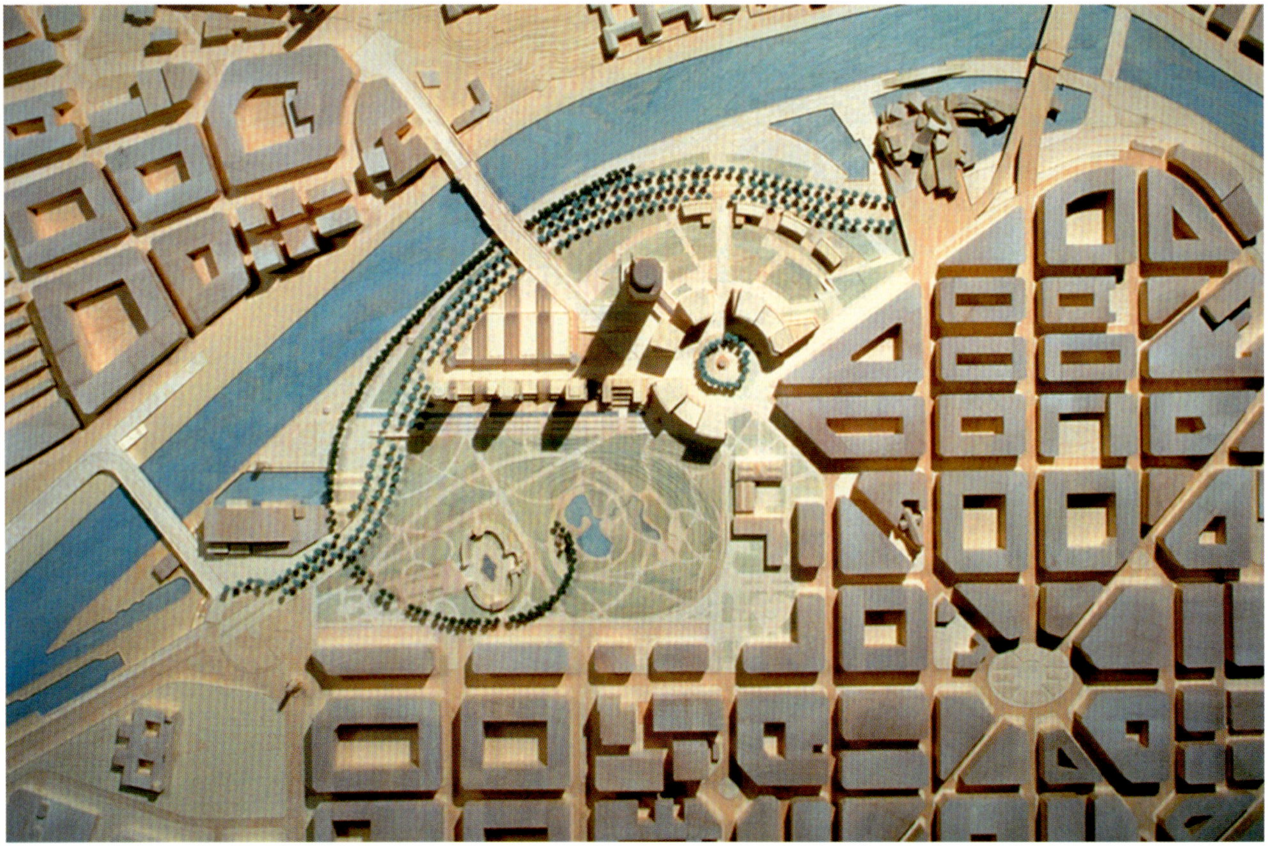

We did the master plan as an extension of the city of Bilbao, with a promenade along the River Nervión that is used extensively. This allows people to reach the river in style, with lots of green space, and a gracious approach to Gehry's Guggenheim.

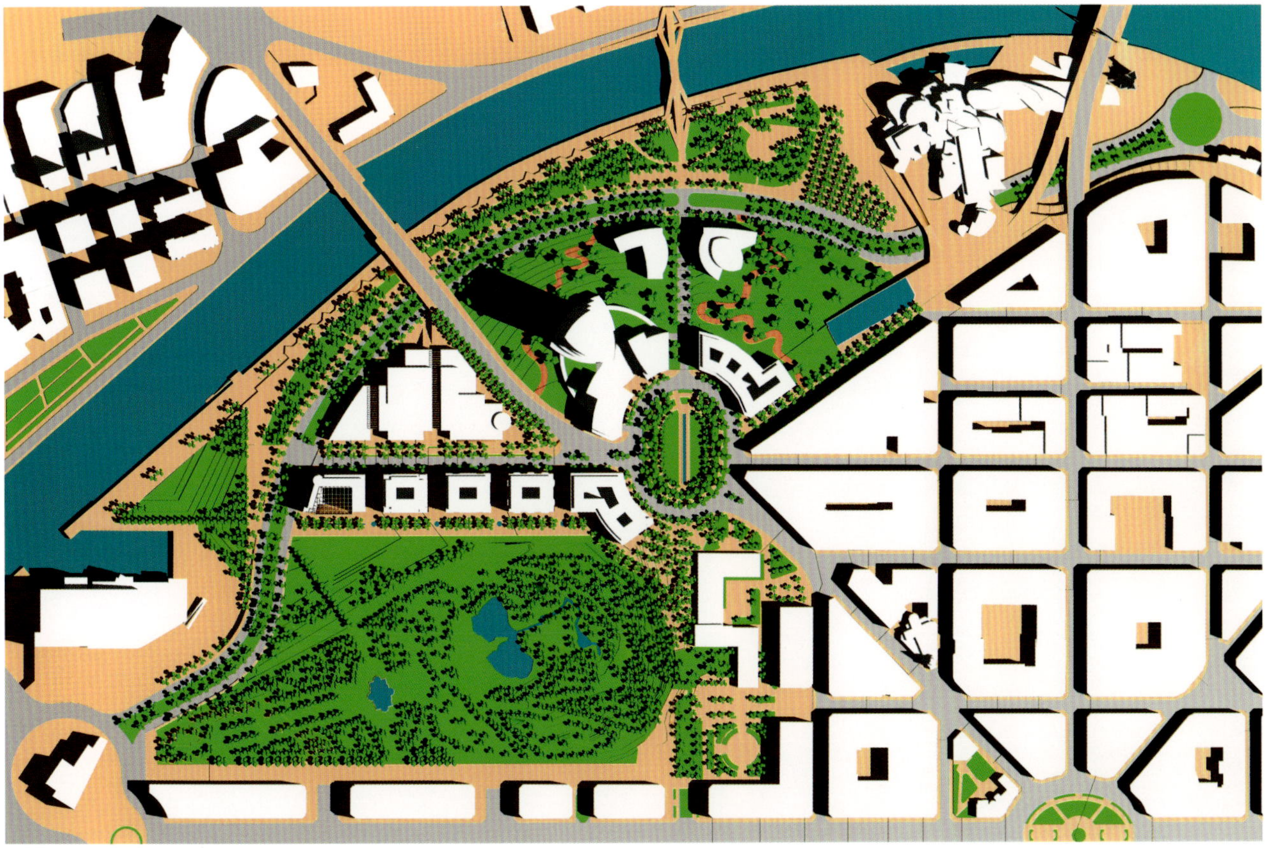

Plan showing evolution of central space and its definition by surrounding building mass with Gehry's Guggenheim Museum at far right in plan.

IBERDROLA

Torre Iberdrola

2011

Bilbao, Spain

Torre Iberdrola is the first tower in Europe to achieve LEED Platinum certification, the US Green Building Council's highest rating in sustainable design. The elegant 41-story glass tower is the headquarters of Iberdrola, an international energy company. It is the terminus of the diagonal Elkano Avenue and is the focal point of Bilbao's Abandoibarra neighborhood. The tower anchors a new public square, the Plaza Euskadi.

Torre Iberdrola has a highly efficient double-wall glass façade. Cool interior air circulates through the cavity between the walls, drawing heat up and into the ceiling plenum, allowing the building to recapture heat from its exposed areas and deliver it to where the demand is greatest.

I conceived Torre Iberdrola as the centerpiece of Abandoibarra. It is the tallest building in Bilbao and the focal point of the view from Plaza Eliptica, the traditional center point of the city. It is an elegant, simple form, a curved triangle that tapers to the sky. The façade is made from clear, non-iron glass and is highly transparent.

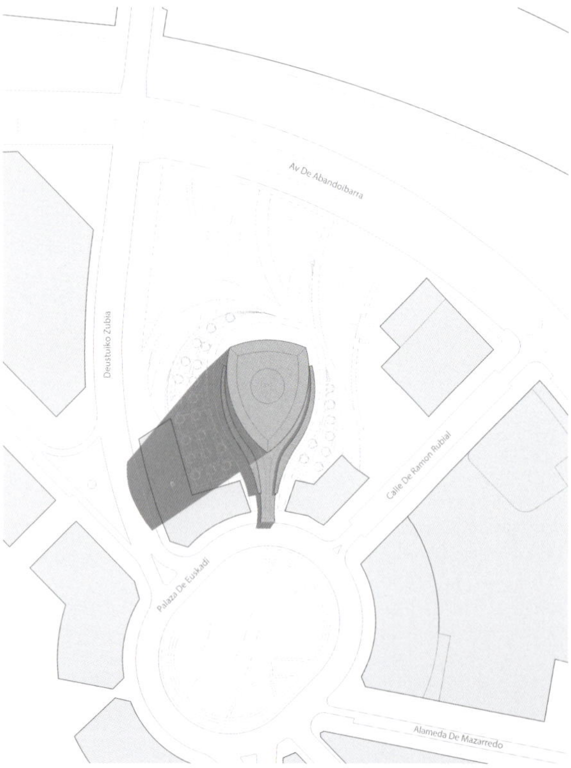
Av De Abandoibarra
Deustuko Zubia
Calle De Ramon Rubial
Palaza De Euskadi
Alameda De Mazarredo

IBERDROLA

IBERDROLA

The tower's siting responds to bridges and green space along the river promenade.

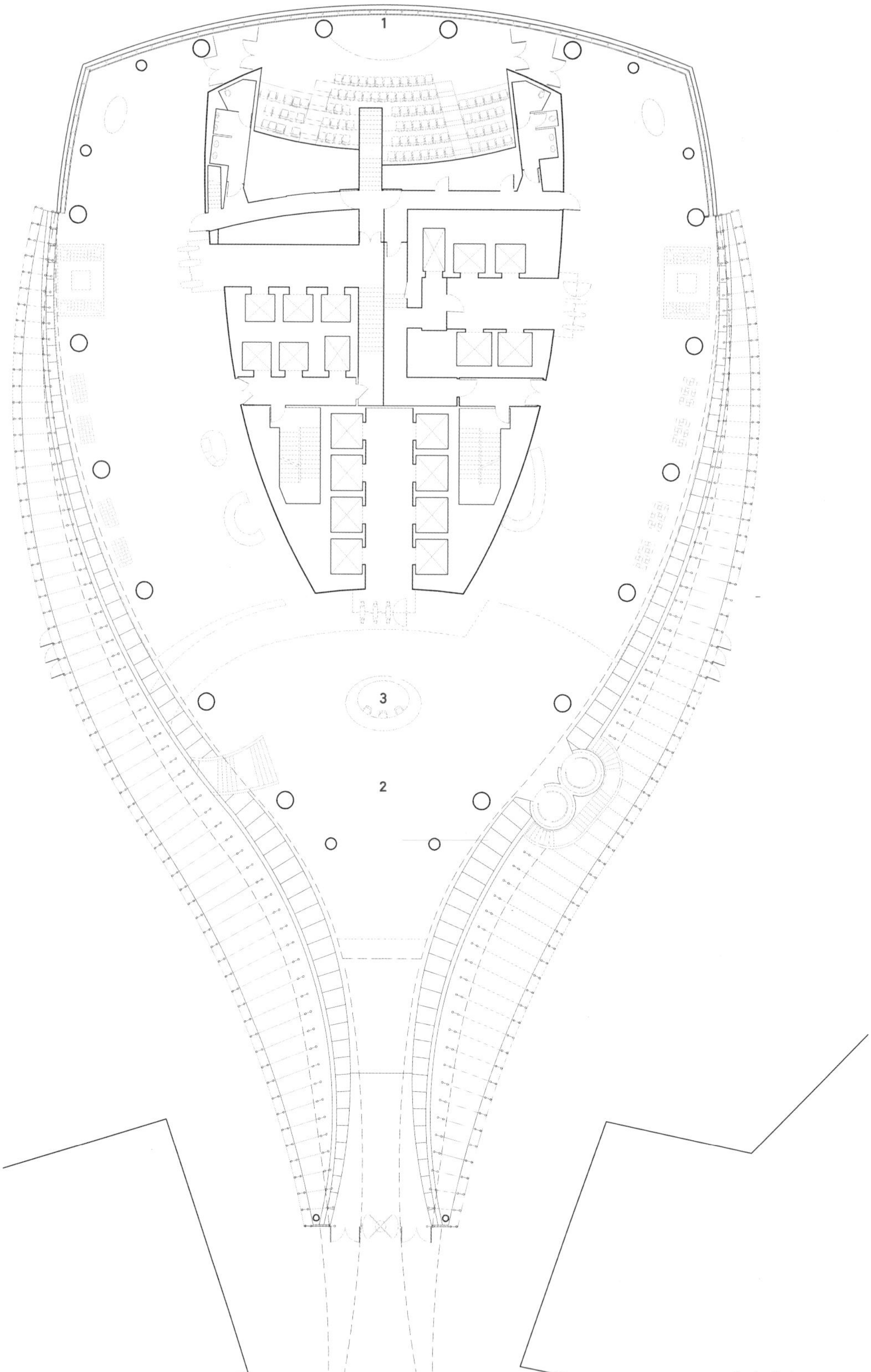

1 Auditorium
2 Lobby
3 Reception desk

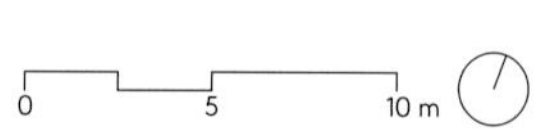

C25

International Finance Centre

2004

Hong Kong, China

The International Finance Centre of Hong Kong occupies a beautiful urban site, adjacent to the narrowest crossing of Victoria Harbour, with the Central District and Victoria Peak as a backdrop. Part of the Hong Kong Central Station Development, the complex includes the 88-story Two International Finance Centre, the 40-story One International Finance Centre, and a four-story retail podium with public roof garden.

Two International Finance Centre is the tallest building on Hong Kong Island, its 412-meter (1,352-foot) height accentuated by its waterfront site. The entire form is visible as it stands apart from the cluster of other skyscrapers.

We designed this tower as a clear and memorable presence, a great obelisk on the scale of the city. With its carefully proportioned setbacks, its centric form tapers as it rises, expressing a vertical ascending movement.

The International Finance Centre captures the spirit of Hong Kong—confident, daring, and in harmony with the natural beauty of its setting.

CHAN CHE KEE
JEWELLERY
陳志記
MAN YEE
Belgian Ban
PAWN SHOP

ance centre

SINOPEC

It is very appropriate for Hong Kong; it is part of the light of the city. It reflects the dynamism of this incredible metropolis.

National Museum of Art
2004
Osaka, Japan

The National Museum of Art of Japan posed an unusual design challenge: we were required to create an iconic image for a museum in which only the entrance lobby was permitted to be built above ground. Fred Clarke (with whom I founded the firm) and I responded to this requirement by creating an entrance that is an enormous stainless steel and glass sculpture. This web of intertwining stainless steel tubes stands against the sky with greater impact than its size would seem to allow.

The entrance structure is designed to resemble the arching stalks of a bamboo grove, a counterpoint to the massive form of the neighboring science museum.

The museum is distributed on three levels below grade. The floors are spacious and receive natural light. Visitors soon forget that they are underground and become absorbed in the art being exhibited.

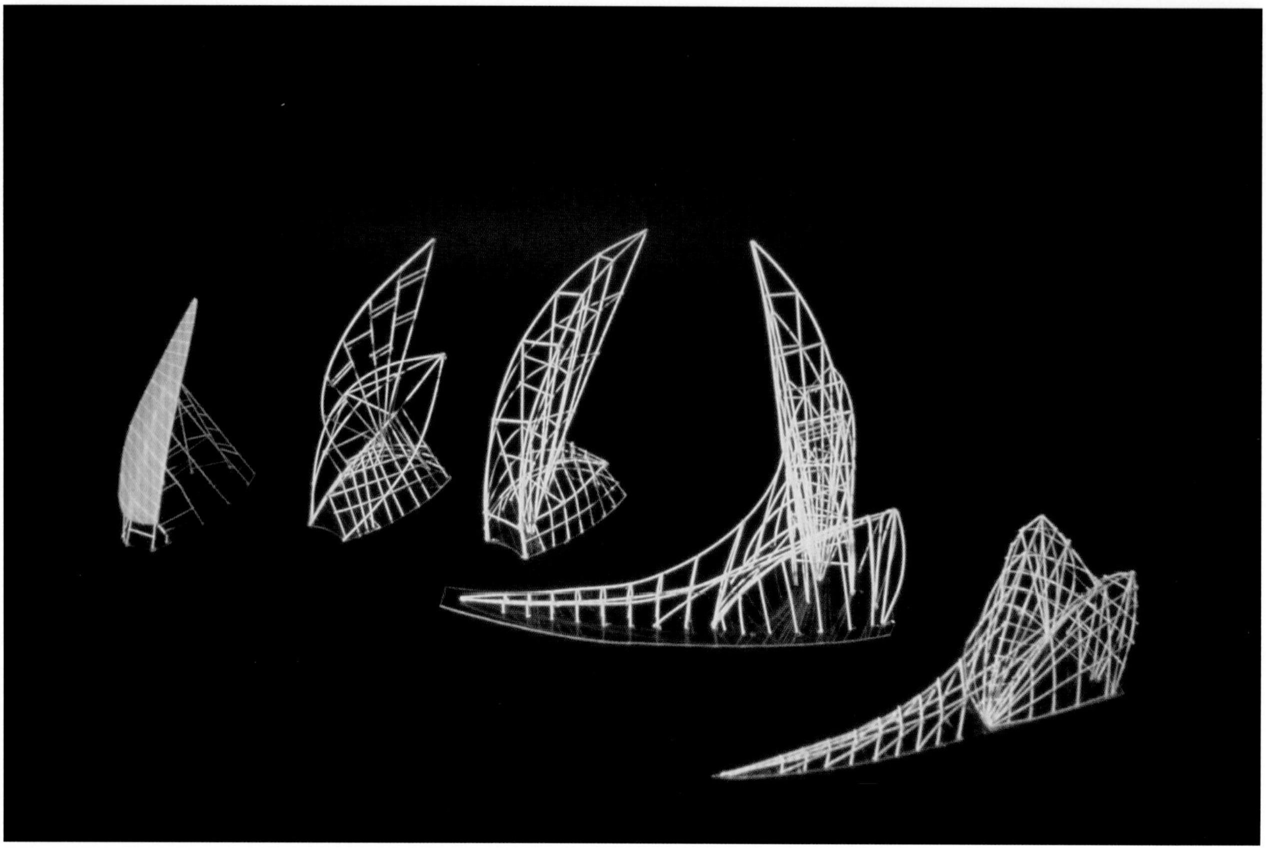

Osaka's sculptural lobby entry was studied in large-scale models, wire diagrams, and impressionistic drawings.

OPPOSITE Entry to the museum lobby is gained through the glass and stainless-steel sculpture at street level. The dramatic stainless-steel columns distinguish the space.

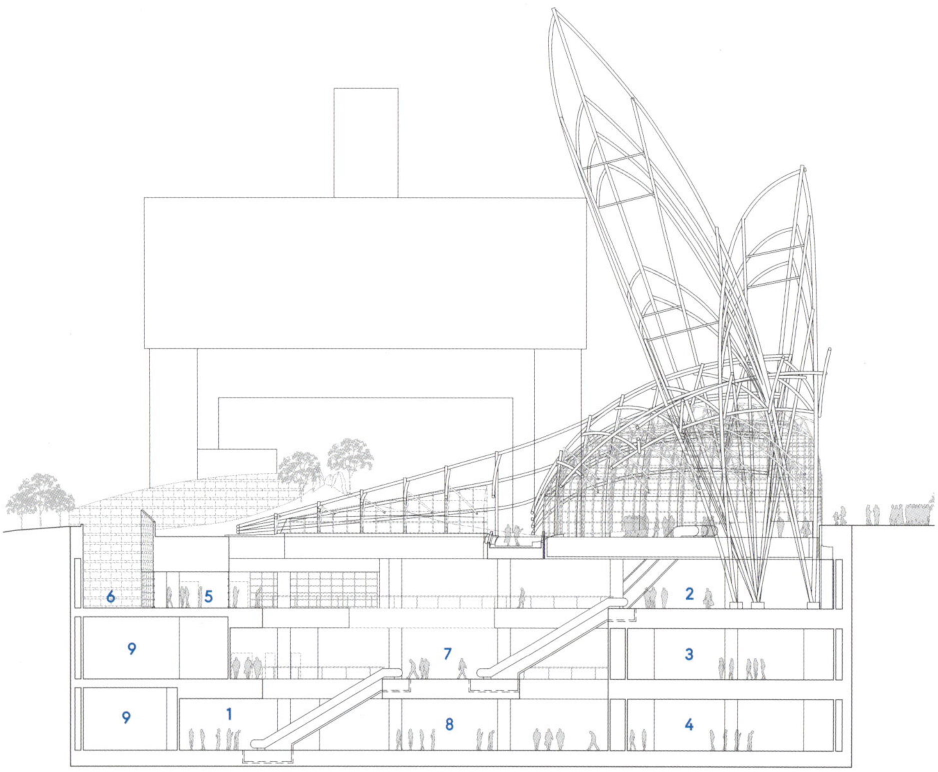

Section

1 Entry lobby
2 Reception floor
3 Temporary Exhibit Gallery 2
4 Permanent Exhibit Gallery 2
5 Restaurant
6 Restaurant Court
7 Temporary Exhibit Gallery 1
8 Permanent Exhibit Gallery 1
9 Mechanical

ABOVE Cascading escalators deliver visitors from street level to exhibit spaces.
OPPOSITE Natural light filters down to the lowest-level galleries.

山文
コウダイ

Cira Centre
2005
Philadelphia, Pennsylvania, US

Cira Centre is a 29-story tower adjacent to Philadelphia's 30th Street Station, along the Schuylkill River. Standing apart from the city's cluster of tall buildings, the tower is visible from a distance on all sides—a singular, sculptural object.

In contrast to the weight and solidity of the train station, the tower is delicate and light. Sheathed in a reflective surface, the crystalline form mirrors the sky, the façade changing according to the time of day and the point of view.

A minimally textured curtain wall reinforces the sense that the tower is a sculpted form. Barely projecting from the façade, the mullion system creates a thin, seemingly two-dimensional grid on the building's exterior.

A grand, light-filled foyer links Cira Centre, the train station, and Amtrak's enclosed parking garage. A suspended mezzanine-level walkway cuts through the foyer and links to a sky bridge over the street and into the train station. The glass curtain wall billows and extends to form a trapezoidal canopy.

In 2006 the Cira Centre won a Project Award from the March of Dimes, and the American Architecture Award from the Chicago Athenaeum.

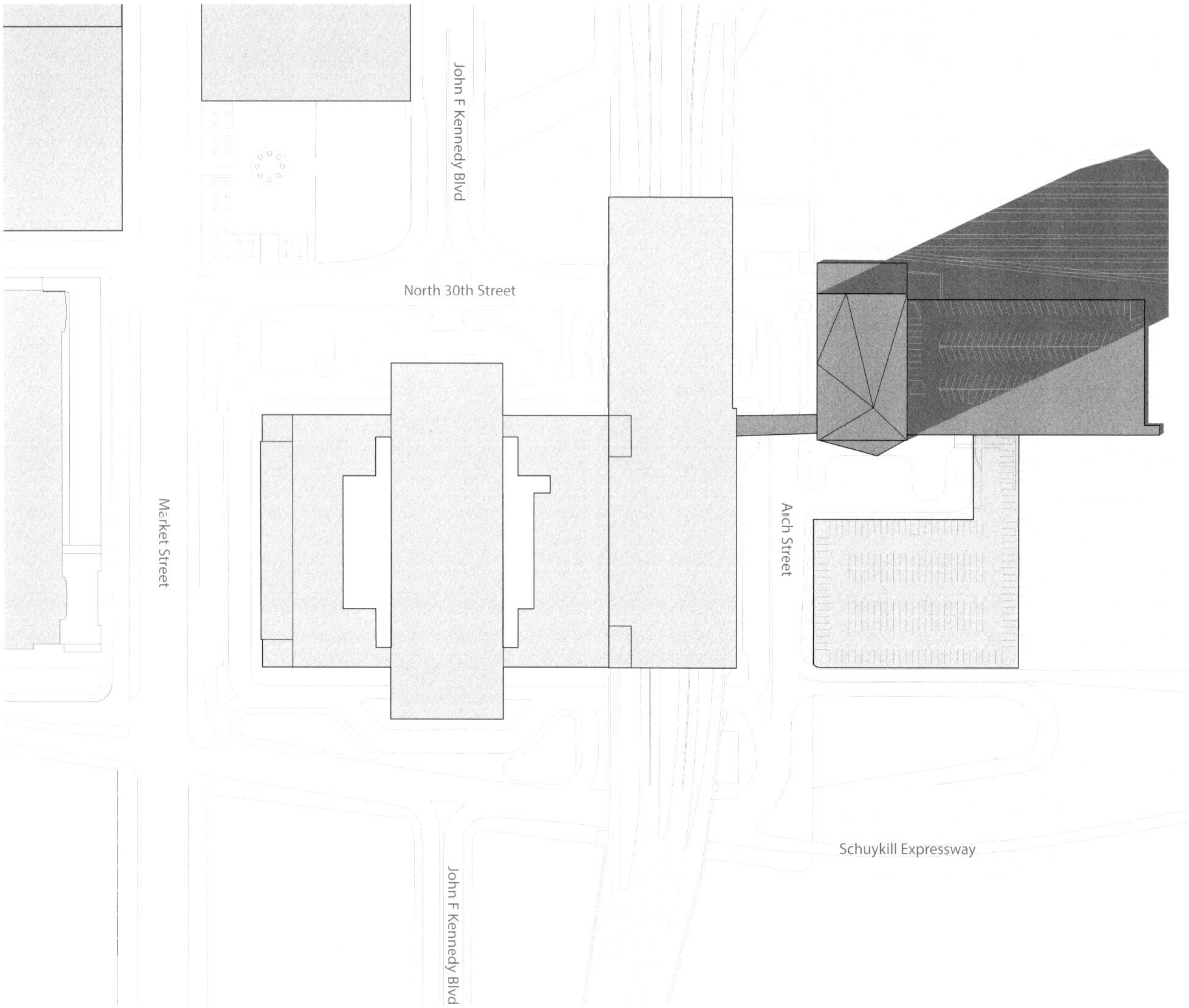
John F Kennedy Blvd
North 30th Street
Market Street
Arch Street
Schuykill Expressway
John F Kennedy Blvd

Abstract crystalline forms are a foil to the train station's classical architecture.

AMTRAK

Entry lobby is flooded with natural light.

Malone Engineering Center

2005

Yale Unversity, New Haven, Connecticut, US

The design of Yale University's Malone Engineering Center balances two very different settings: a city street on one side and a wooded trail on the other. The resulting research building expresses its function while respecting its natural and historic surroundings.

Fronting Prospect Street, one of Yale's main academic thoroughfares, an elegant façade of limestone maintains the rhythm and scale of neighboring buildings. What appears to be a rectangular site from the street is actually a narrow triangle formed where a canal once cut across the block. On the diagonal of the triangle, facing what is now the Farmington Canal Greenway, a gently curving glass wall spans the full length of the building.

The glass wall encloses the building's major circulation corridor and is cantilevered from the main structure to create an open, column-free space. Each research suite is perpendicular to the common corridor, with laboratories at the core of the building and offices adjacent to the hallway. Windows on both sides of the offices bring natural light into the labs. This arrangement encourages interaction among research teams.

In addition to wet and dry labs for biomedical engineering and physical sciences, the Malone Center includes the Frederick P. Rose Teaching Laboratory, seminar rooms, and offices.

The first building at Yale to achieve LEED Gold rating, the Malone Center is designed with key sustainable design strategies. The combination of a high-performance exterior envelope with the use of lighting controls, daylighting, and a highly reflective white roof reduce the demand for cooling and the use of energy. By reusing lab wastewater for toilet flushing, and low-flow faucets, the building consumes 85 percent less potable water than comparable buildings.

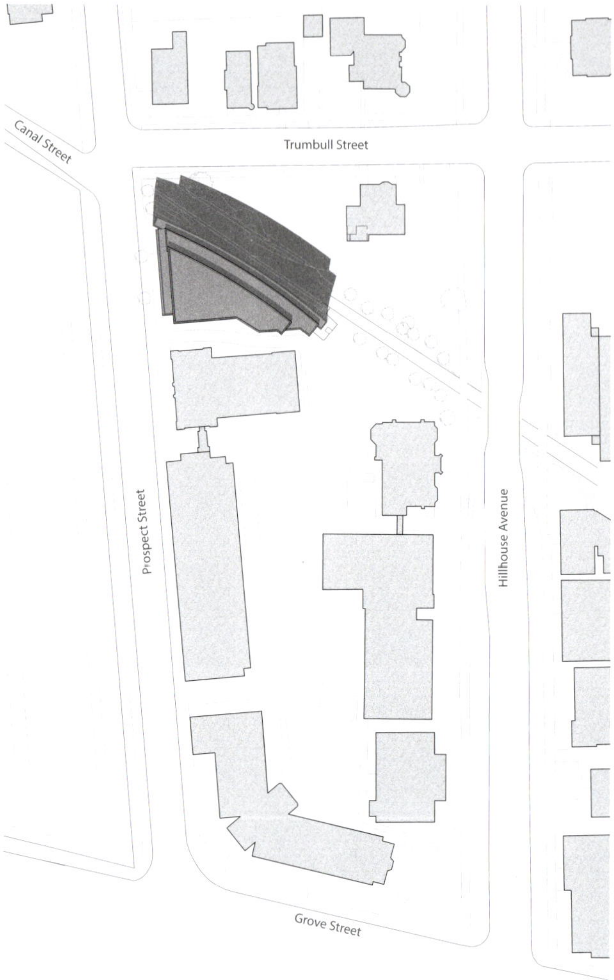

1 Lab
2 Office
3 Support

0 15 30 ft

It is a triangular-shaped lot, and I curved the building to respond to the Farmington Canal Trail and give it life.

Robert Venturi designed a Yale lab building with a curved façade years earlier, and our building recalls that.

Natural light and views penetrate into lab spaces via glazed hallways and lab offices.

JAMA
Science

My Father, My Mentor

by Rafael Pelli

My father, Cesar Pelli, made the entry into architecture easier for me, but he never pushed it or directed my path. Cesar as an employer and mentor feels very natural, and entirely consistent with how I recall my childhood in Los Angeles. He and my mother, Diana Balmori, loved to make things, and so my brother Denis and I grew up in a house full of drawings and paintings.

Papier-mâché masks and creations for Halloween, embroidery, and other artistic pursuits were scattered throughout every room. Soon after a somewhat misguided foray in college into ancient history, I realized I missed this day-to-day creative environment and wanted a career that was visual and about making things.

In the studio, my father's relationship with all the designers is the same. He values good, clear thinking (his highest praise), and creative ideas from anyone. Although he will challenge us if our design ideas follow a consistent conceptual approach, he truly thrives by exploring the broadest range of creative expression. A favorite project was our collaboration on the design for a new business school at the University of Illinois in Champaign-Urbana, the College of Business, in 2001. I had recently founded our New York office, where I would direct the UIUC effort, but Cesar came with me to many design meetings on the campus, trips that evoked small memories and anecdotes about my parents' beginnings that made the family history vivid in a way that it had never been before.

A little background: my father and mother came to the US in 1952 on a one-year scholarship to the university from a small city in northern Argentina, Tucumán. Every expectation had been for them to return, but one year led to two at the university, and then a connection by the Dean led to an interview and temporary job, which eventually led to a life and career in the US. (My father still only buys American-made automobiles.)

That first year was an incredible adventure for my parents, who had arrived in this foreign country at a time when even a phone call home was impossible without a dime or knowing a single other person. Growing up, I had not only heard this story many times, but also the significant importance of the University's Student Union the first year there—a great room and a place where they could spend hours away from their Quonset hut temporary housing, looking at the beauty and bustle of the main quad of the campus. Nothing like this existed in the Universidad Nacional de Tucumán where they had studied in Argentina.

Not surprisingly, the Student Union was the first place Cesar wanted to see when we arrived at UIUC together (I imagine they had long ago torn down the Quonset huts). I then understood the genesis of the persistent idea throughout my father's career of the importance of public spaces within private projects, such as the Winter Garden in New York. I saw, too, how deeply that experience had affected and informed his thinking about buildings. Though the particulars were different and specific to the project, our design for the new College of Business would also take shape around a great public room facing a quad, though in this case more of a great reading room than a lounge space.

In hindsight, I treasure most the experience of working on that one project with my father. Through our frequent site visits together, it allowed him the chance to relive one of the most formative moments in his life during our long walks through the campus; for me, it offered again the chance to learn directly from his experience and his mentorship.

RENÉE AND HENRY SEGERSTROM CONC

Renée and Henry Segerstrom Concert Hall and Samueli Theater

2006

Costa Mesa, California, US

The design of the Renée and Henry Segerstrom Concert Hall was a pleasure for us. The place, the purpose, and the client all engaged us in an intense and ultimately fruitful effort. The building reflects our enthusiasm. It is a magical music box that comes alive in the sunlight of southern California. The Concert Hall is, I believe, a building that expresses the energy, optimism, and aspirations of the people of Orange County. Together with the Segerstrom Hall of 1986 and the South Coast Repertory, they form a new world-class performing arts center.

The Concert Hall is a composition of creamy sandstone cubic forms outlined by their shadows. Towards the north end of the building where we find the main entrances to the Concert Hall, the forms explode in an undulating wall of clear glass which appears to ripple, shimmer, and dissolve as you walk in front of it. The waves of the glass wall are, for me, recollections of the waves of the Pacific Ocean.

The Concert Hall is like a great musical instrument on which to produce sublime music. We consider it the Stradivarius of classical music venues.

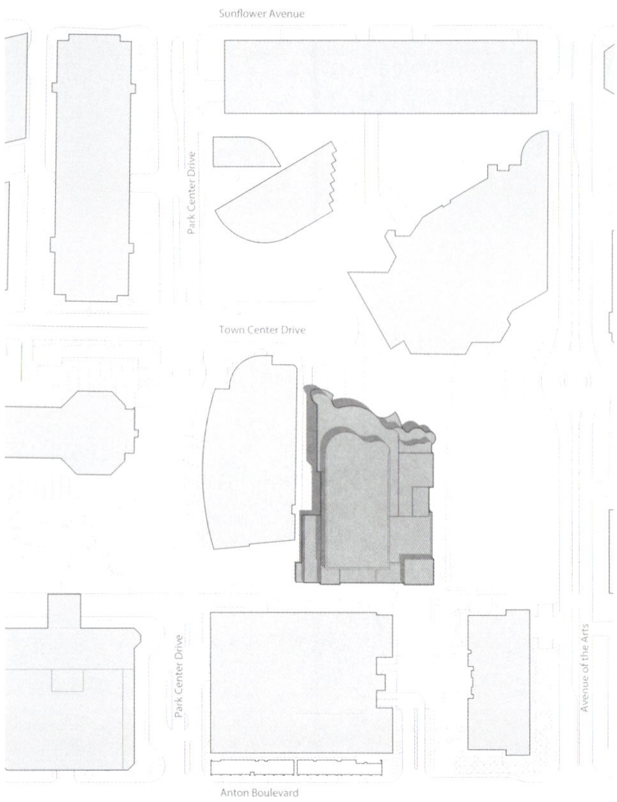

We created a beautiful wall with a single layer of curved glass. The climate is benign, it is very sinuous, and the glass faces north so the sun doesn't hit it.

ENRY SEGERSTROM CONCERT HALL

AND HENRY SEGERS

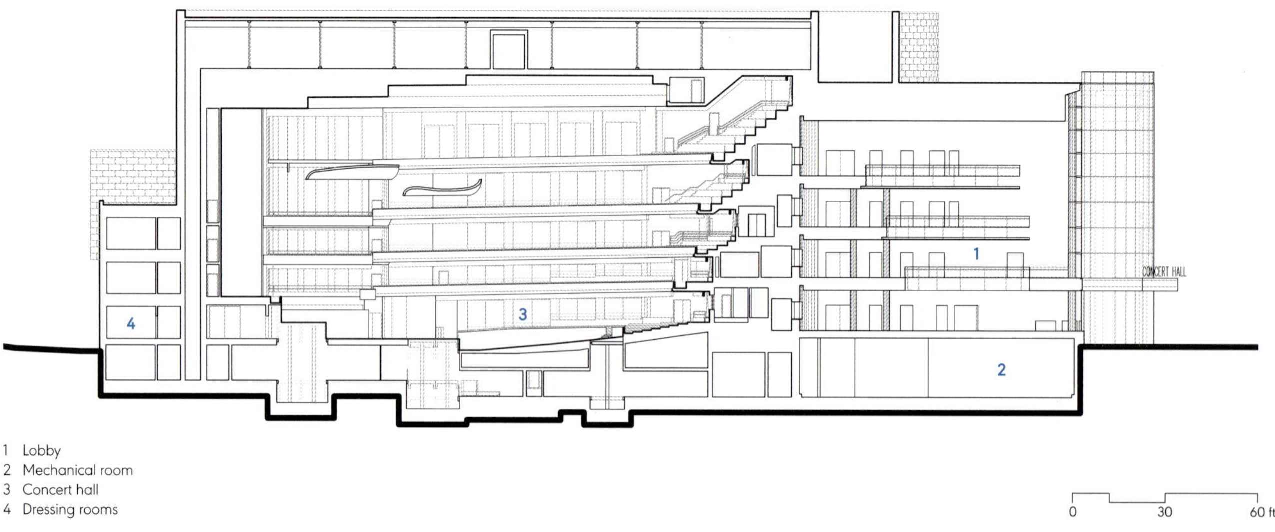

1 Lobby
2 Mechanical room
3 Concert hall
4 Dressing rooms

OPPOSITE TOP Performance space features seating that extends behind the stage. OPPOSITE BOTTOM Section looking west. ABOVE The lobby's curving forms, including the chandelier, echo those in the performance hall.

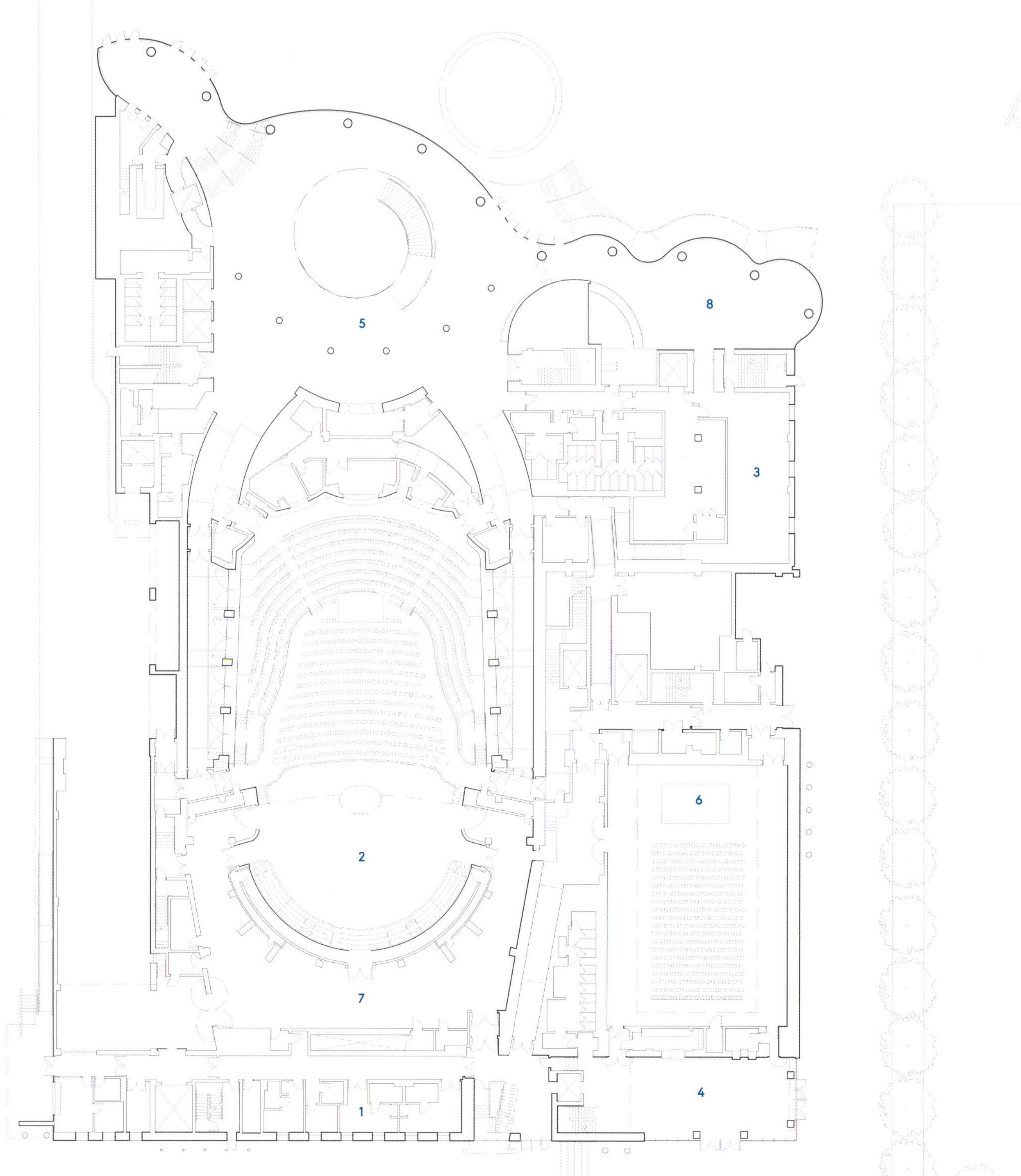

Site plan

1 Artist suites
2 Concert hall
3 Kitchen
4 Lobby–music theater
5 Lobby–orchestra
6 Music theater
7 Platform area
8 Restaurant

Performance space ceiling design (opposite) suggests elements of musical instruments, such as the organ (above).

The layered planer form of the entrance to Samueli Theater is a counterpoint to Segerstrom's curved front façade.

SAMUELI THEATER

Adrienne Arsht Center for the Performing Arts

2006

Miami, Florida, US

We were selected to design Miami-Dade County's Adrienne Arsht Center for the Performing Arts in an international competition. From the beginning, in a five-day-long competition charette in Miami in 1995, the project was very engaging. We had to create two world-class theaters: one for concerts and one for opera and ballet, now called the Knight Concert Hall and the Ziff Opera House, respectively. This goal alone would have made this a very special architectural commission, but we were also strongly attracted by the fact that these two grand theaters were meant to help Miami take a leap forward in its quest of becoming a great world metropolis—the informal capital of the Americas.

The County and the City expected these theaters to generate new development and bring new life to this part of town, which had been lagging behind its neighbors for too long. This goal has been achieved and surpassed. The Concert Hall and the Opera House are on two sides of Biscayne Boulevard, each one occupying a full block. Together they define a magnificent elliptical plaza—the Parker Thomson Plaza of the Arts—with landscaping by Balmori Associates. The plaza straddles Biscayne Boulevard and its form is completed by a pedestrian bridge which connects the two halls on the second level.

The plaza, shaded with trees and surrounded by sheltering colonnades and cascading garden terraces, was conceived as the third public venue in the complex, and is a space for open-air performances. The two theaters have been carefully placed on their sites, the Concert Hall facing north and the Opera House facing south, with the main public entrances opening to each one of the four sides bordering the Adrienne Arsht Center, knitting them tightly in the city fabric.

We were required to preserve the tower of the old Sears Building because it is considered to be the first Art Deco building in Miami. This was a difficult request but we took it to heart and made the tower into a marker and pivot point on the plaza. It is now an essential element in the composition. The two theaters rise like mountains on the flat Miami landscape. The faceted forms appear to swirl and dance as you move around them. The lobbies are great glass windows, opening every balcony level to views, and the two audience chambers are large but feel intimate and welcoming.

The street passing through the site is Route 1, and we crossed it with a plaza for the arts, which is used extensively. It is a truly free, public space. They close the street for performances.

Site plan

1 Key office pavilion
2 Classroom
3 Foyer
4 Green room
5 Lobby
6 Rehearsal room
7 Stage door
8 Theater

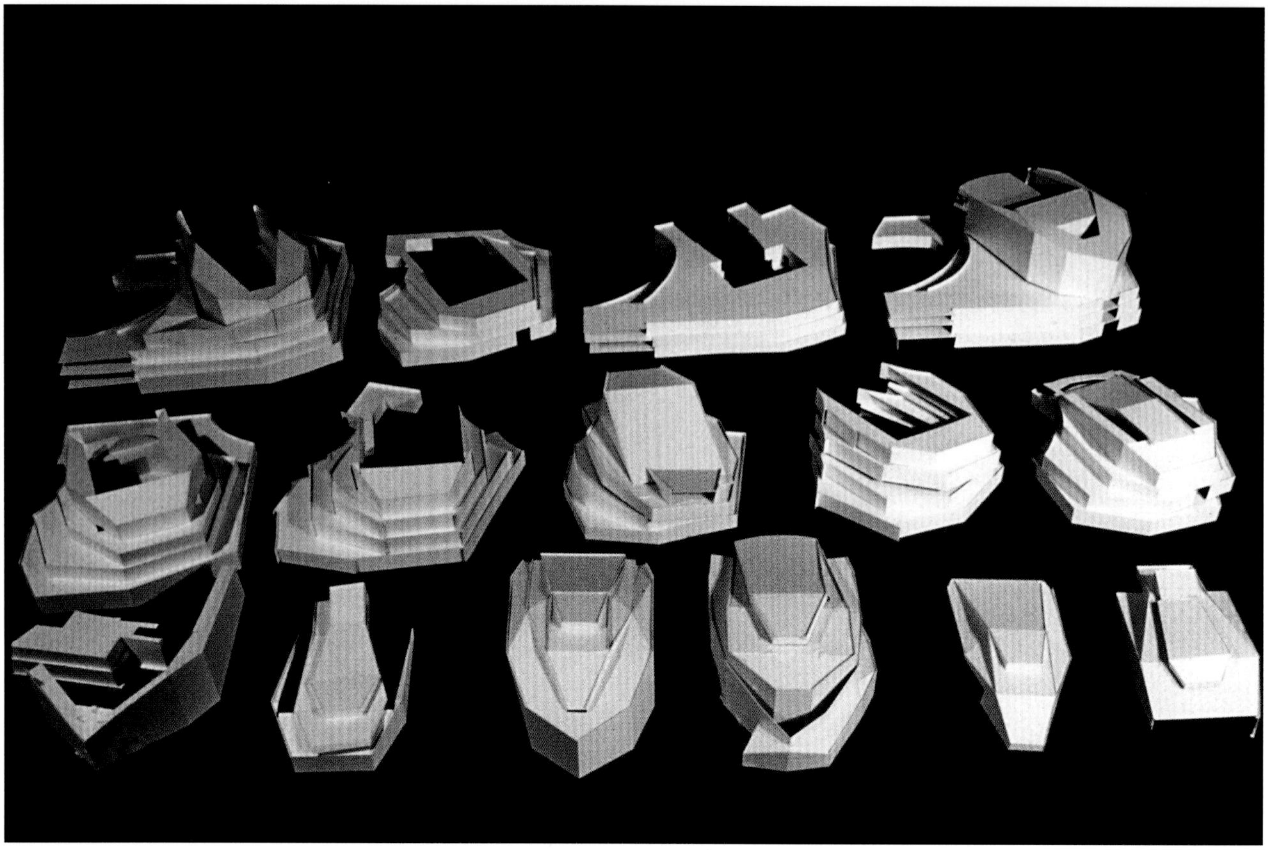

The Adrienne Arsht Center crosses Biscayne Boulevard with an arts plaza, framed by two theaters that were studied extensively in model form.

The arts plaza features the fountain *Water Scores* by Anna Valentina Murch.

ABOVE AND OPPOSITE The lobby of the Opera House features mosaics and balustrade panels by artist José Bedia.

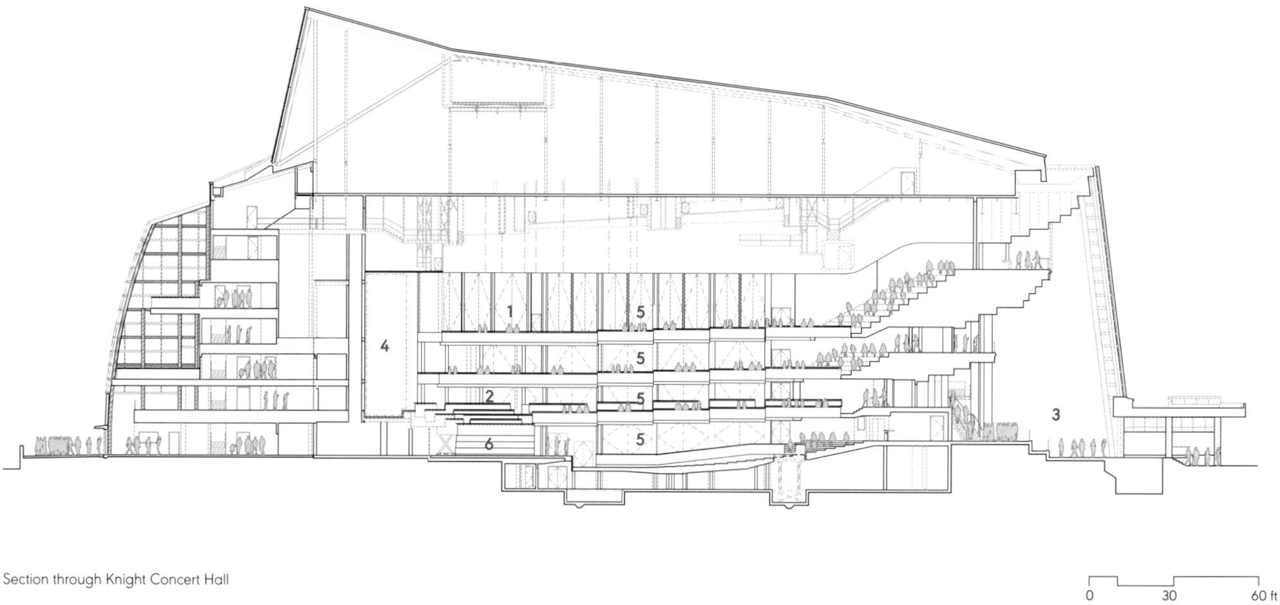

Section through Knight Concert Hall

1 Acoustic canopies
2 Choral risers
3 Lobby
4 Organ chamber
5 Reverberation chamber
6 Stage

ABOVE AND OPPOSITE José Bedia's mosaics and balustrade panels in the Concert Hall lobby are companion pieces to those in the Opera House.

Section through Ziff Opera House

1 Concessions
2 Lighting gallery
3 Lobby
4 Orchestra pit
5 Rear stage
6 Stage

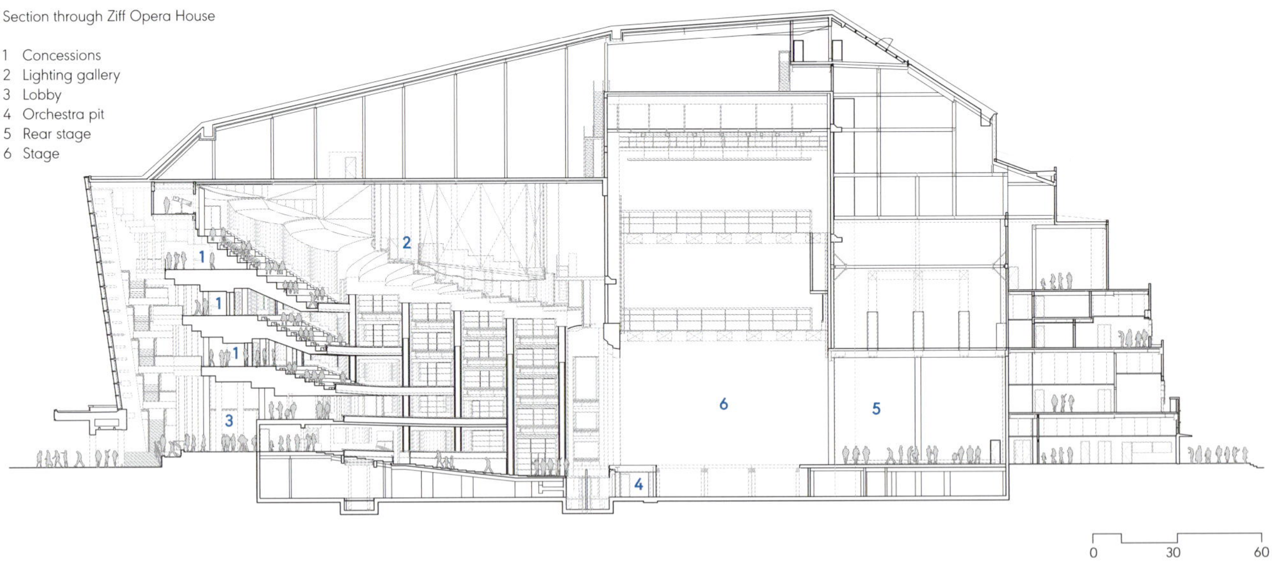

OPPOSITE The Opera House is crowned with an acoustical dome with swirling, sound-reflective forms.

COMMITMENT
SANFORD AND DOLORES ZIFF BALLET OPERA HOUSE

2008

Minneapolis Central Library

2006

Minneapolis, Minnesota, US

Our design for the Minneapolis public library tries to answer a difficult question: What is the future of public libraries? The traditional function as the main repository of knowledge is being challenged by the internet. Libraries will probably not survive for long unless they reinvent themselves, and some are already becoming social centers of culture and learning.

These new functions are already quite important: the library is heavily committed to computer teaching and training and provides special areas conceived as social centers for children, teenagers, and new immigrants. A planetarium has been designed but not yet completed.

We have designed as flexible a building as possible with simple loft-like spaces that can be reconfigured to accommodate new programs. Flat slabs are supported by a widely spaced grid of columns with mushroom capitals, constructed without beams.

The loft-like nature of the design is clearly expressed in the exterior and its simplicity is given life by a floor-to-ceiling glass wall modulated in several ways. The slab edges are covered in ochre-colored Minnesota stone, while the size, transparency, and depth of the windows vary in a complex rhythmic pattern.

Library Commons is now the heart of the building—a dynamic triangular space six stories high and very luminous. It separates the most accessible elements of the library (such as reading rooms and open-shelf stacking) from the more private workrooms and the compact storage of less accessible books. Both halves are well connected, with bridges at both ends of Library Commons and the floors functioning as one, with natural light introduced into the very center of the building.

The roof is a metal wing that appears to float above the space, extending at both ends to become the marker of each entrance. The wing broadens toward Nicolet Mall where it creates a large floating roof over the entrance, like a giant porch. The narrow end cantilevers over the sidewalk and street like a delicate metal finger.

East-facing main entrance includes a cantilevered metal canopy, which extends across the roof to the west façade (opposite).

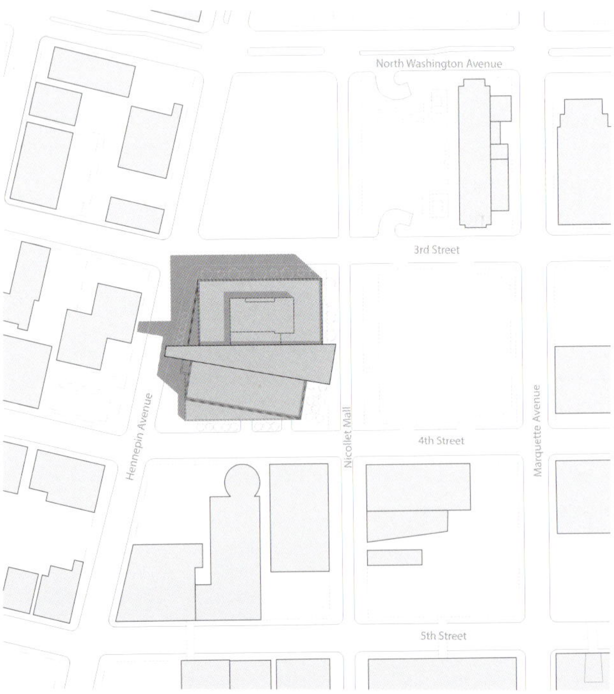

The library incorporates many sustainable design strategies. The roof is planted with drought-resistant ground cover, creating a 1,720-square-meter (18,500-square-foot) roof garden that slows storm-water run-off and reduces the urban heat island effect. The under-floor ventilation system reduces cooling costs, and the generous daylight and energy-efficient light fixtures exceed the state's energy code requirements.

In 2006 the library won a Design Award from the American Institute of Architects Connecticut, and in 2009 a Library Building Award from the American Institute of Architects/ American Library Association.

DUNN BROS COFFEE

MINNEAPOLIS
LIBRARY
CENTRAL LIBRARY

I had always wanted to design a library. The way we use books is changing rapidly, and the functions are changing. We gave them a flexible space, in terms of the structure and systems below the floor, so it is very easy to change the form to adapt to the new functions.

3

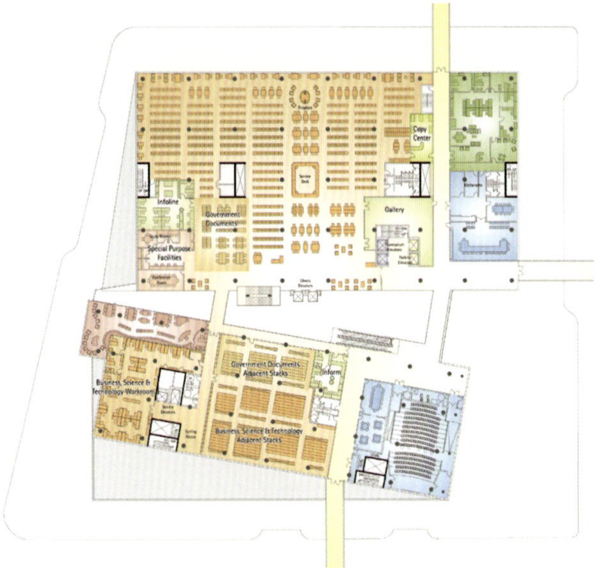

Second-floor plan

Ground-floor plan

ABOVE Artist Ben Rubin's *Four Stories* LED work climbs the elevator in the Library Commons.

2

Overture Center for the Arts
2006
Madison, Wisconsin, US

The Overture Center for the Arts gathers nearly all of Madison's arts organizations in a single place—a full city block near the state capitol and the University of Wisconsin. This exemplary undertaking by an enlightened donor and client was intended to create a unified arts center comprising the renovation of a theater, the redesign of another, the design of a major performance hall, and the expansion of an art museum.

The main piece of the project is the new Overture Hall. Seen from downtown, the hall is a crisp geometric form in limestone and glass with a grand lobby that extends over the sidewalk to shelter the entrance.

The complex maintains the pedestrian-friendly character of downtown Madison. The 1920s stone façade of the former Kessenich-Yost's Department Stores, which had to be retained, is now an entrance to the entire Overture Center. A new glass dome brings sunlight to all levels of the building through a four-story rotunda. On the lowest level is the Rotunda Stage, an indoor amphitheater.

The two existing theaters were substantially redesigned. The Capitol Theater, built as a movie palace, retains original details including its Grand Barton Organ, ornate ceiling, wall niches, proscenium arch, and chandelier lighting. To create a more intimate and acoustically improved 800-seat venue, some seating was removed and replaced by a new lobby in the character of the original theater. The interior of the Isthmus Playhouse, now a 350-seat thrust theater known as The Playhouse, is almost entirely new. Three flexible black box theaters were also added.

The Madison Art Center, renamed the Madison Museum of Contemporary Art, was expanded. Designed as a clear iconic form, the museum is a landmark for the flatiron corner of the block. The museum's triangular four-story glass lobby is a prismatic form visible along State Street. The monumental scale of its glass stair recalls the great entrances of contemporary museums around the world.

ORPHEUM

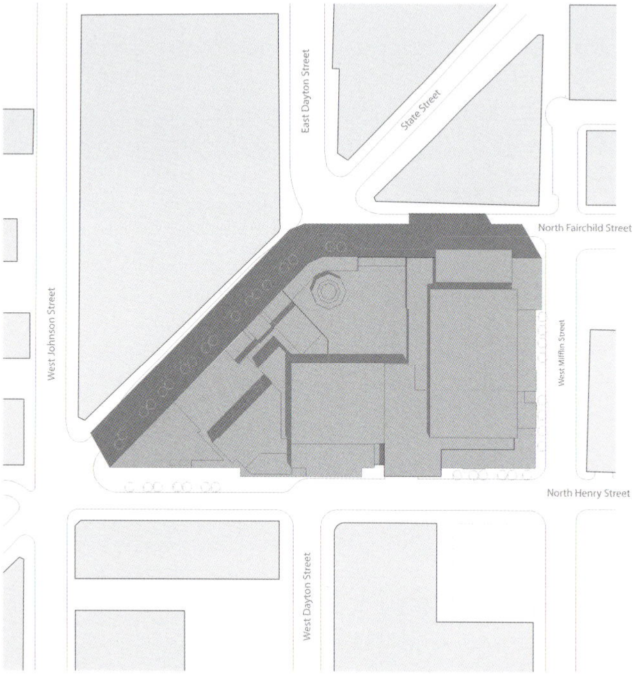

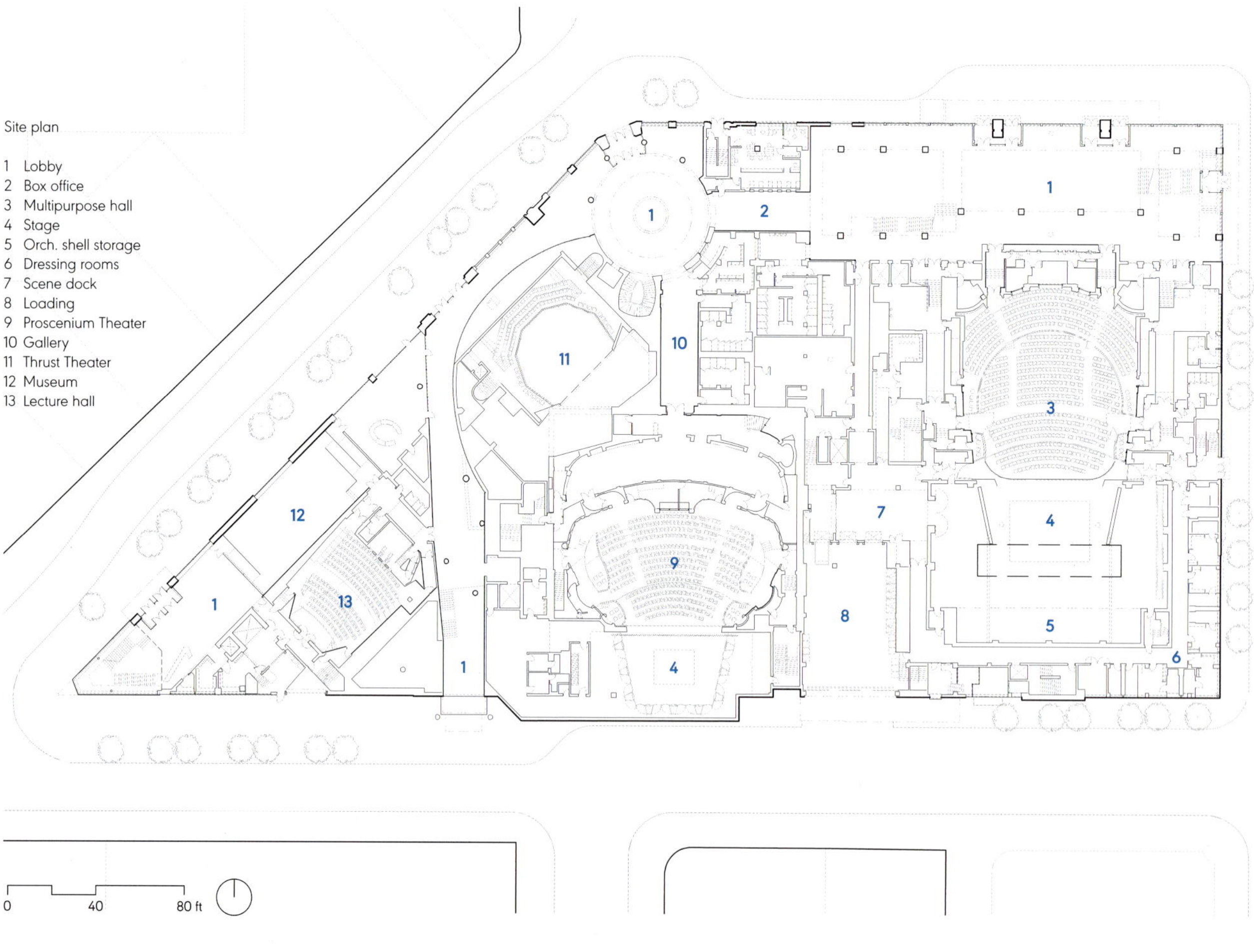

Site plan

1 Lobby
2 Box office
3 Multipurpose hall
4 Stage
5 Orch. shell storage
6 Dressing rooms
7 Scene dock
8 Loading
9 Proscenium Theater
10 Gallery
11 Thrust Theater
12 Museum
13 Lecture hall

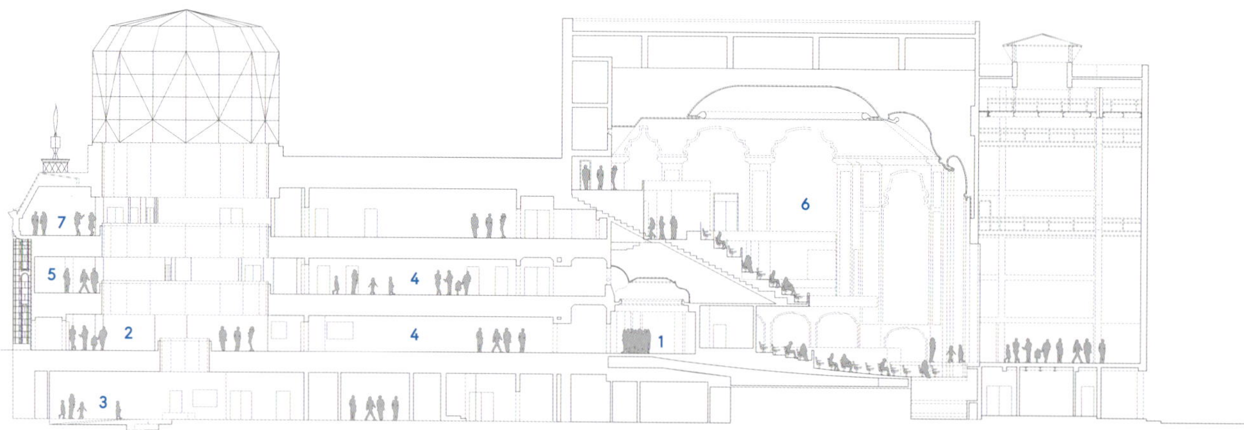

1 Capitol lobby
2 Capitol room
3 Circle Stage
4 Community Gallery
5 Promenade room
6 Renovated Capitol Theater
7 Academy of Sciences & Arts

0 25 50 ft

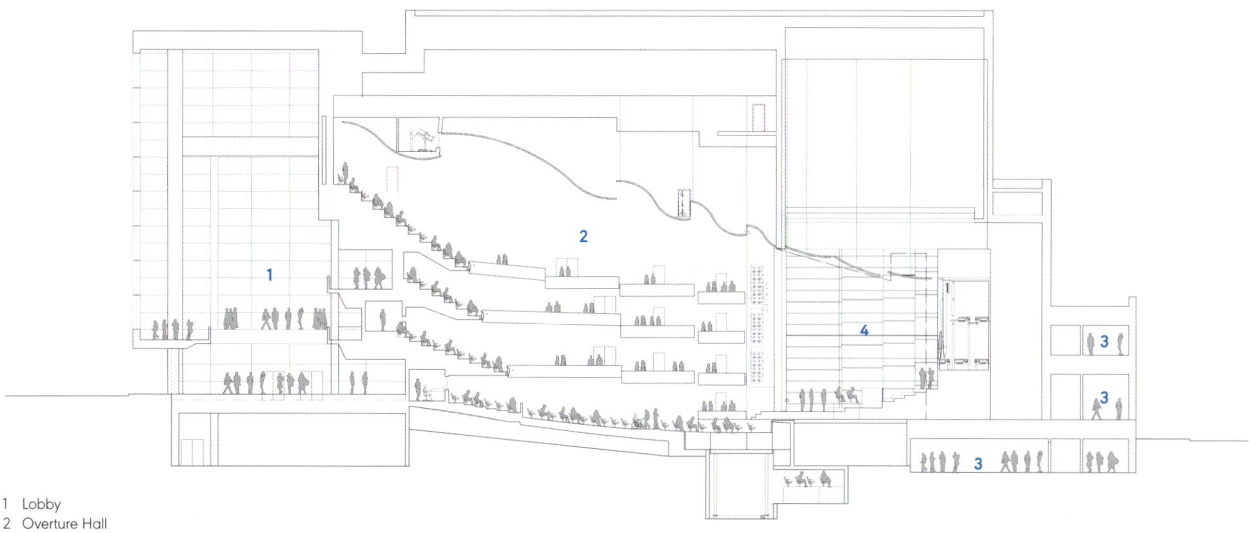

1 Lobby
2 Overture Hall
3 Performance support
4 Stage

The complex includes a variety of performance spaces, from the renovated Playhouse (opposite top) and Capitol Theater (opposite bottom), to the new Overture Hall with its undulating balconies (above).

BOK CENTER

BOK Center
2008
Tulsa, Oklahoma, US

The BOK Center is an 18,000-seat sports and entertainment venue that gave Tulsa the performance and sports center it had always wanted, and which has become an architectural icon. The design is a sweeping spiral of walls of stainless steel and glass that tilt inward as they swirl around the arena.

Wrapping the southern façade of the BOK Center is a very large curving glass wall. The icon wall, as this outer wall is known, reaches more than 30 meters (100 feet) above grade. The glass wall gives the BOK Center an unusually strong connection to the city for an arena. Visitors can look out over Tulsa from many places in the building, including some of the arena seats. Although the large expanse of glass appears transparent, about half of the icon wall is covered in a subtle ceramic frit pattern to prevent glare. The glass wall fills the building with light during the day. Exceeding local building code requirements in a tornado-prone region, the glass wall can withstand winds of over 160 kilometers (100 miles) per hour.

The BOK Center incorporates several site-specific artworks commissioned for the building: *Dreamland,* a multi-story painting of horses by celebrated Tulsa and New York City painter Joe Andoe; *Stratum,* a cloud-like installation by sculptors Kendall Buster and Siemon Allen; *Realms,* four 7-meter-diameter (22-foot-diameter) medallions embedded in the terrazzo floors by Cherokee Nation father and son Bill and Demos Glass; and *The Tallgrass Prairies*—25 scenes of the Tulsa prairie by local painter Mark Lewis.

The BOK Center won a 2009 Innovative Design in Engineering and Architecture with Structural Steel (IDEAS2) Award from the American Institute of Steel Construction; a 2011 Design Award from the American Institute of Architects New England; and a 2012 American Architecture Award from the Chicago Athenaeum.

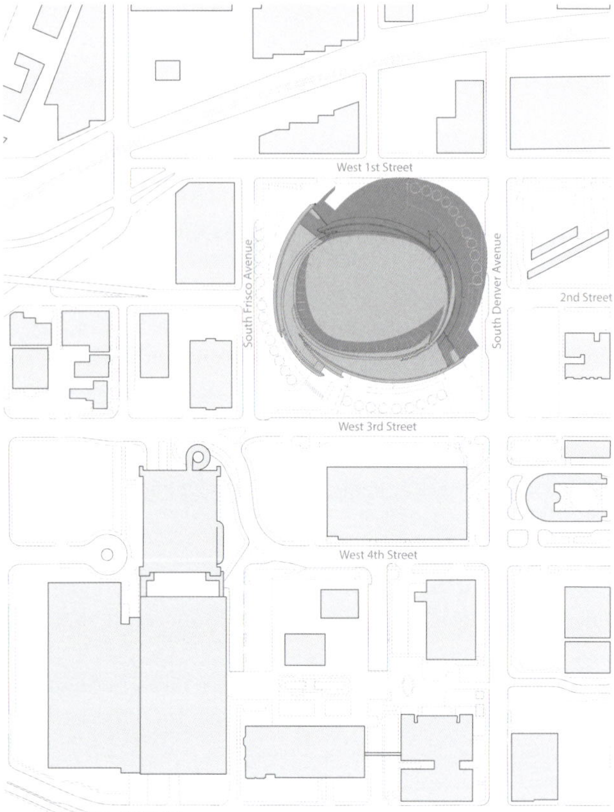
West 1st Street
South Frisco Avenue
South Denver Avenue
2nd Street
West 3rd Street
West 4th Street

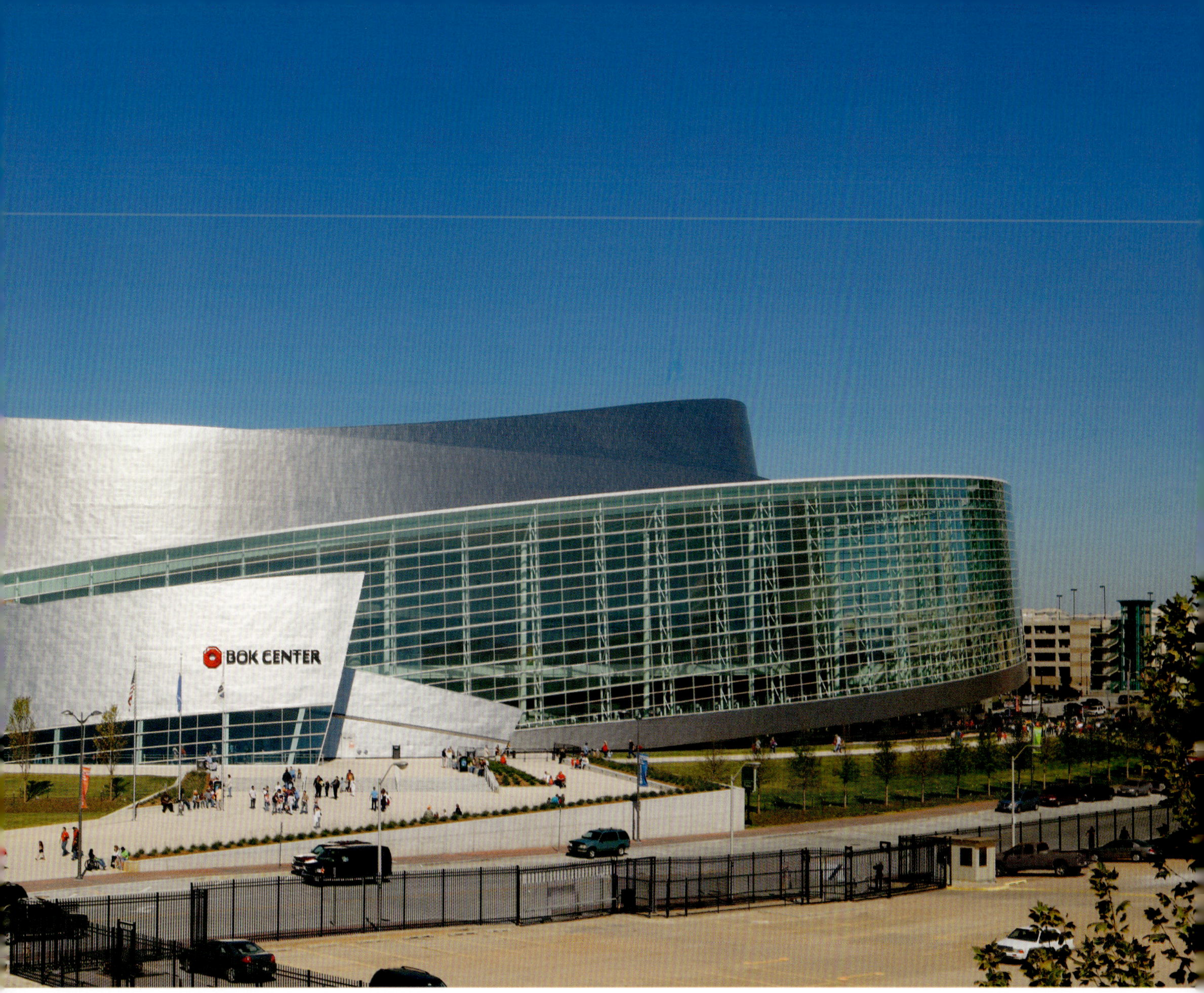
BOK CENTER

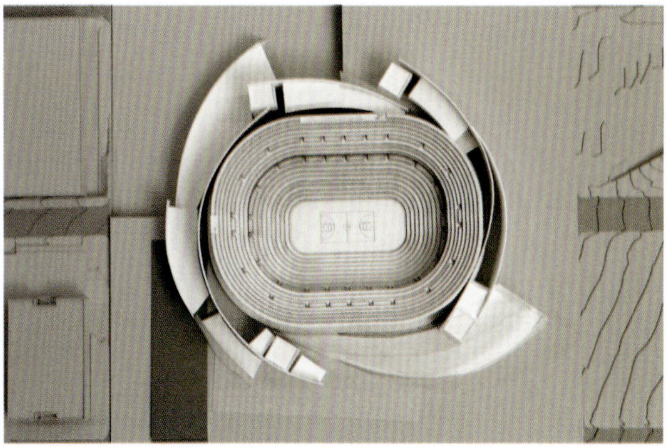

The new element is the ramp. You enter on the lowest level and gently rise to the upper level. People always prefer the ramp. It is more inviting and social, and it reflects the movement of people inside.

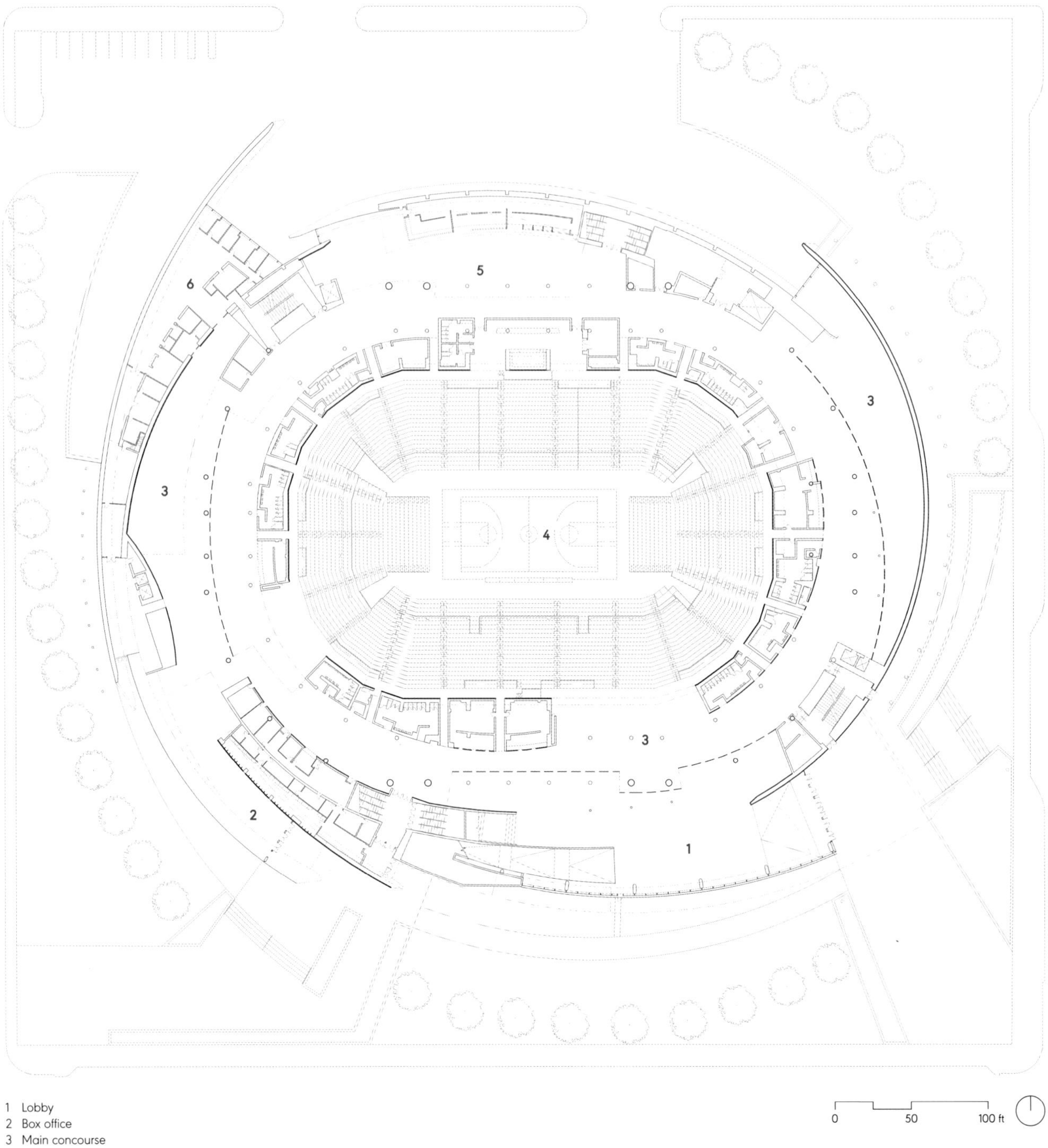

1 Lobby
2 Box office
3 Main concourse
4 Multipurpose arena
5 Concessions
6 Offices

1 Club Lounge
2 Commissary
3 Concessions
4 Concourse–main
5 Councourse–upper
6 Locker room
7 Restroom
8 Storage
9 Suite level

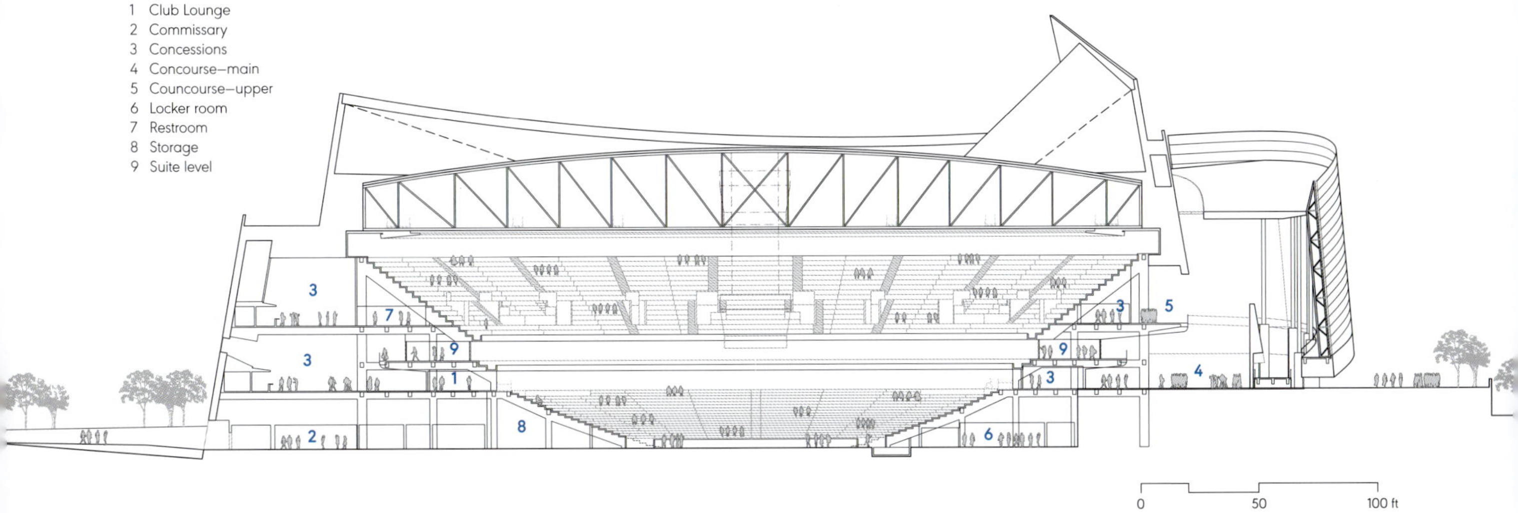

BOK CENTER

Torre YPF

2008

Buenos Aires, Argentina

The 37-story YPF Tower stands apart from the busy streets and avenues of Buenos Aires, its full height visible from all sides. Located in the new neighborhood of Puerto Madero, it is visible from the historic Plaza de Mayo. With its clean lines and dramatic winter garden, it is a dignified corporate symbol and a modern landmark for Buenos Aires.

I gave the tower the form of a curved rhomboid organized on its diagonal. The two sides facing the Rio de la Plata are made entirely from glass in horizontal bands, echoing the water of the river. The two sides facing the city are clad in glass and stainless steel, forming over-sized windows that create a relationship between the tower and the urban site. A distinctive feature in the tower is the six-story winter garden. Located near the top of the tower and facing the city, the garden's huge window is an emblematic presence on the façade. Several large jacaranda trees occupy the space. At night, lit from within, the tower is visible from afar, a proud and beautiful edifice.

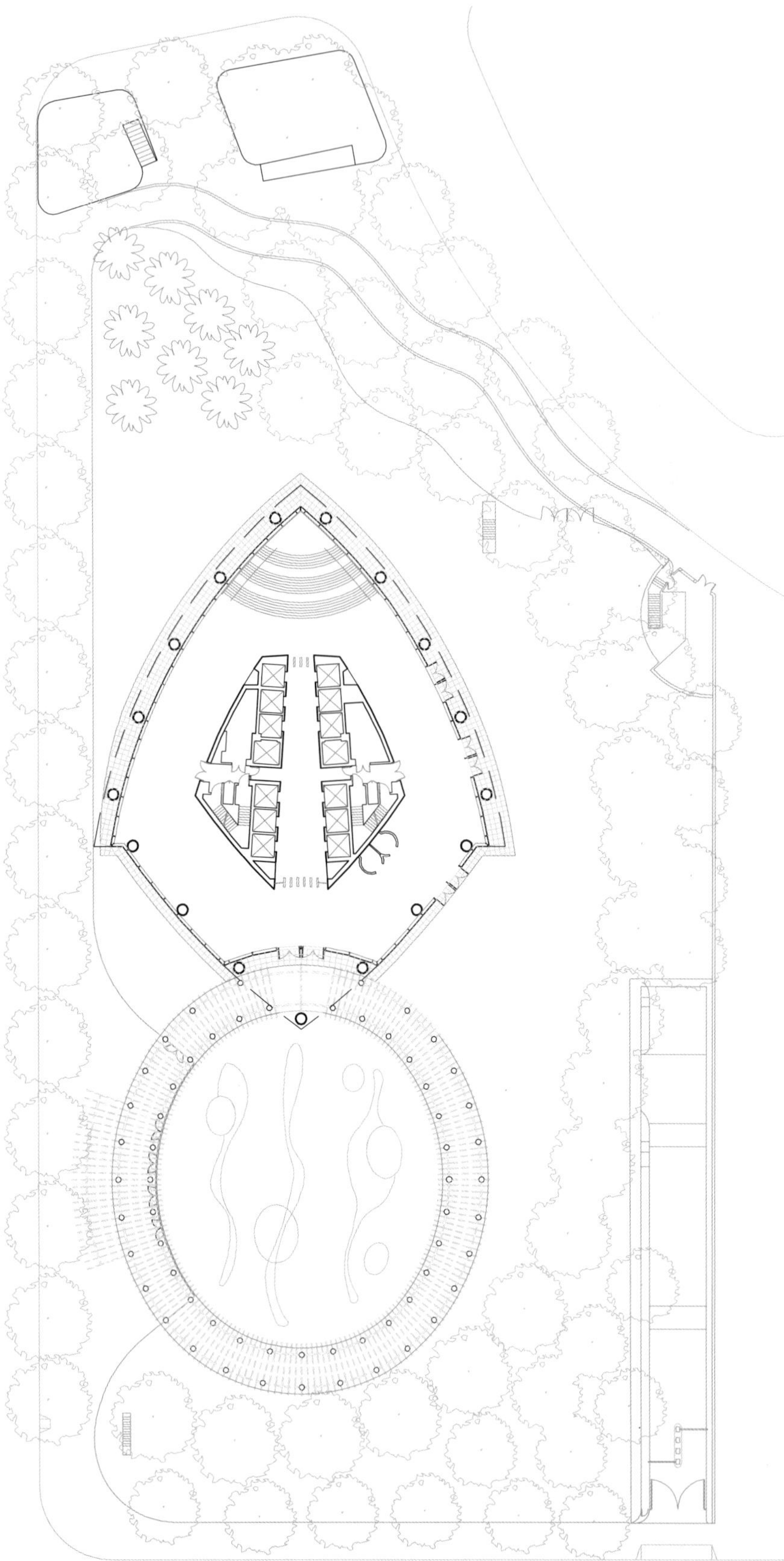

ARIA Resort and Casino

2009

Las Vegas, Nevada, US

The ARIA Resort and Casino is the centerpiece of CityCenter, an urban development fronting the Las Vegas Strip. The 4,000-room hotel and casino is the tallest structure in CityCenter.

The hotel form is composed of two counterpoising, curvilinear towers joining to form an open center. The curved plan allows the guest rooms to have light and natural views within a limited height.

East of the towers is a casino and retail area. West of them is a 1,800-seat theater with a layered, three-dimensional façade. Just past the theater is a three-level conference center. With its glass façade, the conference center is filled with natural light and has views of the landscaped pool area. Opposite the conference center is a two-level spa building clad in the red metaquartzite stone that is synonymous with Las Vegas.

ARIA is the world's largest hotel to achieve a LEED Gold rating. Its curtain wall uses a new generation of glass coatings which allow maximum daylight, while blocking internal heat gain. Sunshades reduce sun and glare and give life to the hotel forms.

Water efficiency is also a key achievement. More than 117,000 cubic meters (31 million gallons) of water are saved throughout the resort each year. This includes savings of 40 percent in the hotel and 60 percent for landscape irrigation, by US standards. In addition to LEED, ARIA received the highest rating from the Green Key Eco-Rating Program for sustainable hotel operations.

STOP

Cesar Pelli

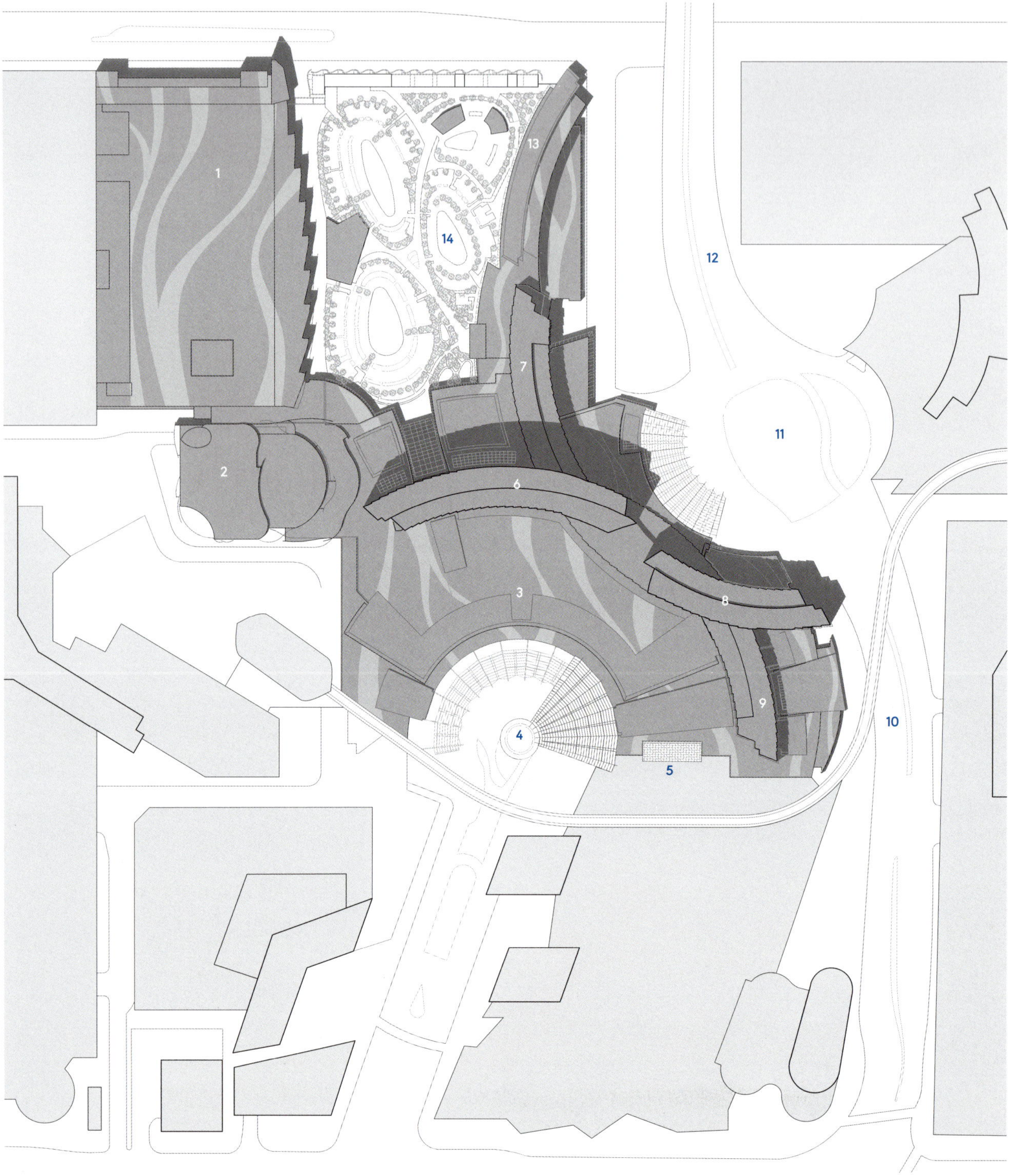

1 Convention center
2 Theater
3 Casino
4 Casino Circle
5 Registration
6 South Hotel Tower
7 West Hotel Tower
8 North Hotel Tower
9 East Hotel Tower
10 Harmon Drive
11 Hamron Circle
12 West Harmon Avenue
13 Spa
14 Pool

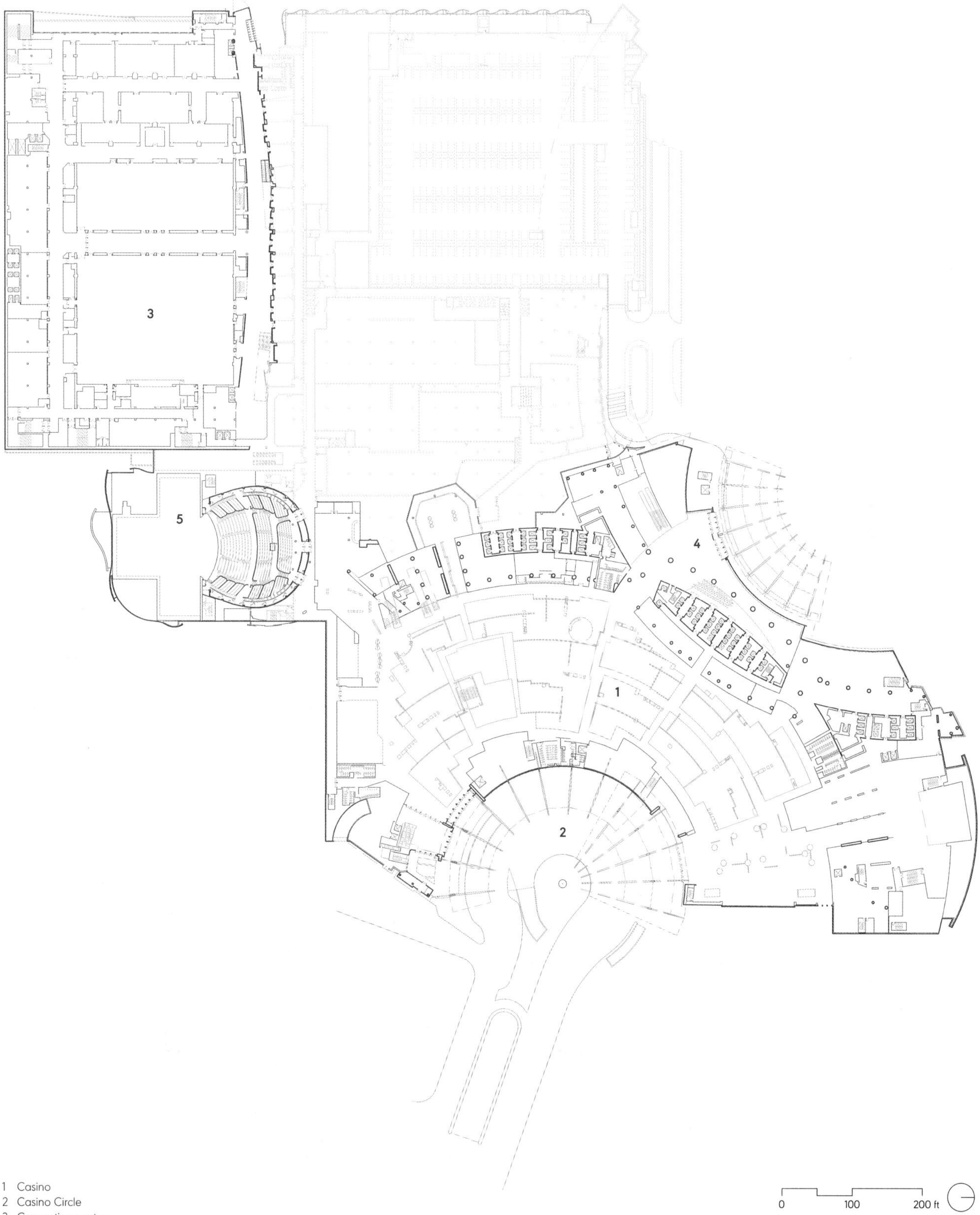

1 Casino
2 Casino Circle
3 Convention center
4 Hotel lobby
5 Theater

Behind ARIA's front desk is *Silver River*, a sculptural work by Maya Lin; hotel corridors have natural illumination, graceful curves, and views of the strip to enrich the visual journey to and from one's room.

They wanted something elegant and contemporary. The two towers undulate and dance with each other.

ABOVE The hotel provides a dramatic backdrop to one of four pools.
OPPOSITE Across from the convention center, with its colorful metal panels and glass-wedge walls, the parking garage is screened by metal mesh.

planet hollywood

Connecticut Science Center

2009

Hartford, Connecticut, US

We were selected to design the Connecticut Science Center in an international competition. I tried to capture the excitement and wonder of science in its design.

The Science Center comprises three major elements: two enclosed volumes that house the exhibits, and Science Alley, a narrow six-story space between the two. Science Alley is covered by an iconic S-shaped roof—the building's signature image of the "magic carpet." The building is clad in transparent glass, lightly reflective metal panels, photovoltaic panels, and a large LED screen.

Visitors enter the Science Center at street level on the west side of the building, and immediately ascend a generous staircase into Science Alley, a grand hall crisscrossed by pedestrian bridges. This striking space serves as a central circulation point from which visitors can discover all of the museum's exhibitions and attractions. With its soaring, east-facing glass wall, the space draws visitors out to a landscaped plaza on the Connecticut River.

The building uses multiple strategies to achieve its LEED Gold rating. Energy-saving mechanisms, locally manufactured building materials, recycled content building materials (including 95 percent of the steel from recycled cars), high-performance glazing on the exterior envelope, and a fuel cell that generates energy on-site are some of the features that contribute to the sustainability concept of the center.

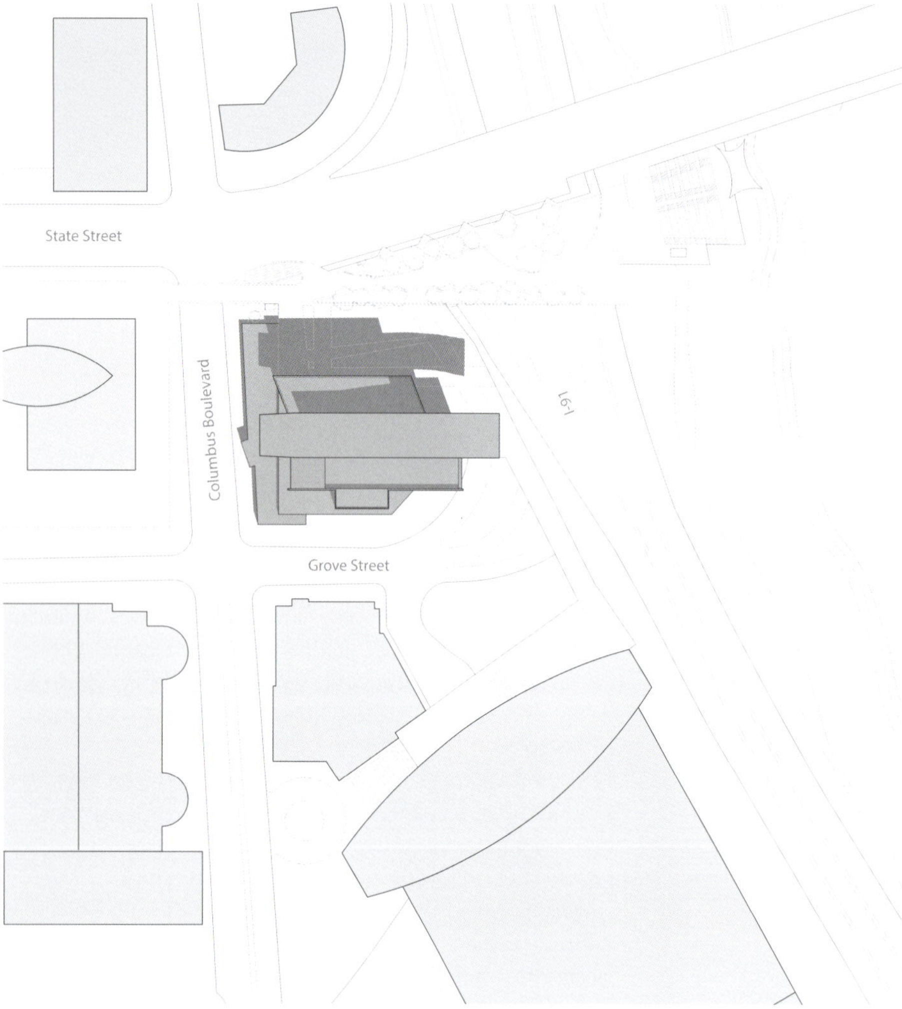
State Street
Columbus Boulevard
I-91
Grove Street

CTCSE

The roof is a flying carpet.
We wanted to suggest that it could
fly over the Connecticut River.

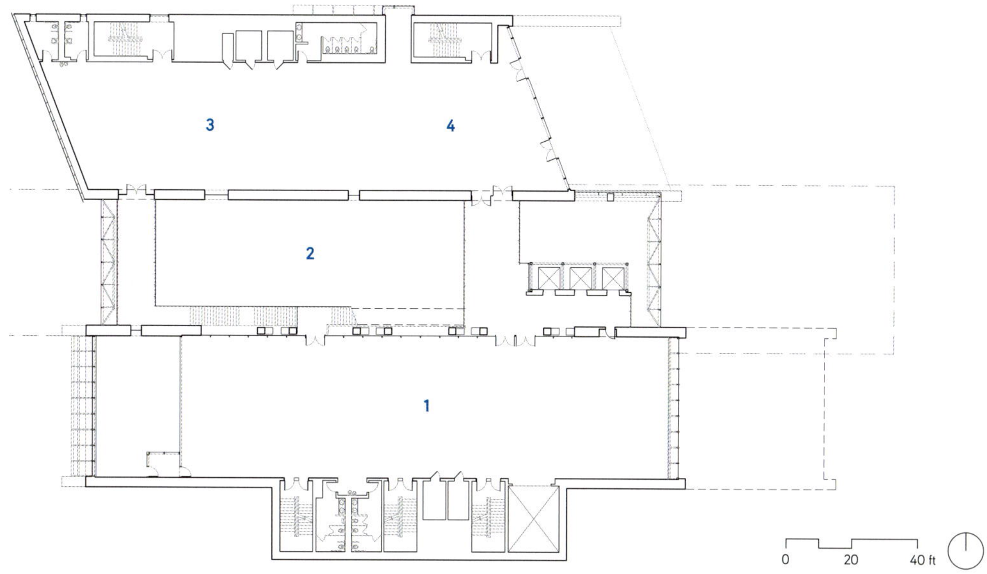

Fourth floor

1 Traveling exhibits gallery
2 Open atrium
3 Forces in Motion exhibit gallery
4 Sight and Sound exhibit gallery

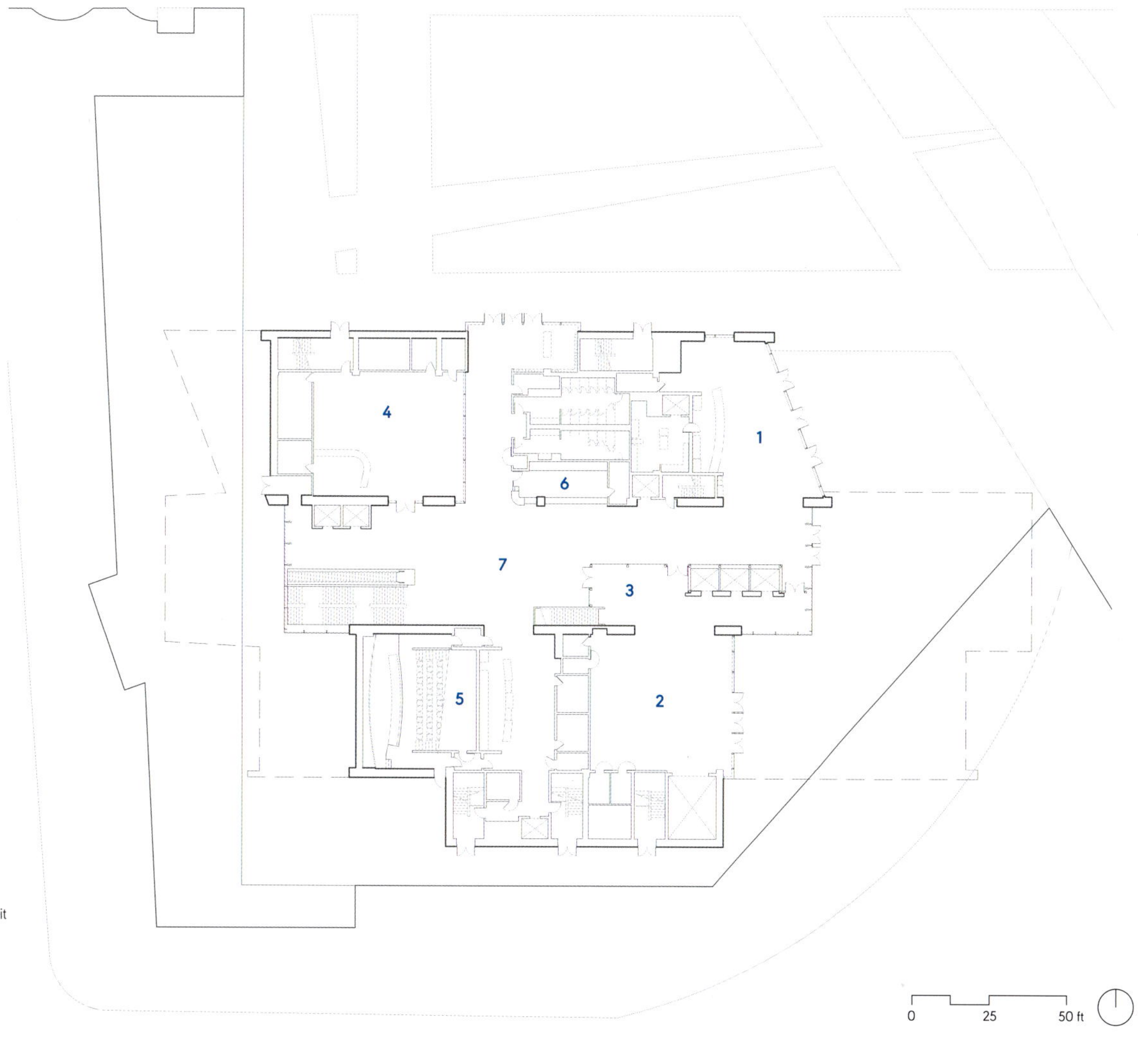

Plaza level

1 Café
2 Children's exhibit
3 Exhibit Hub
4 Gift shop
5 Theater
6 Ticket counter
7 Science Alley

OPPOSITE At the heart of the museum in Science Alley, one can view interactive demonstrations and visitors circulating through the building. ABOVE A glass room projects from the east façade as an oriel window, offering views over the Connecticut River.

Marriott

Cooperative Arts and Humanities High School

2009

New Haven, Connecticut, US

The Cooperative Arts and Humanities High School is dedicated to art education and performance, and lies at the heart of New Haven's arts and entertainment district. It includes a full-sized public theater, a black box experimental theater, exhibition spaces, as well as all the elements of a traditional high school. To maintain a lively street presence, on the ground floor the building hosts retail stores and public entrances to the theater lobby and galleries.

One block from the New Haven Green, the school is close to theaters, art galleries, and Yale University's architecture, art, music, and drama schools. The high school's theaters, exhibit spaces, and studios are shared with local arts institutions, encouraging collaboration.

The design strives to be a high school, a good neighbor to the buildings of downtown New Haven, and an exciting place in which to start a career in the arts. The long College Street façade is a composition of brick masses, glass volumes, and copper planes. At the corner of College and Crown Streets, a double-height glass dance studio announces the arts-focused program. Similarly, the abstracted maple, oak, and elm leaves silkscreened on the insulated glass panels of the College Street façade reference the drawing, painting, and printmaking studios inside. This patterned glass helps reduce the building's energy consumption by allowing views, letting in light while reducing solar gain, and giving privacy. It is a handsome, inviting, and daring building.

In 2014, the building received a citation from the American Institute of Architects Connecticut.

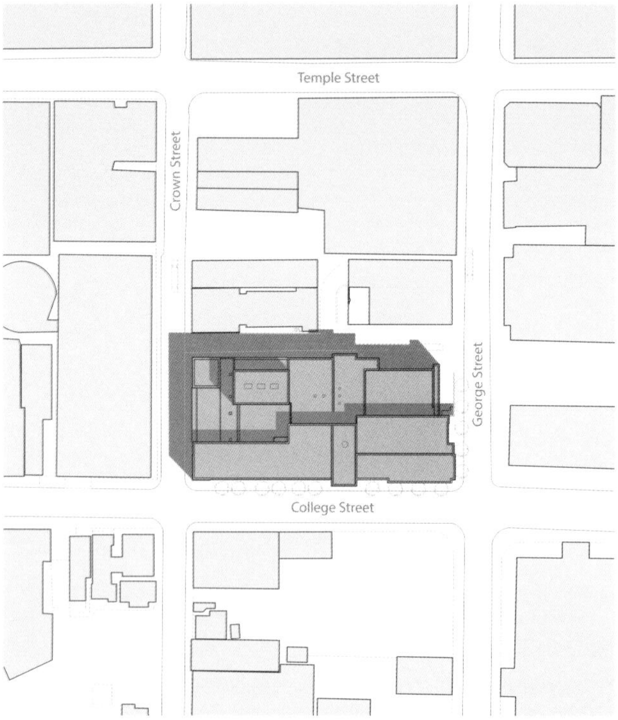

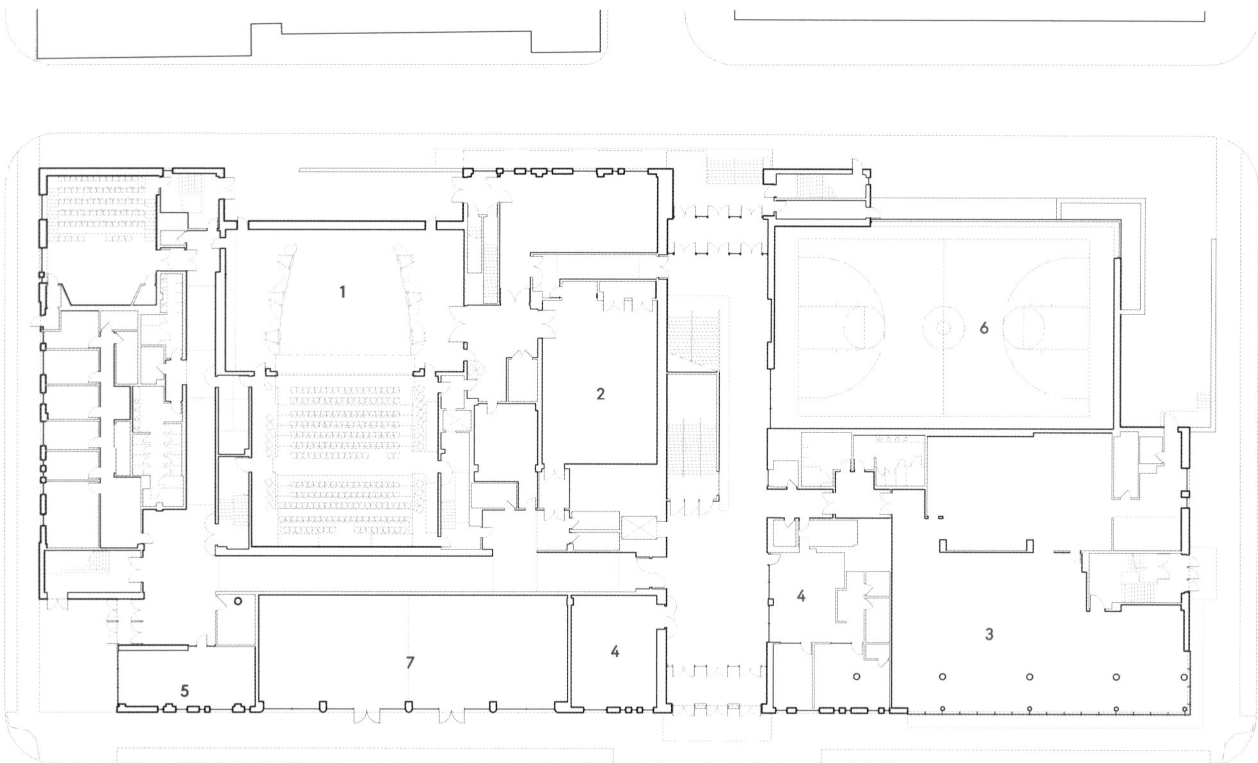

1 Auditorium
2 Black Box
3 Cafeteria
4 Classroom
5 Exhibit
6 Gymnasium
7 Retail

OPPOSITE Theater spaces are flexible and adaptable. ABOVE The school's long façade faces College Street to the west, and includes generous interior stairs.

This school is very dedicated to the arts, and the building's marquee announces that.

OMNI HOTEL
park

Park Here
NEW HAVEN HOTEL

Torre Libertad
2009
Mexico City, Mexico

Torre Libertad is a simple and sculptural form—an equilateral triangle with curved sides pointing towards the Diana Fountain in a gesture of respect. To strengthen this relationship, I made the corner that addresses the fountain an undulating facet that presents a dramatic face towards it and marks the entrance to the building. At this corner, the tower rises from the earth and soars towards the sky.

The exterior is an elegant, delicately proportioned wall of clear floor-to-ceiling glass and white aluminum sunshades wrapping the curved forms of the triangle. The curved walls of glass catch the changing light with their multiple facets. The shape of the tower harks back to ancient civilizations, yet is a contemporary presence fully in keeping with modern Mexico.

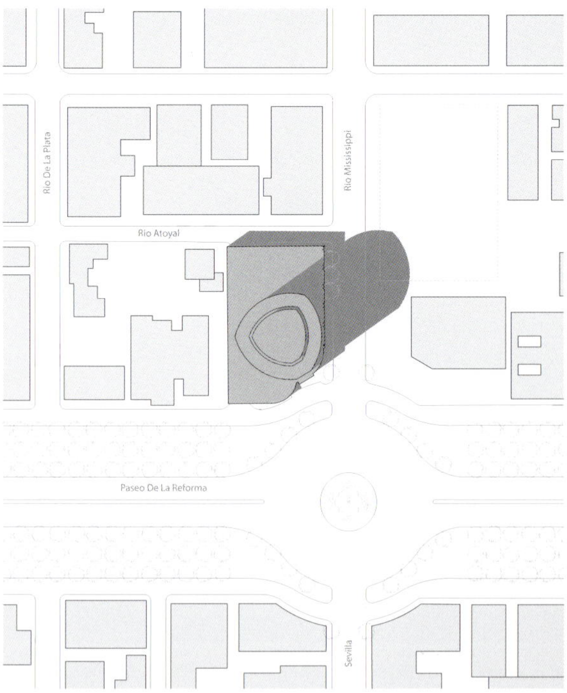

The tower is sited along the boulevards with their monumental circles and sculptures, which create vistas across the city.

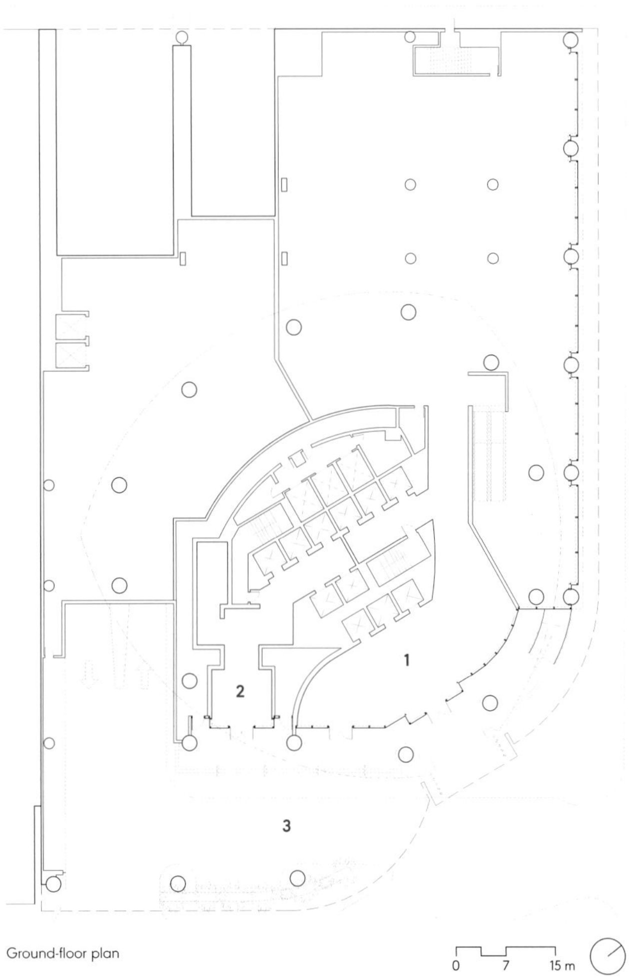

Ground-floor plan

1 Hotel shuttle lobby
2 Residential lobby
3 Taxi drop-off

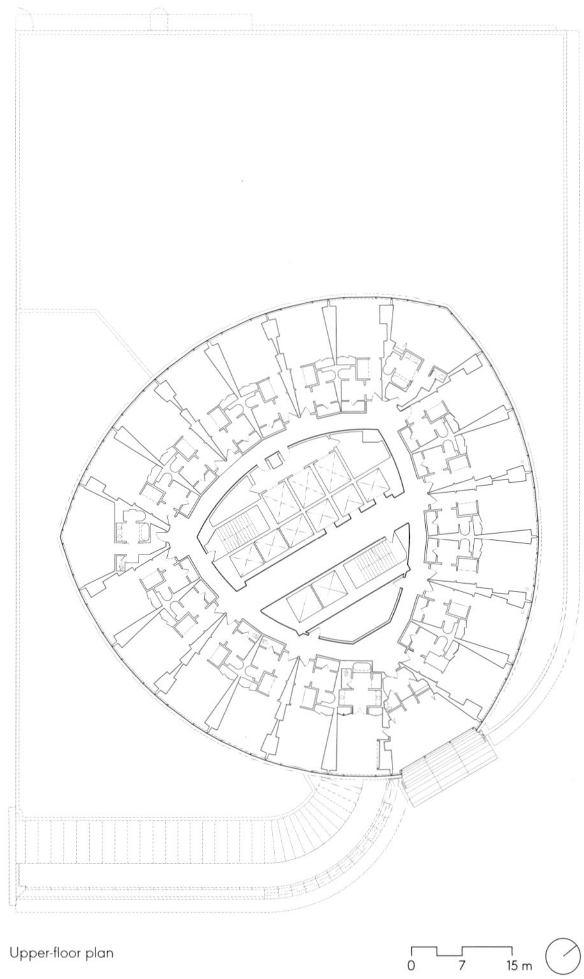

Upper-floor plan

AEROMEXICO

Hillhouse Avenue Pedestrian Bridge

2010

Yale University, New Haven, Connecticut, US

Hillhouse Avenue is one of New Haven's best-preserved historic districts, home to mansions by Henry Austin and Alexander Jackson Davis. As part of the replacement of a vehicular bridge there, Yale University commissioned two pedestrian bridges, designed in collaboration with structural engineer Guy Nordenson and Associates, to align with the existing Hillhouse sidewalks. Spanning 18 meters (60 feet) over the Farmington Canal Greenway, the two bridges offer unobstructed views of the tree-lined street which, according to legend, both Charles Dickens and Mark Twain called the most beautiful in America.

With their diamond-shaped perforations, the new bridges recall a lattice truss, a bridge type once widely used throughout New England. Patented in 1820 by New Haven architect Ithiel Town, the lattice truss uses a diagonal arrangement of thin bars. The primary structure and handrails (the main load-carrying members) are two steel-plate girders with 6-millimeter (quarter-inch) corrugated, perforated webs.

Like the lattice truss, the Hillhouse bridges represent an advance in bridge design. These cutouts lighten the structure and allow sunlight to reach the walking and cycling trail below. The wave patterns of these girders vary in amplitude across the bridge spans, according to structural demands, creating an efficient design. Web sections with the greatest amplitudes are located at the bridge ends and at mid-span, allowing for thinner web plates and eliminating the need for stiffeners.

Details of the pedestrian bridge are derived from lattice-truss bridge technology developed by a Connecticut architect in the 19th century. The undulating, perforated railings provide structural support.

Watching the Teacher Learn
by Fred Clarke

On a humid spring evening in Austin in the late 1960s, I wandered among the guests at a faculty party, a bit lost, when peals of laughter drew me across the lawn. It was then that I first met Diana Balmoral—source of the joyful sounds—and Cesar Pelli, a guest critic at the University of Texas at Austin School of Architecture, where I was a student. I joined an animated conversation but, interestingly enough, architecture wasn't the topic. Instead, a cascade of ideas and opinions about photography, painting, the Beatles—the hot cultural topics of the day—engulfed us. I have an indelible memory of this bright, handsome couple. Their broad knowledge and energy was infectious. I felt an immediate connection.

A few weeks later, unexpectedly, I received a letter from Cesar with an open-ended offer of a position in his design department at Gruen Associates in Los Angeles. I must have read the note a hundred times. I called Cesar to be sure the offer was real and accepted without hesitation. I then embarked on what would become one of my life's most important journeys.

Nearly fifty years have passed—fifty years in which Cesar and I have worked closely and continuously—and the simple kindness in that letter resonates today. It was just a few lines typed on Gruen letterhead with Cesar's distinctive signature etched in black marker—but somehow it conveyed his decency and warmth, and an offer of something more than a job—an invitation to discover the practice of architecture in its highest form.

Cesar is a natural teacher and our relationship grew within that context. Initially, at Gruen, it was something akin to an apprenticeship, with Cesar guiding me and others in the studio in our day-to-day work as young designers. At some point, however, I became a colleague—someone who could participate as a trusted collaborator in discussions and decisions. This happened quite naturally, which I see in retrospect was due to Cesar's magnanimity—he has never been territorial, but always open to any contribution, even those coming from the youngest team member.

In architecture, mentoring is sometimes a silent process. As a young designer, Cesar gave me the opportunity to quietly watch and learn about the craft of architecture in a supportive and nurturing environment. It was something much grander and more powerful than anything I could have imagined as a student in 1969. The result was a deep connection between two people working in concert toward a common goal.

In 1977, when Cesar became Dean of the Yale School of Architecture, I came to New Haven to help him found an architecture firm and continue my own teaching. Remarkable commissions followed, allowing the office to grow and, in many ways, the mentorship has continued. Nearly every day, working side by side, I have witnessed Cesar discovering something new about architecture. His curiosity and perceptiveness allow him to constantly evolve, ever open to new ideas. My opportunity to witness this—to observe the teacher learning—has been a powerful experience.

Architecture is certainly about talent and skill, but it is also about the development of character and values, and one of the most important ingredients is time. Over many years, I have had the satisfaction of mentoring younger designers and watching them become talented professionals and true friends. Perhaps one of mentorship's greatest qualities is that it spreads through time, like ripples on a pond, extending its subtle influence, providing a powerful vehicle for the development of deeply held beliefs which will inform an entire career.

I am profoundly grateful to my great friend and partner Cesar Pelli for his offer to work together all those years ago. He gave me what Eero Saarinen had given him and I, in turn, have tried to give to my younger colleagues. In this way, through generations of optimistic, young architects, Cesar's admirable character and talent has shaped our buildings and shaped us.

St. Katharine Drexel Chapel, Xavier University of Louisiana

2012

New Orleans, Louisiana, US

Named for Xavier University's founder, the St. Katharine Drexel Chapel is a new central place of worship on campus. It has an octagonal plan, respecting the liturgical directions of Vatican II, with a limestone base crowned by a faceted copper roof topped with a 4.5-meter-high (15-foot-high) cross. The building acknowledges the materials and colors of Xavier's campus buildings and the architectural tradition of centric religious structures.

The building is raised 1.2 meters (4 feet) above grade, as required for flood protection. A 24-meter (80-foot) ramp edged with raised planters creates a ceremonial procession to the chapel.

Inside the 430-seat sanctuary, the height of the space rises to 20 meters (65 feet). Sunlight enters the space through a ring of skylights and is diffused through a perforated aluminum chancel screen. It is a soaring nave with diaphanous walls that form a sacred and joyous space. Colored glass windows surround the main chapel. Windows designed by artist José Bedia depict the Stations of the Cross; the rest have a tapestry-like texture and were designed by New Orleans glass artisan Laurel Porcari.

Directly adjacent to the main sanctuary is the 40-seat day chapel, expressed on the exterior below the bell tower as a smaller octagonal form. A meditation garden surrounds the day chapel outside the building.

The chapel is designed to be highly sustainable. Design strategies include abundant daylight to reduce artificial lighting and energy demand, and low-maintenance native plants for landscaping to decrease potable water consumption. The orientation of the building and the location of its windows minimize solar heat gain, reducing energy used for cooling. All the timber used for furniture and millwork is from certified sources, while low-VOC materials are specified to maximize indoor air quality.

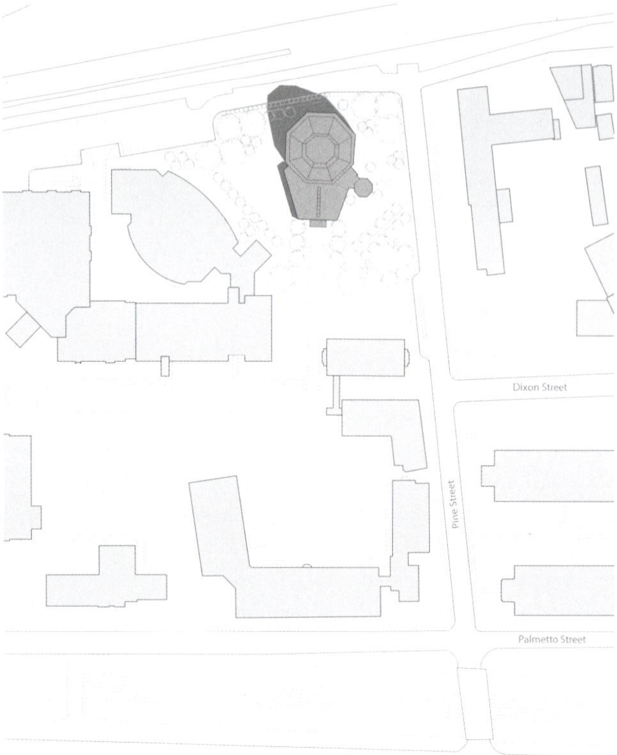

BOTTOM AND OPPOSITE The chapel's limestone walls and their coursing pattern provide a sense of lightness, topped with a faceted copper dome.

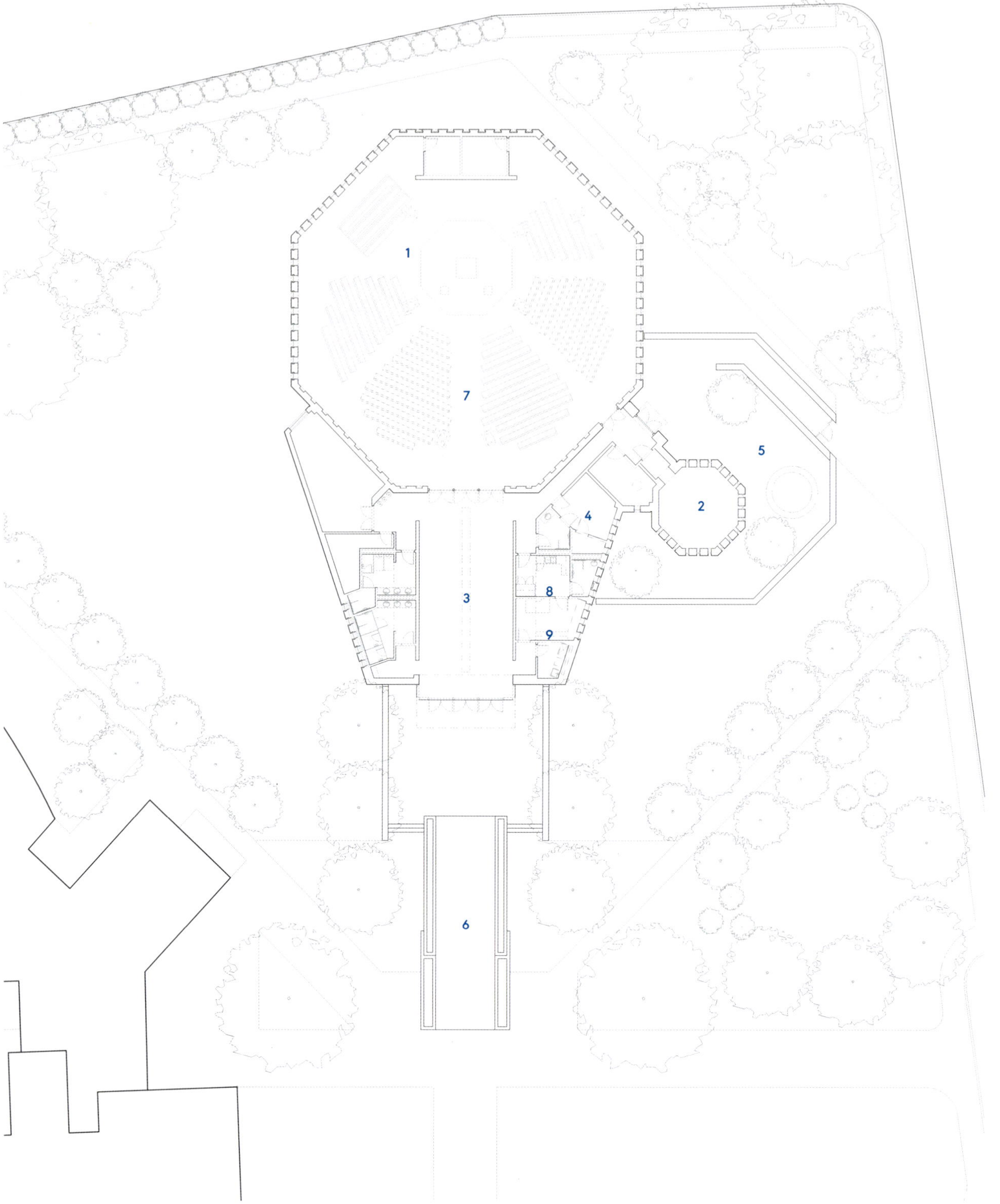

1 Choir
2 Day chapel
3 Narthex
4 Office
5 Outdoor gathering space
6 Processional approach
7 Sanctuary
8 Vesting sacristy
9 Work sacristy

The sanctuary dome interior is defined by a luminous screen, upon which floats the 3.65-meter-tall (12-foot-tall) *Risen Christ Corpus* by Stuflesser Studio.

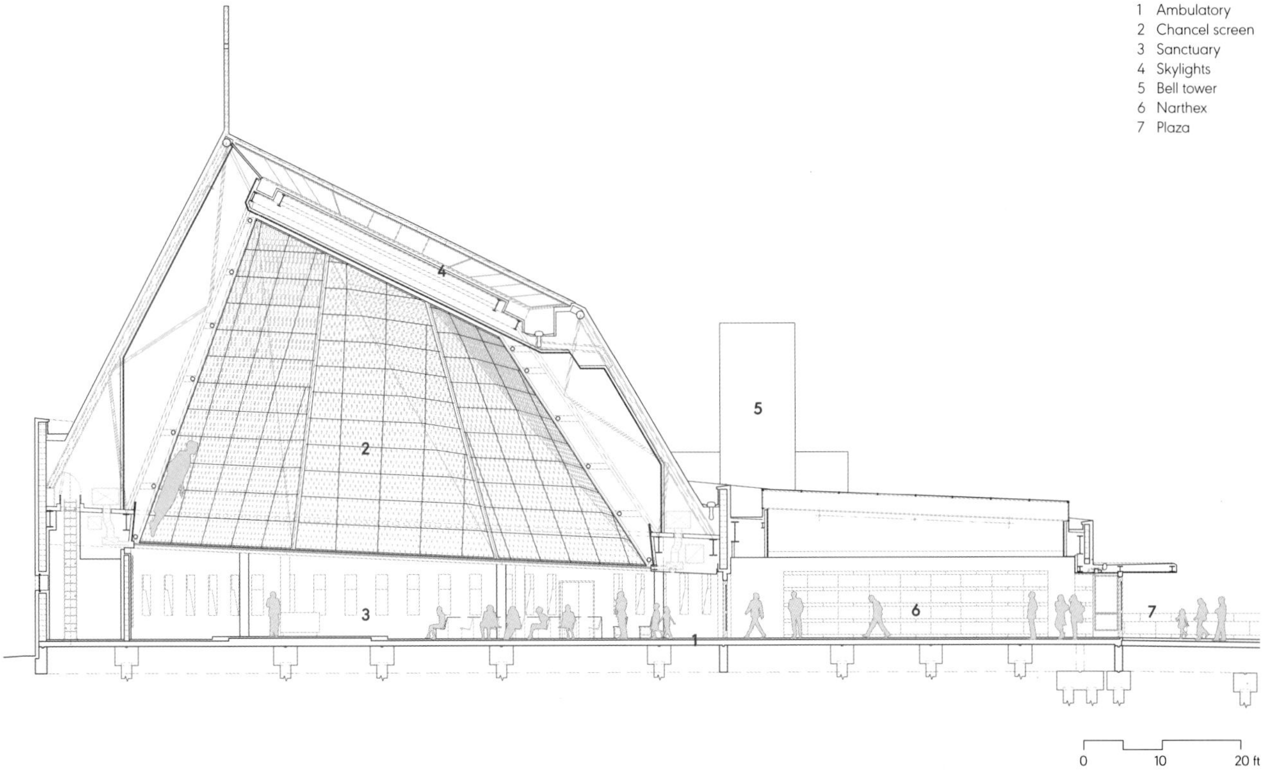
1 Ambulatory
2 Chancel screen
3 Sanctuary
4 Skylights
5 Bell tower
6 Narthex
7 Plaza
1
2
3
4
5
6
7
0
10
20 ft

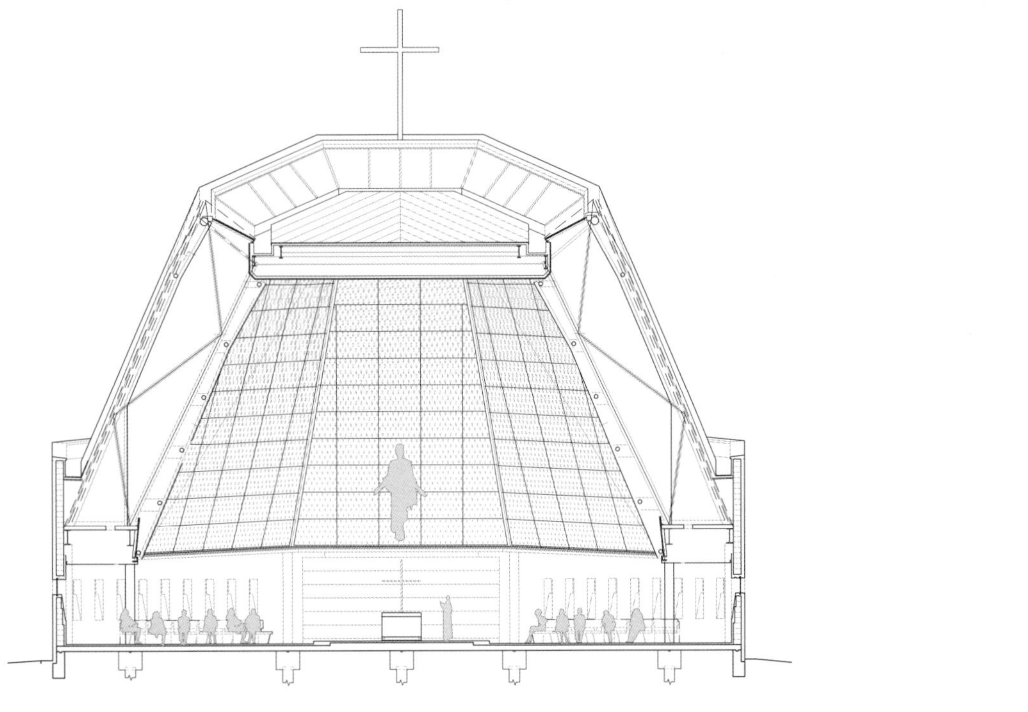
0
10
20 ft

Art glass windows by Caribbean artist José Bedia (above) and New Orleans artist Laurel Porcari (opposite) are inspired, respectively, by the Stations of the Cross and West African textiles.

In designing a sacred space, you must put yourself in the mood to receive the sacred.

he Theatre School at DePaul University

The Theatre School, DePaul University

2013

Chicago, Illinois, US

The Theatre School is a gateway to DePaul University's Lincoln Park campus. Used for instruction and performance, the building welcomes students, faculty, and staff during the day, and theatergoers at night. The building's openness and transparency put the excitement of a theater education on view for the whole neighborhood.

We designed the five-story building as a composition of rectangular forms clad in limestone, translucent glass, and transparent glass. Projecting from the building at the corner is the experimental theater, serving as a sign for the university. Its north façade softly glows at night, a beacon for the Theatre School. Similar to a scrim, the translucent glass wall can reveal the 100-seat flexible theater behind it, when illuminated.

Behind-the-scenes activity is visible to both theatergoers and passersby. Floor-to-ceiling glass on the ground floor places the scene shop, metal shop, and paint shops on display. Theatergoers gathering in the glass-enclosed lobby for the Fullerton Stage, a 250-seat thrust theater, are also visible from the street. The Theatre School is a beautiful building, a great theater school, and very good neighbor.

We wanted to make a very theatrical building that the users would participate in, with a great staircase in the middle where they can make their entrance.

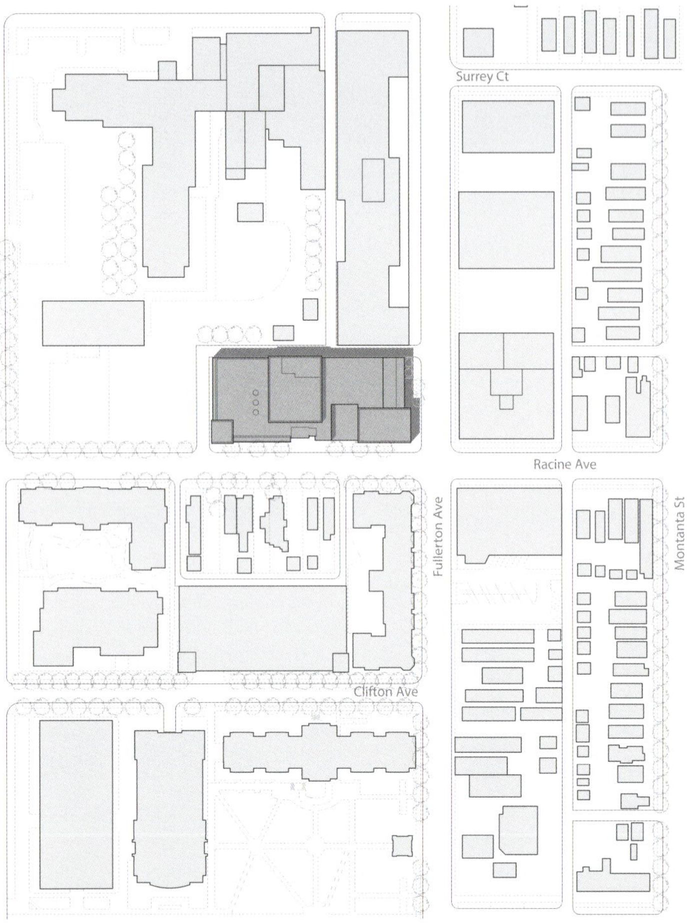
Surrey Ct
Racine Ave
Fullerton Ave
Montanta St
Clifton Ave

atre Scho

THE THEATRE SCHOOL
UHAUL

ABOVE AND OPPOSITE Views into and from the lobby allow activities inside the building and in the neighborhood to enliven the urban context.

1 Box office
2 Concessions
3 Lobby–public
4 Lobby–student
5 Painting shop
6 Platform
7 Shop

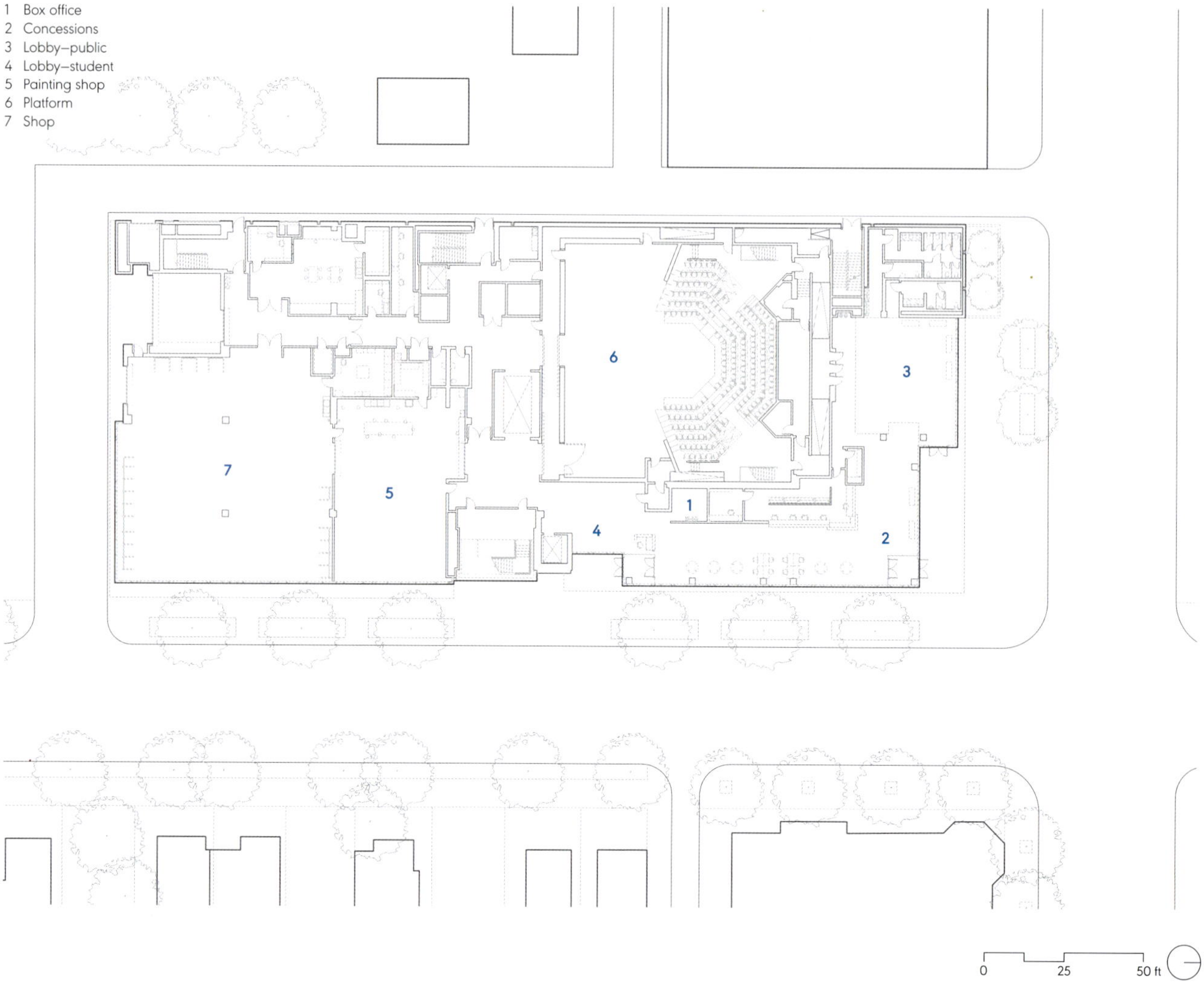

THE THEATRE SCHOOL FOUNDED IN 1925 IN HONOR OF KENNETH

Ample spaces throughout are geared toward rehearsals (opposite top), make-up (opposite bottom), and costume design and fabrication (above).

Hydraulic folding bridge allows circulation connectivity on the second floor with the option of moving large pieces of scenery through the first floor.

EXIT

543210

Theater production activities throughout the building become a performance for those on the street, as glass walls allow spectators to take in the action, such as in the scenery shop.

FREEDOM
FREEDOM
FREEDOM
FREEDOM
FREEDOM
FREEDOM
FREEDOM
FREEDOM
FREEDOM
FREEDOM

Porta Nuova Garibaldi and UniCredit Headquarters

2013

Milan, Italy

Our master plan for a mixed-use development north of Milan's historic city center was selected in an international competition. It redevelops an area of abandoned railyards adjacent to the Garibaldi train station, creating a new and grand gateway to the city. One of the largest redevelopment projects in Milan, it includes residential, office, retail, and hotel components, with a strong focus on pedestrian activity at the base of the buildings.

We designed the largest components of the development: office and retail complexes totaling 70,600 square meters (759,900 square feet) and a podium with 60,000 square meters (645,800 square feet) of retail, restaurants, and parking. The development creates new, continuous pedestrian connections between neighborhoods that were once quite isolated from each other. Porta Nuova also includes a new public space, Piazza Gae Aulenti. The piazza connects with the Corso Como, a well-known pedestrianized street full of fashion boutiques, restaurants, and cafés.

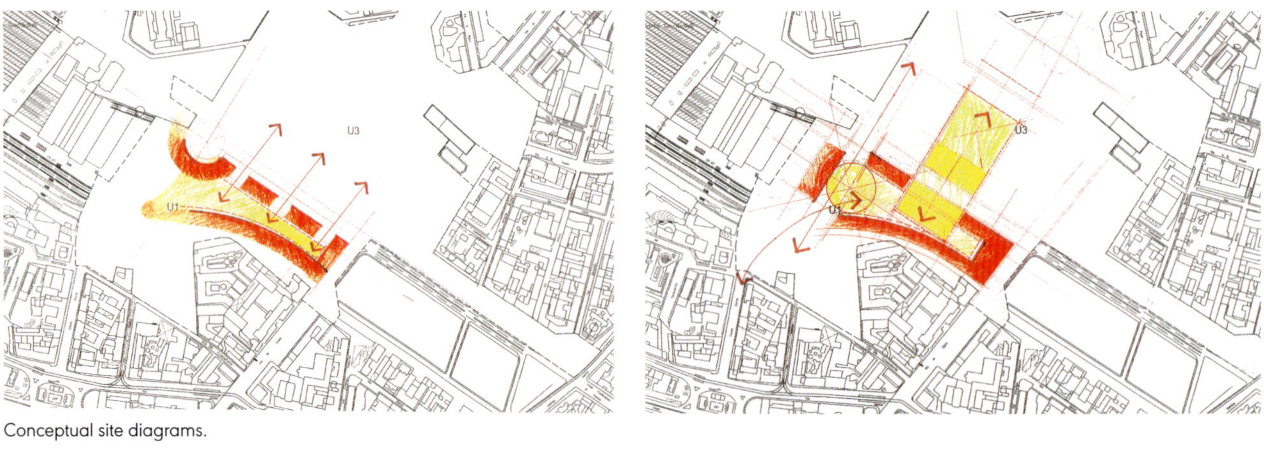

Conceptual site diagrams.

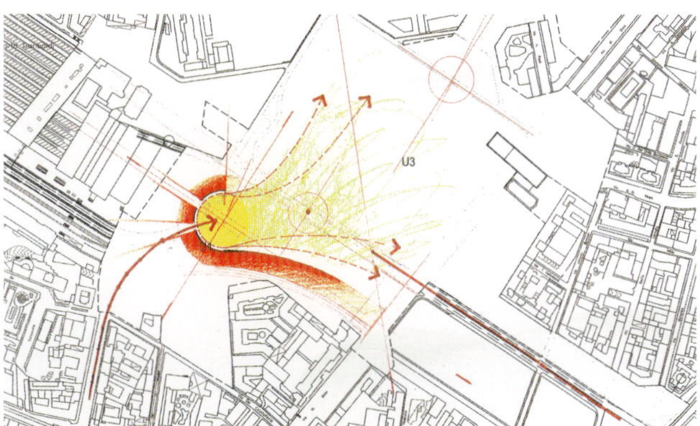
U3

U3
U1

UniCredit

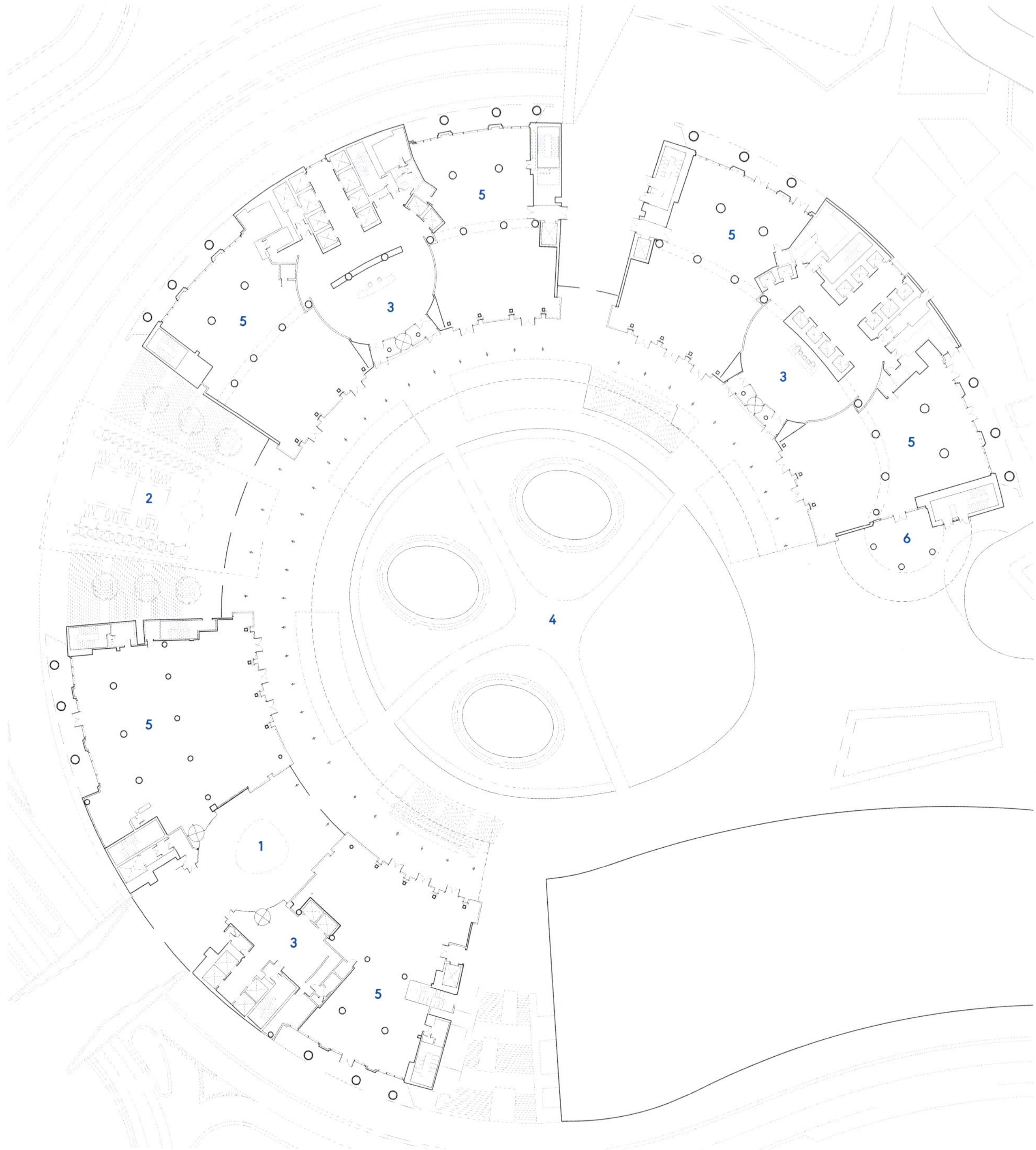

1 Corso Como Passage
2 Garibaldi stairs
3 Lobby
4 Piazza Garibaldi
5 Retail
6 Taxi drop-off

UniCredit Headquarters

These three office towers and their podium are the largest components of Porta Nuova Garibaldi, a mixed-use development north of Milan's city center. We were selected to design the master plan for the 7-hectare (18-acre) development in an international competition. It creates a new and grand gateway to the city.

The narrow, curved forms of the towers—31, 22, and 11 stories tall—enclose a circular piazza, a new public space that links the buildings to their surroundings. Facing the piazza, the façades incorporate sunshades, emphasizing the buildings' fluid shape.

Around the piazza, a canopy connects the podiums of the three towers. Two levels of shops sit above the piazza, with additional retail and dining at the sunken level. In addition to retail, the combined podium contains parking and a direct connection to the Stazione Garibaldi railway station. Extending south, the piazza meets Corso Como, a pedestrian street of fashion boutiques, restaurants, and cafés.

Sustainability was a major design consideration for the project, and all of the buildings are certified LEED Gold. The potable water demand was reduced by 30 percent through such measures as efficient drip-irrigation systems, climate-based controllers, extraction of groundwater for non-potable water supply, and low-flow fixtures. Energy consumption is 37 percent lower than a comparable building in Milan through the use of high-performance glazing, dedicated outside air units with heat recovery, localized fan coils for space heating and cooling, river-water heat extraction/rejection, water-to-water heat pumps, and high-efficiency lighting and daylight controls. Recycled-content building materials were used and at least 50 percent of construction debris was diverted from the waste stream.

Inside the buildings, filtered outside air helps to achieve high air quality, while building monitoring systems ensure thermal comfort. To enhance the desirable working environment, a direct line of daylight reaches 90 percent of all occupied areas.

The project won a Top 10 Skyscraper Award from Emporis in 2012.

The center of this urban complex is Piazza Garibaldi, surrounded by the towers and a lower canopy that rings the public gathering space.

RIPLEY

Torre Costanera
2016
Santiago, Chile

At 300 meters (985 feet) high, Torre Costanera is the tallest building in Santiago and indeed the whole of South America.

Torre Costanera's location so close to the Andes creates a unique setting for the design of a tall building. No human-built form can compete with the power and beauty of these mountains. The building that we designed is a part of the city, its tallest element against the backdrop of the Andes.

Torre Costanera is a true skyscraper. All good skyscrapers share some characteristics, such as a strongly defined vertical axis—the 'axis mundi' that connects heaven with earth. The tower, occupied by Chilean retail giant Cencosud, has a slightly tapered, slender form which aspires to the heights of the mountains, and culminates in a simple crown. It is a beautiful, strong form. Against the backdrop of the Andes, in this unique context, it was important that the form of the tower be simple and clear.

RIPLEY

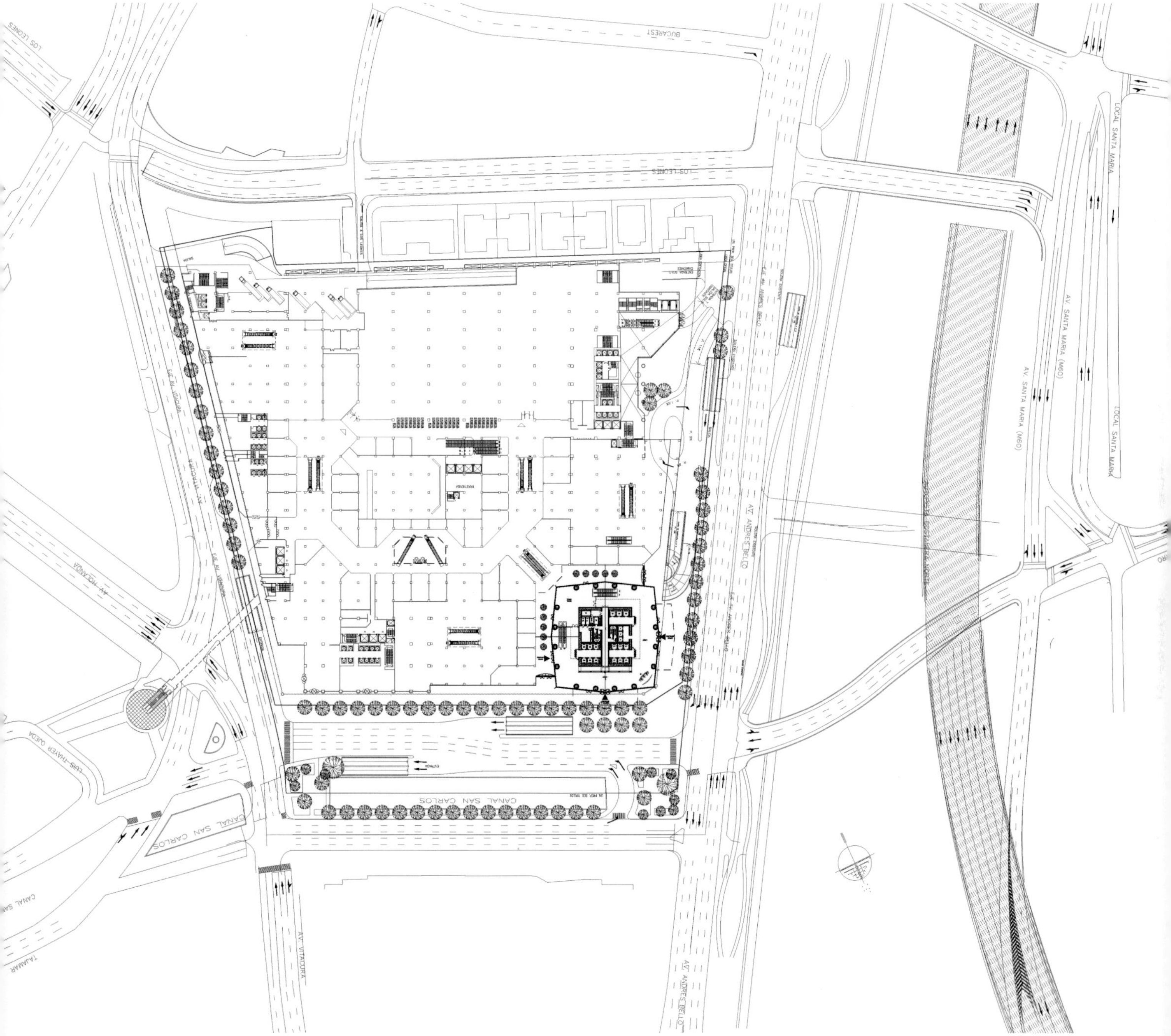
BUCAREST
LOS LEONES
LOS LEONES
AV. SANTA MARIA (M60)
AV. SANTA MARIA (M60)
LOCAL SANTA MARIA
LOCAL SANTA MARIA
AV. ANDRES BELLO
AV. ANDRES BELLO
AV. VITACURA
AV. VITACURA
AV. HOLANDA
CANAL SAN CARLOS
CANAL SAN CARLOS
LUIS THAYER OJEDA
TAJAMAR

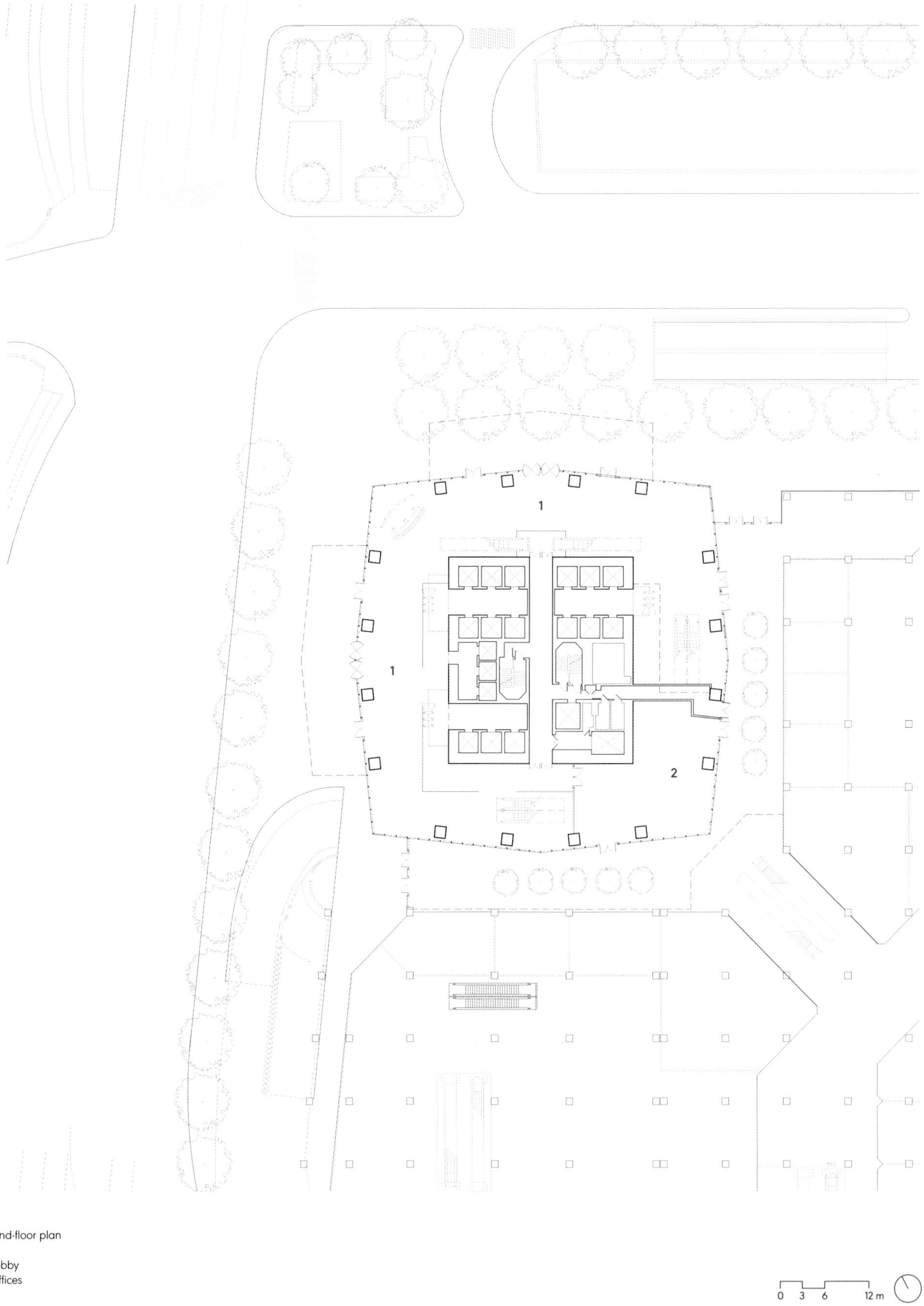

Ground-floor plan

1 Lobby
2 Offices

An observation deck at the tower top allows panoramic views of the city; at night the deck is bathed in a purple light.

MEDEL
17

Hancher
2016
Iowa City, Iowa, US

Hancher reaches audiences beyond the University of Iowa and it is widely recognized for commissioning new works of dance and music. The new home for this renowned institution is on a rise on the ground, high above the Iowa River floods which are increasing in intensity and frequency.

We designed sweeping horizontal forms that echo the landscape and the curve of the river, and the design draws from the building's natural surroundings.

The building creates a strong focal point across the Iowa River from the main campus. Cladding on the auditorium's main structure is stainless steel with a brushed satin finish, which glows gently under the Iowa sun.

The new Hancher Auditorium is a vision of beauty and a promise of extraordinary performances.

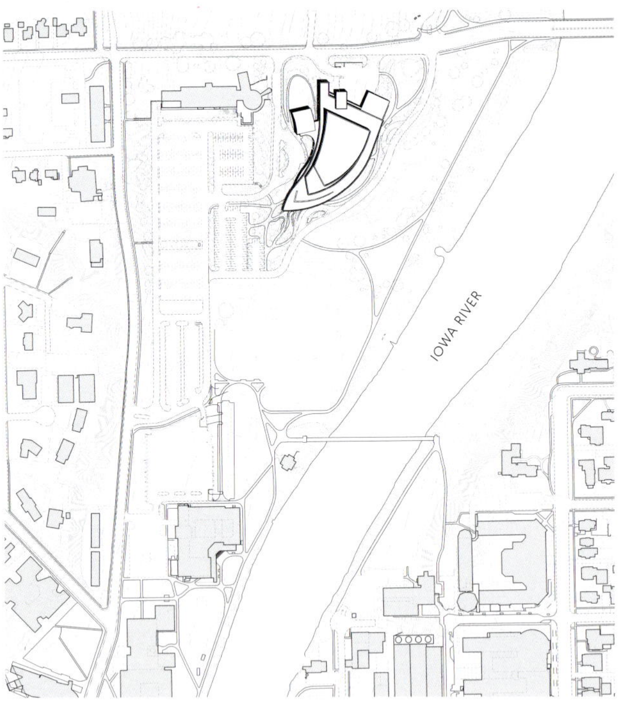

Hancher offers sweeping views of the Iowa River from its ample terraces.

HANCHER

OPPOSITE The lobby's dramatic layering of spaces with views to the landscape.
ABOVE Exterior and interior of the rehearsal room with the backdrop of the campus.

Ground-floor plan

1 Scene shop
2 Receiving
3 Stage
4 Rehearsal room
5 Hall
6 Lobby

Building section

1 Stage House
2 Hall
3 Lobby

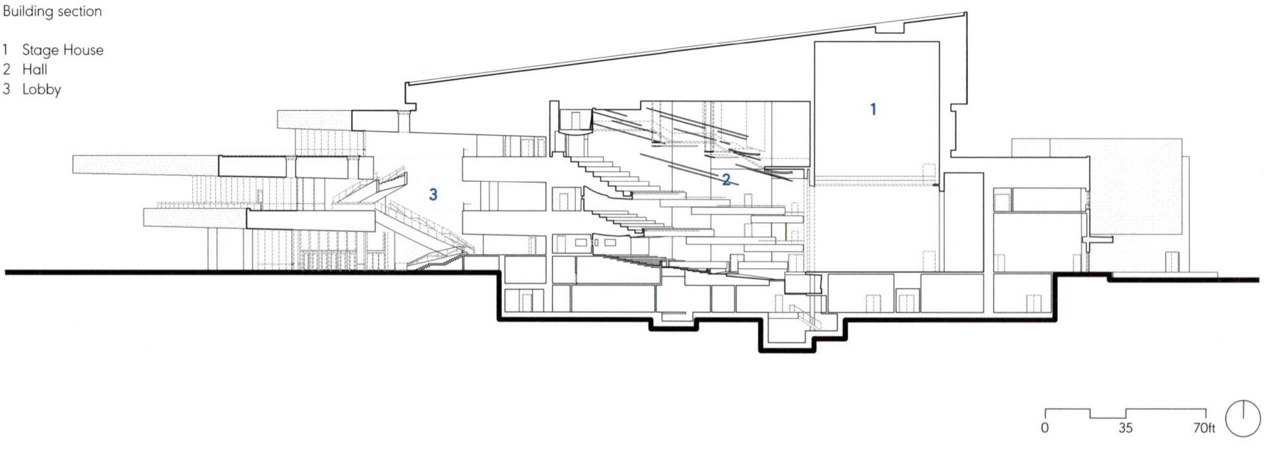

Arced lighting over the performance space, inspired by circular geometry, echoes the exterior form of the building.

Maral Explanada
2016
Mar del Plata, Argentina

Located by the sea in Argentina's largest beach resort city, Maral Explanada consists of three residential towers. The towers sit above the rocky Atlantic shoreline at Playa Chica, one of Mar del Plata's best-known beaches. With their pleasant setting and well-designed amenities, the towers offer the promise of easy living by the sea.

Our design for the towers is based on a curving, pinwheel-shaped plan which creates a lively silhouette. The dynamic plan allows for four apartments per floor, all with sea views and generous balconies. The towers are three svelte, sculptural forms on a cliff at the water's edge, which will appear to dance with each other.

The towers are on a steep site. The landscape design by Balmori Associates mediates the incline with a series of terraces which recreate the natural coastline. The terraces include spaces for walking and leisure, as well as an outdoor swimming pool.

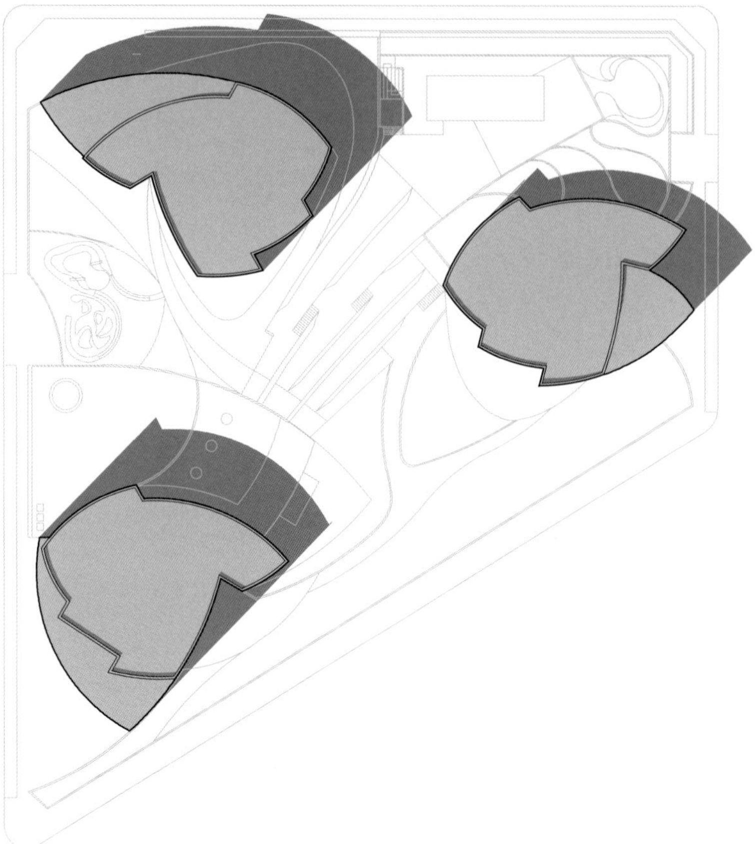

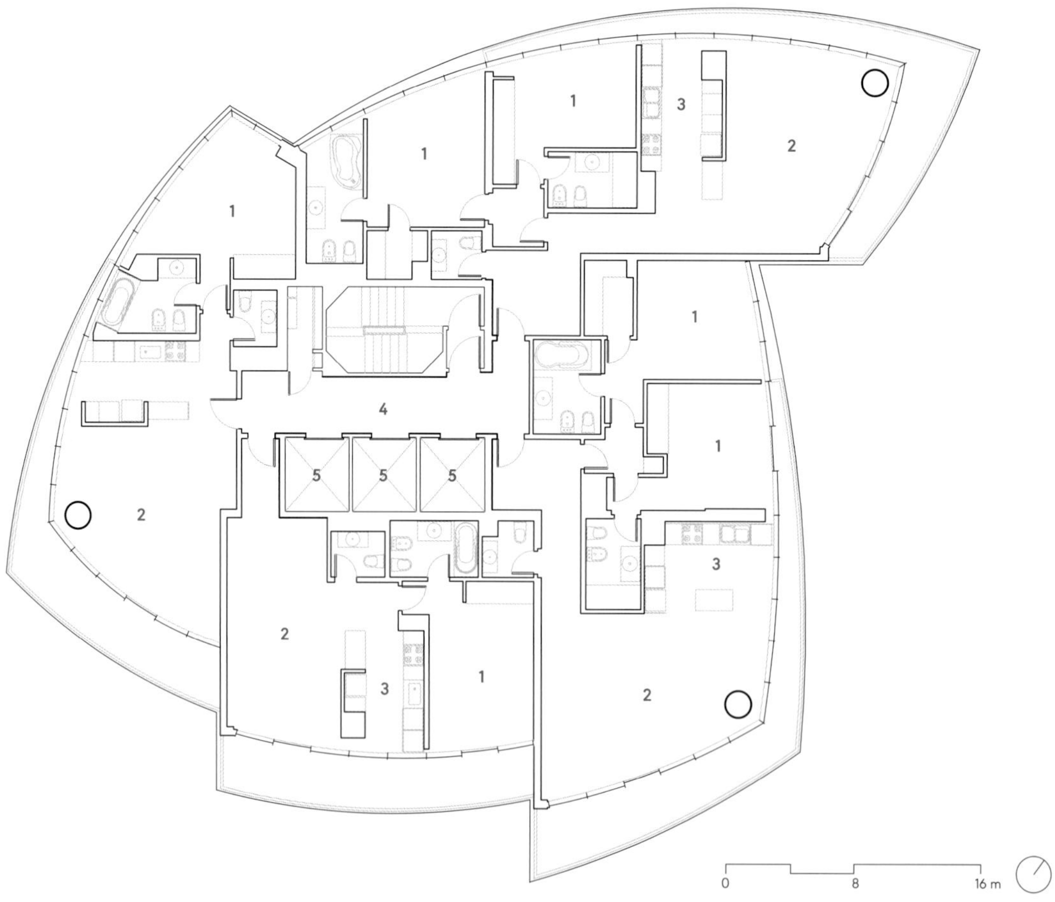

Upper-floor plan

1 Bedroom
2 Living/dining room
3 Kitchen
4 Lobby
5 Elevator

WINTRUST
ARENA

Wintrust Arena
2017
Chicago,
Illinois, US

We won the Wintrust Arena commission in an international competition. This project adds a mid-size venue to McCormick Place, the country's largest convention center. The new arena, which doubles as an arena for DePaul University basketball, is part of a redevelopment plan to transform the neighborhood into a vibrant entertainment district.

The arena has a roof that swells upward over the arena seating. With this elegant curving, light gray membrane roof and lightweight glass walls, the building follows in the Chicago tradition of architecture with strong roots in engineering. The smooth, arching canopy has long dramatic rising arcs that will be lit at night, creating an instantly recognizable image for the new arena.

CHOOSE
CHICAGO
WINTRUST
ARENA

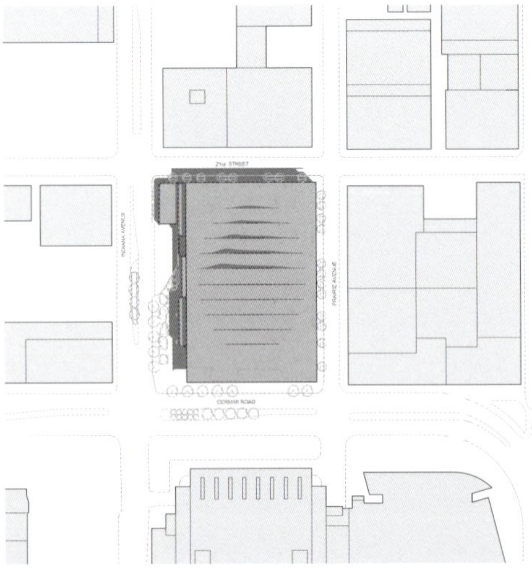

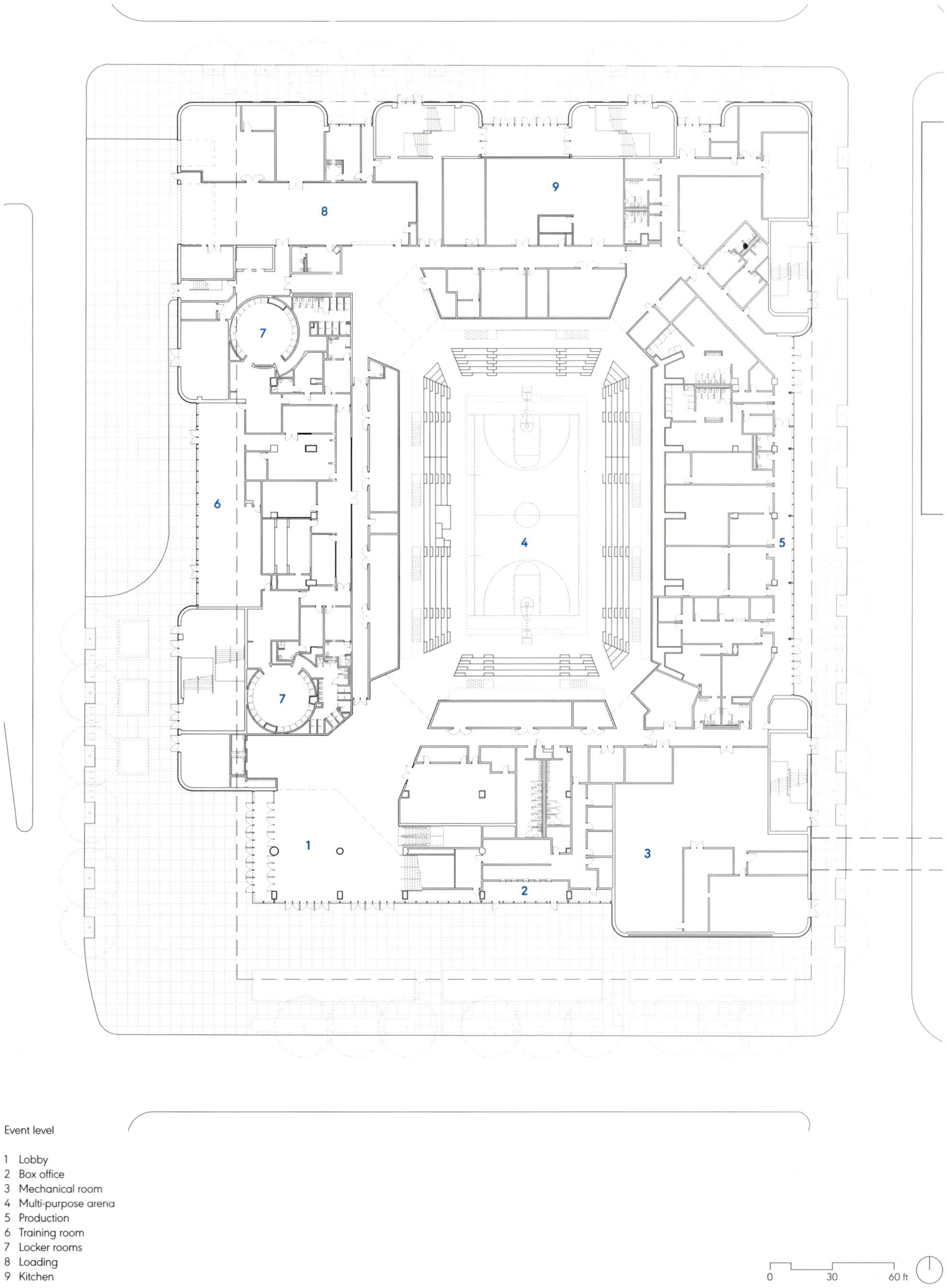

Event level

1 Lobby
2 Box office
3 Mechanical room
4 Multi-purpose arena
5 Production
6 Training room
7 Locker rooms
8 Loading
9 Kitchen

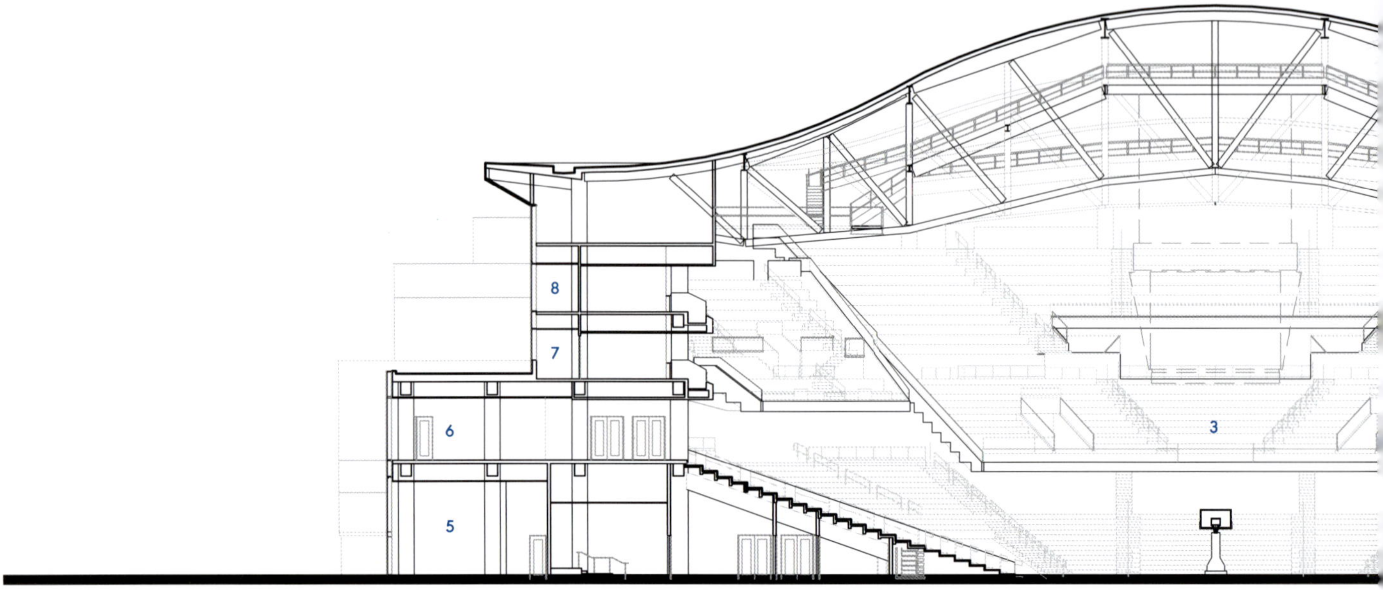

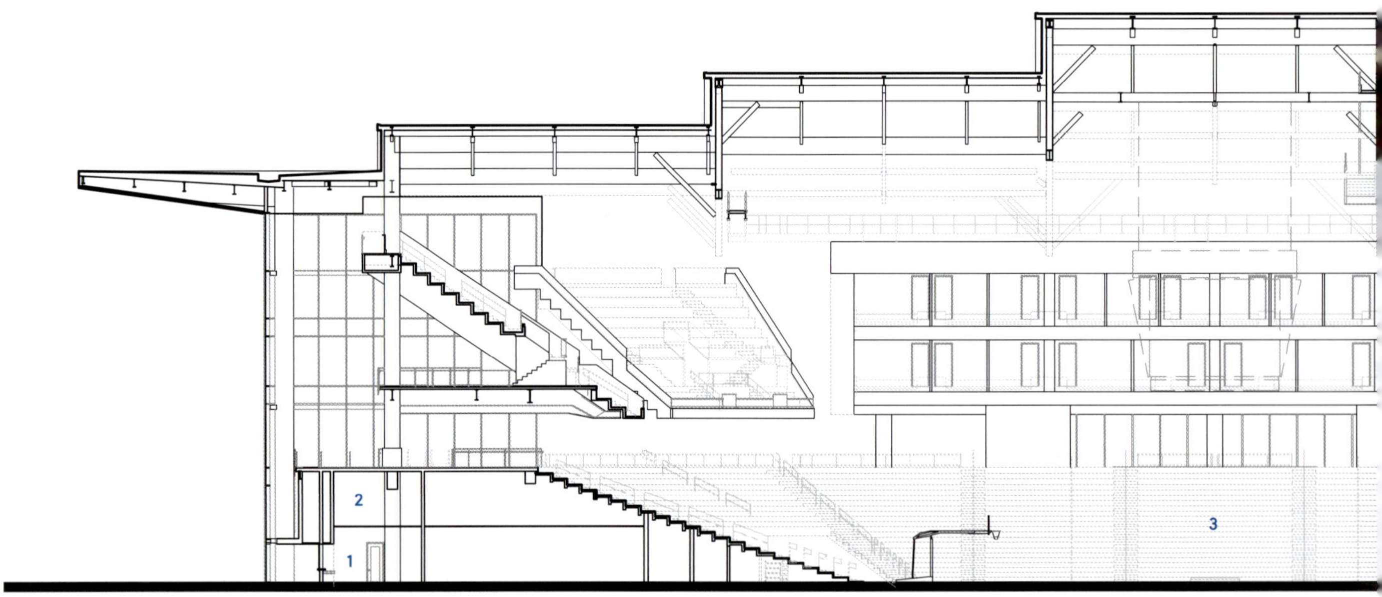

1 Box office
2 Main concourse
3 Multi-purpose arena
4 Kitchen
5 Training room
6 Club
7 Lower suites
8 Upper suites
9 Production

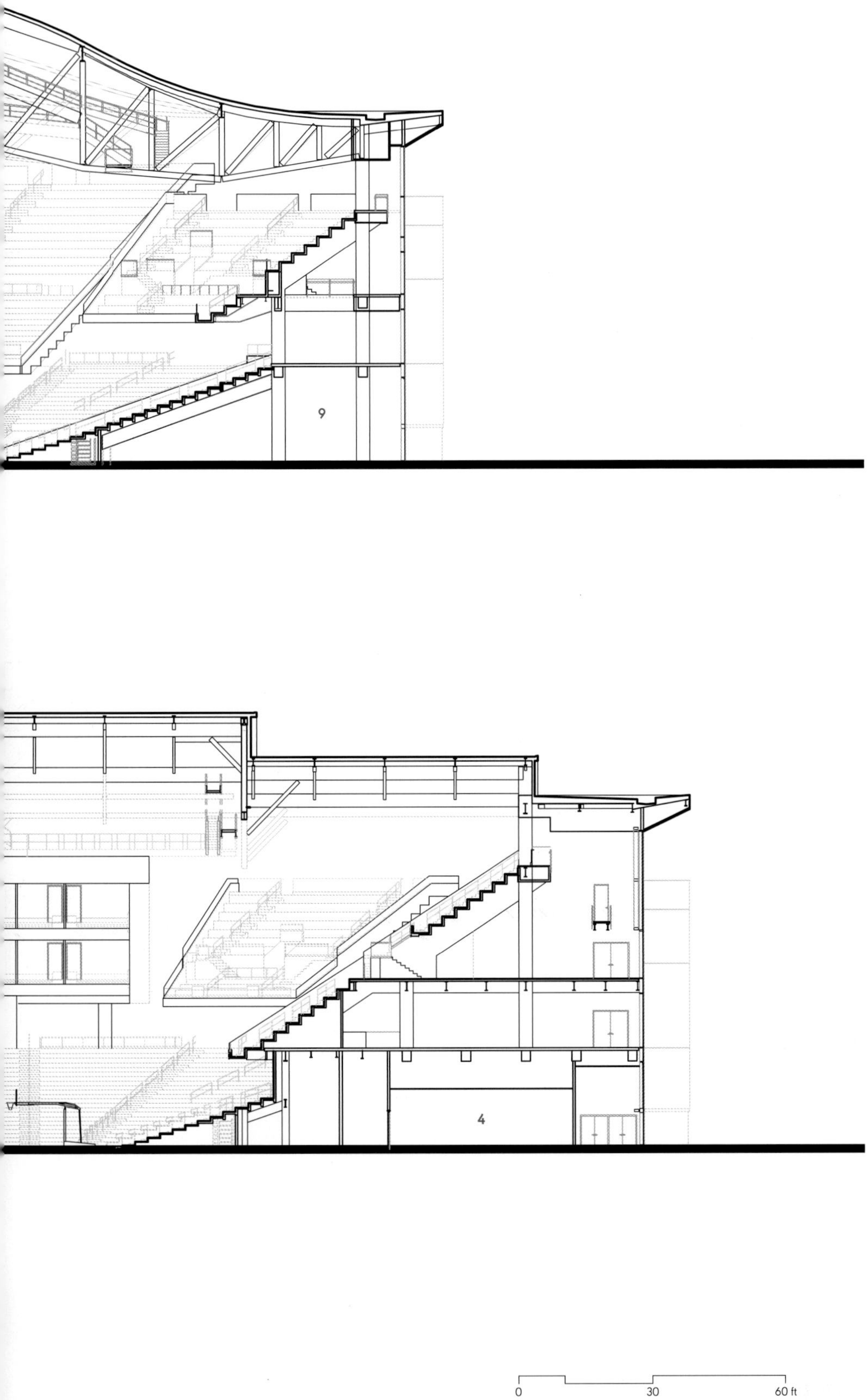
9
4
0
30
60 ft

MARQUETTE
PROVIDENCE
ST. JOHN'S

Floor Seating
Courtside
Lounge
EXIT

WINTRUST
ARENA

Torre Sevilla
2017
Seville, Spain

We were selected to design Torre Sevilla in an international competition. Located on part of the site of the 1992 World's Fair in Seville, the project consists of a 37-story hotel, office tower, and four-story retail podium. The tower defines the new skyline of Seville and engages in a dialog with La Giralda, the city's landmark cathedral.

Seville is a wonderful city with a unique charm which preserves the beauty of past centuries while striving to find its place in the 21st century. My intention was to design a modern but very Sevillian tower, contemporary yet rooted in the city's history and character in its design. Fortunately, the site is located across the old Guadalquivir River, on the former site of the 1992 World's Fair, and this gave us a certain degree of freedom in the design of the project.

As for almost all of the buildings in Seville, providing sun protection was a major issue that contributed to the character of the tower, shielding it by multiple strategies that provide shade and a unique character. The slabs on each floor cantilever to shade the south, east, and west elevations, but almost disappear towards the north. The cantilevering slabs are supplemented by horizontal and vertical sunshades, which will prevent the sun's rays from striking the building during the middle of the day.

The site is approximately 4 hectares (10 acres) and almost all of it will be accessible to the public: the extended plaza, the lower buildings' green roofs, and the tower observation deck. I hope that the roof garden trails will becomea well-used promenade for Sevillians and visitors alike. The tower culminates in a public space—an ample observation deck that offers spectacular views of Seville to the east, Triana to the south, and the countryside to the west and north.

The lower buildings open up like arms greeting visitors to the public space. As you walk towards the tower, the space gently descends and narrows to create a typical narrow Sevillian street that will be protected from the sun by a retractable canvas awnings during the summer. The narrow street finally opens up to embrace the tower.

The tower with its sun-shaded elevation is already perceived as a slender, vertical, and vibrant city landmark.

Low wings under construction feature landscaped public roof spaces.

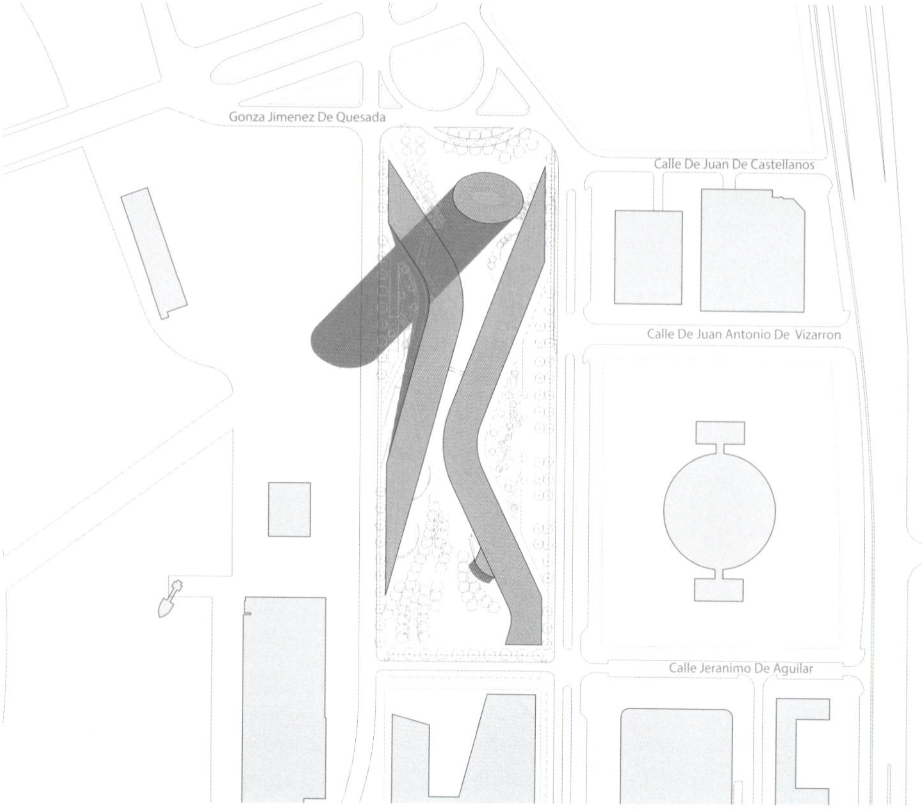

Fixed sunscreens on the lower wings are positioned to block solar gain at critical times throughout the day.

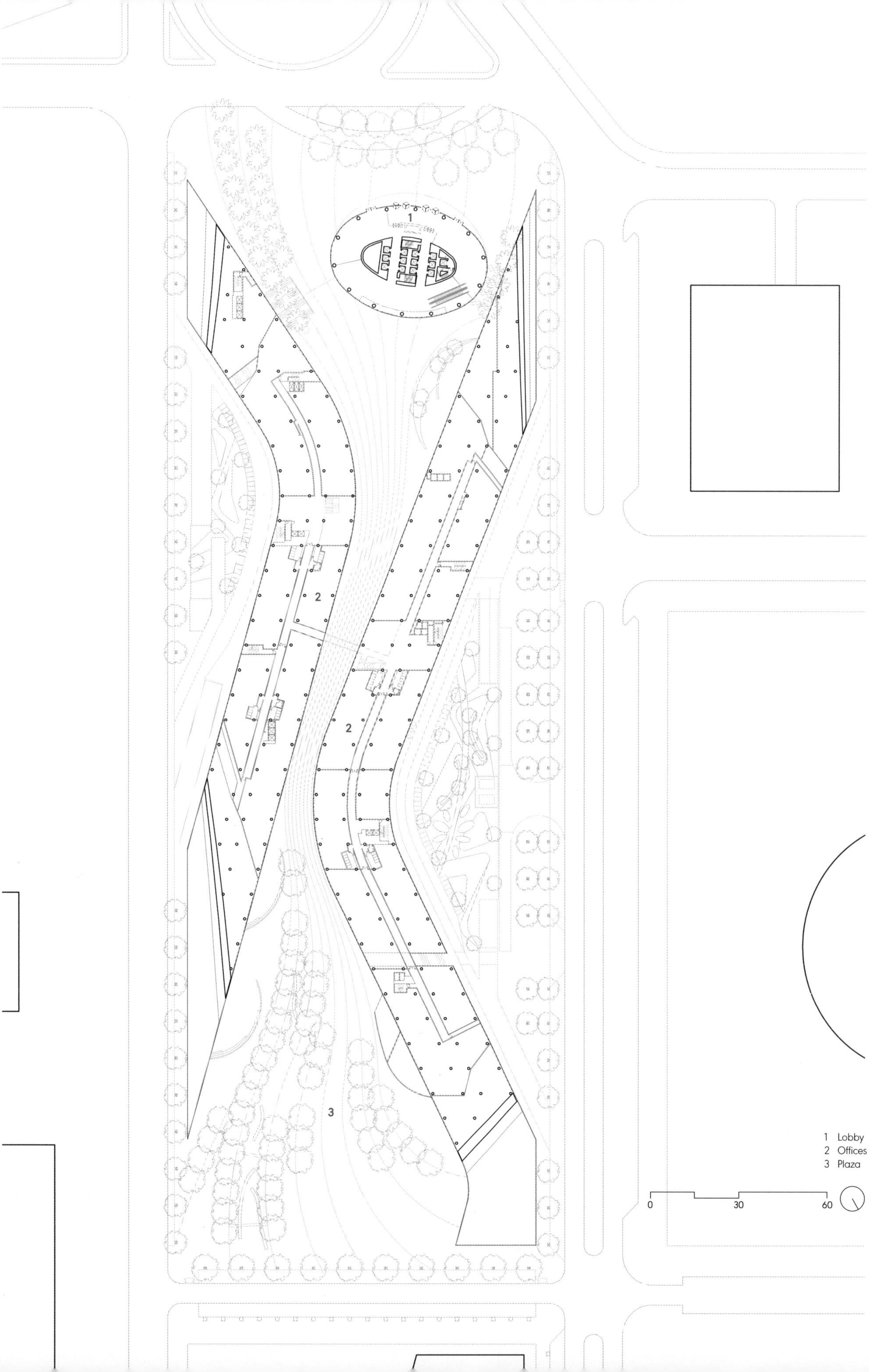
1
2
2
3
1 Lobby
2 Offices
3 Plaza
0
30
60

NH HOTELS

Torre Banco Macro
2016
Buenos Aires,
Argentina

The 30-story headquarters for Banco Macro is being built on one of the last vacant lots of Catalinas Norte, a prominent planned business district in downtown Buenos Aires.

The design of this tower is very dear to me. It is nearly oval in plan with a gentle inward curve as the tower rises. This shape is sculptural and efficient, fitting the building well into an irregularly shaped site. The sloping apex of the tower gives it a strong personality.

The reflective glass curtain wall has a smooth and taut appearance. The 1.0-meter-by-3.8-meter (3-foot-by-12-foot) glass panels are held in place with vertical silicon glazing. Stainless steel cylindrical mullions mark each floor on the exterior, while the narrow panes of glass make the tower look like a sculptured object made of curved glass.

The building is being designed for a LEED Gold rating, incorporating high-performance building systems and sustainable materials.

The Torre Banco Macro is already an eye-catching building and it promises to be one of the most beautiful buildings in Buenos Aires.

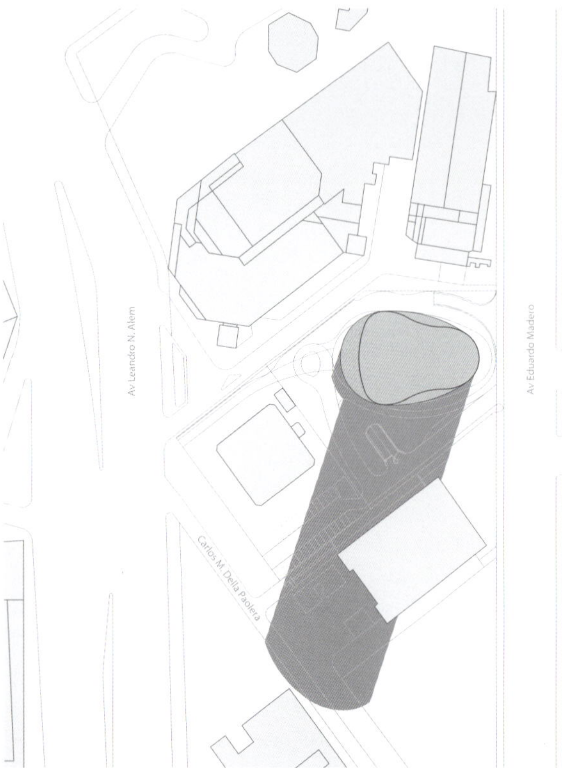

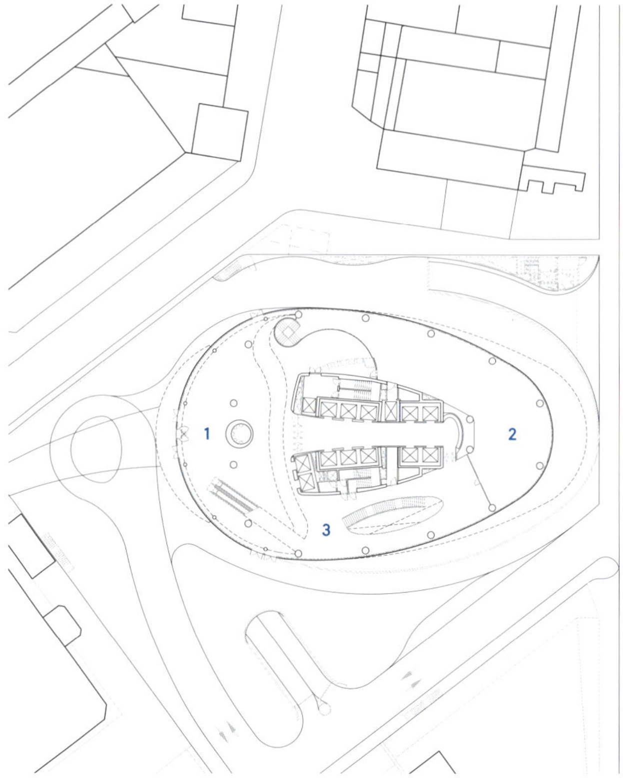

1 Main lobby
2 Bank branch
3 Access to auditorium below

HAMBURG SÜD

Salesforce Tower and Transit Center

2018

San Francisco, California, US

Salesforce Tower is the tallest building in San Francisco, joining the Golden Gate Bridge as one of the skyline's defining elements. We won an international competition in 2007 to design the tower and the the transit center at its base.

The Transbay Joint Powers Authority, a public entity created by the City of San Francisco to develop the new transit center, sponsored the competition. To help fund the building, part of the site was offered for sale to teams of developers and architects in an invited competition. Pelli Clarke Pelli and Hines, its development partner, submitted a design that focuses on sustainability, neighborhood development, and financial feasibility.

Standing 326 meters (1,070 feet) tall, the tower, which I designed with Fred Clarke, has the simple, timeless form of the obelisk, giving the 60-story tower a slender, tapering silhouette. The walls are composed of clear glass within a pearlescent metal grid. The horizontal and vertical accents gradually taper in depth to accentuate the curved glass corners. The walls rise past the top floor to form a transparent crown which appears to dissolve into the sky.

At its base, Salesforce Tower connects to the transit center, which will house 11 Bay Area transit systems. On top of the Transit Center and linked directly to the tower is a 2.2-hectare (5.4-acre) public park, which will offer recreational, educational, and nature activities.

Each floor of the tower has integrated metal sunshades, calibrated to maximize light and views while reducing solar gain. High-performance, low-emissivity glass helps reduce the building's cooling load. Cooling is provided in part by heat-exchanging coils wrapped around the tower's foundations.

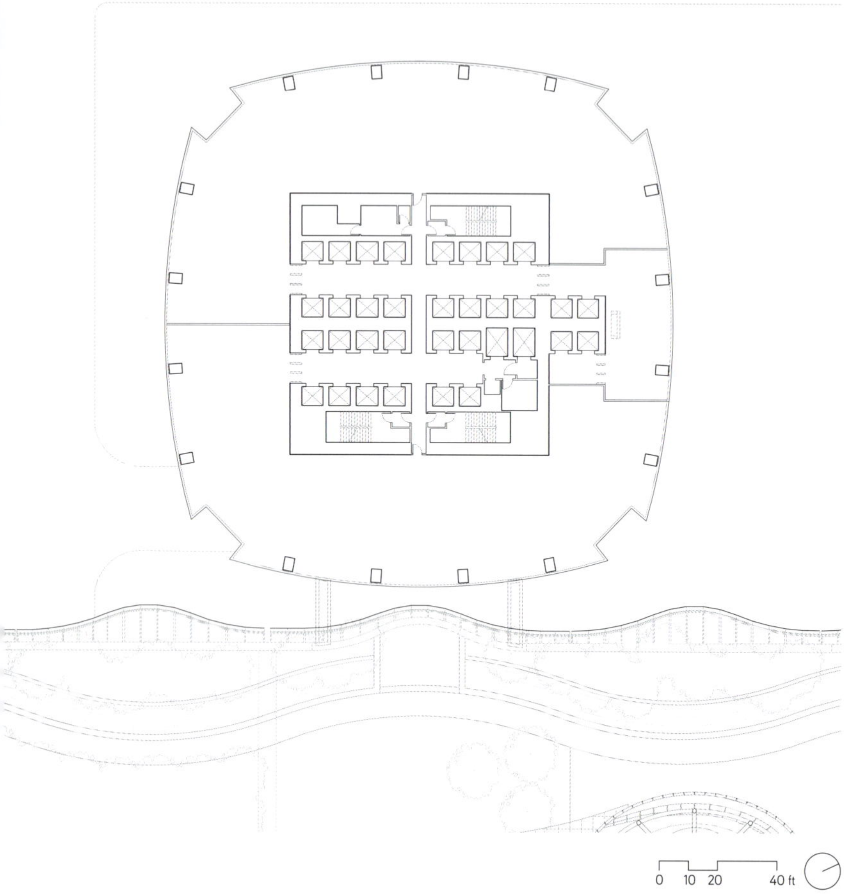
0 10 20 40 ft

DO NOT
BLOCK
INTERSECTION

Salesforce Transit Center

We won the commission to design the Salesforce Transit Center in an international competition. Fred Clarke and I led the design. When it opens, the transit center will be a state-of-the-art multi-modal transit station in downtown San Francisco, linking eleven transit systems and connecting the city to the region, the state, and the rest of the country. The highly sustainable design includes a 2.2-hectare (5.4-acre) park on its roof which will anchor the growth of a new mixed-use neighborhood. The transit center's soaring light-filled spaces will give San Francisco a grand entrance which befits its status as one of the world's great cities.

The new Transit Center will stretch for four blocks along Mission Street, one block south of the city's Financial District. A gently undulating perforated wall, floating above the street on angled steel columns, creates a graceful, luminous, and welcoming image. At street level, shops and cafés attract visitors and energize the surrounding neighborhood, while high above, the trees and flowers of the rooftop park invite people to visit for longer periods, transforming the Transit Center from a commuter hub into an urban destination.

The heart of the transit center's design is the rooftop park. Dense with nature and activities, it has over a dozen entry points, as well as bridges to surrounding buildings. Active and passive uses are woven into the landscape, including an amphitheater, cafés, and a children's playground, in addition to quiet areas for reading, picnicking, or simply taking a break. Designed by Peter Walker Partners, the park presents a wide variety of Bay Area ecologies, from oak trees to a wetland marsh.

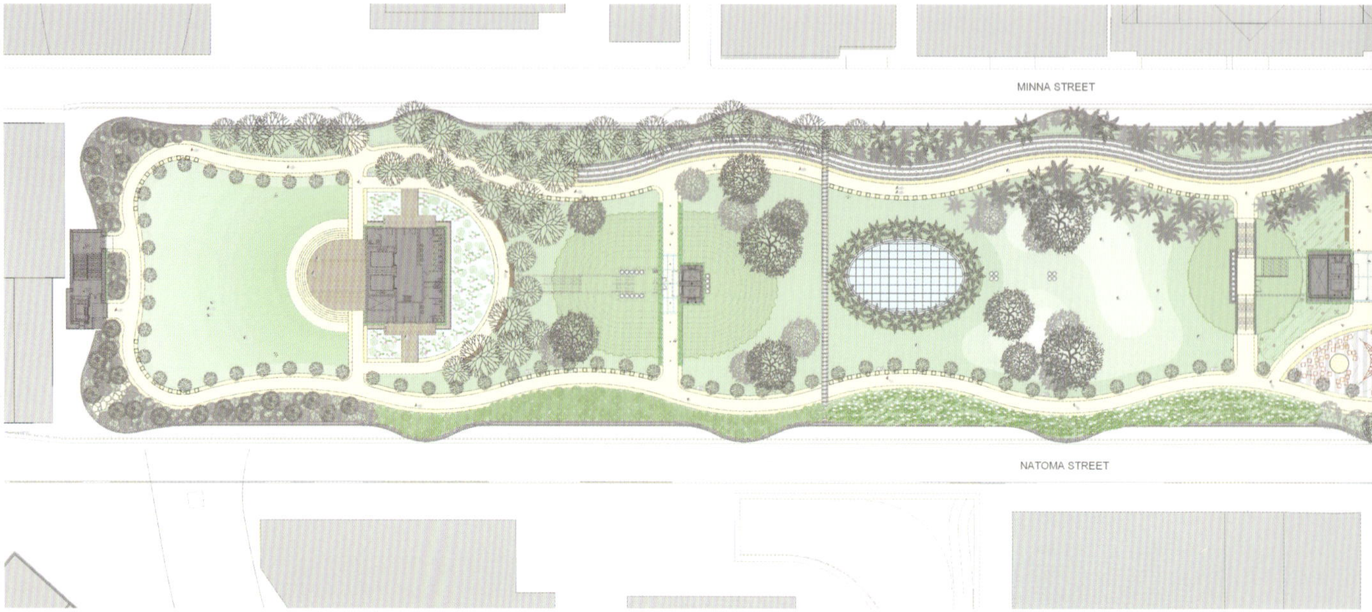
MINNA STREET
NATOMA STREET

Park Level
Bus Deck Level
Ground Level
Grand Hall
Mission Square
Retail
Retail
Lower Concourse Level
Public Concourse & Waiting Area
Train Platform Level
CHSR Platform
Caltrain Platform

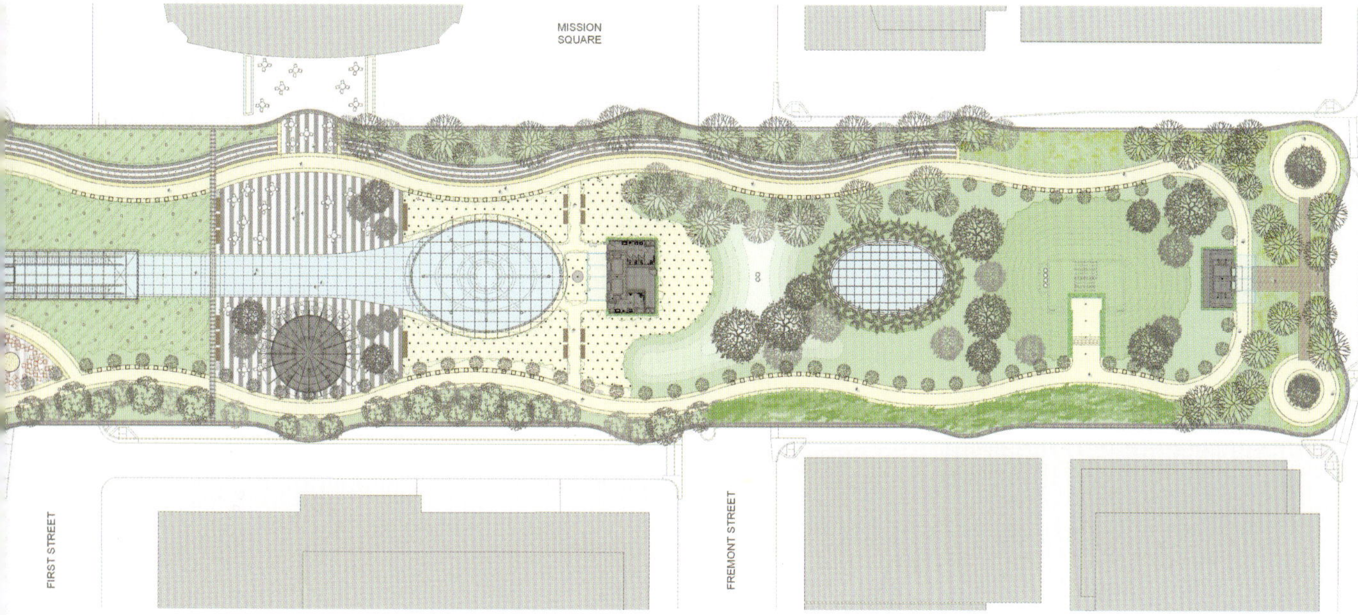
MISSION
SQUARE
FIRST STREET
FREMONT STREET

OPPOSITE The four-block-long building takes the form of an urban park in the air with multi-levels below, punctured by light columns that will deliver natural illumination throughout.

Salesforce Transit Center's structural frame is sheathed with a perforated metal panel system, designed by English mathematical physicist Sir Roger Penrose, who developed the "Penrose tiling" pattern. Salesforce Transit Center connects with the Salesforce Tower and extends over streets.

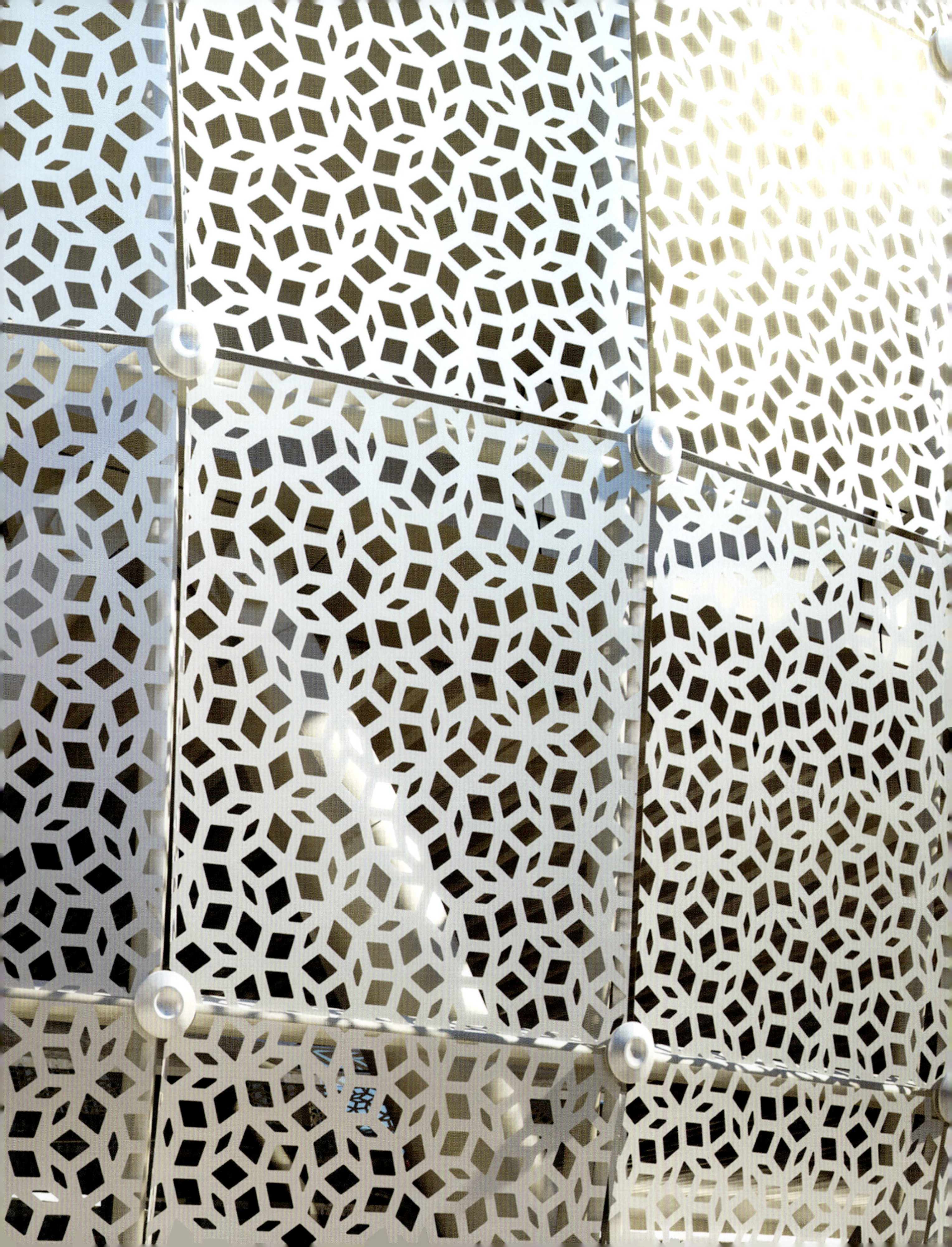

ABOVE AND OPPOSITE TOP Construction photos of Salesforce Transit Center, which slips behind the Salesforce Tower. OPPOSITE BOTTOM Cesar Pelli in front of a light column that will deliver illumination through multi-levels.

Salesforce Tower

Reflections
by Cesar Pelli

I knew I wanted to be an architect when I understood that it meant that I could contribute to making better cities with my building designs and that, at the same time, my architecture could aspire to be a work of art. I was was not even 20, but I felt that I could dedicate my life to such endeavors. I still do.

From the beginning, after architecture school in Argentina and the US, and experience working with Eero Saarinen, I wanted to design my own buildings, but I believed that I could never have my own office because I did not have connections here that are often very important in building a practice. I also knew that I did not have the character or skills to solicit work from others. Therefore, to be able to design I believed that I would need to be in charge of design in a group with others that would obtain the commissions.

I was recommended to DJMM in Los Angeles, which was looking for a Director of Design. After negotiating my freedom of action, I accepted. My first opportunity at DJMM was to propose alternatives to a master plan for the Santa Inez Canyon in the Santa Monica Mountains, in LA. This was the Urban Nucleus, an original design that I produced with Tony Lumsden, then my Assistant Director of Design. The project was very well received in the profession.

I designed other well-noted buildings at DJMM, such as the headquarters for COMSAT Laboratories and for Teledyne Labs, and Kukui Gardens (public housing in Honolulu). My work caught the attention of the architectural critic Esther McCoy, who recommended me to Victor Gruen and Associates, an LA firm that was looking for a new Partner for Design. After four years, I left DJMM and joined Gruen.

Some young designers that I had attracted to Gruen and I decided to enter an open international competition to design headquarters for the UN in Vienna. We developed an exciting and novel scheme that was selected for First Prize by the jury. We all went to Vienna to receive the prize, but the government decided to give the commission to the 4th-prize winner, a Viennese architect. His design, a banal grouping of heavy buildings, was built to Vienna's great loss.

At Gruen I had greater freedom and better support, and I was able to design some beautiful and daring buildings, such as the San Bernardino City Hall, the American Embassy building in Tokyo, and the Pacific Design Center.

After nine years at Gruen I realized that my potential was limited within the partnership, and I resigned from my position as partner to gain flexibility although I continued to work for the firm.

With news of my resigning from Gruen, I received several offers to head schools of architecture. One of those was Yale, a school that I knew and admired. I accepted to come to New Haven and assume the deanship of the School of Architecture of Yale University. I had taught most of my life and I love teaching as much as I do design.

This was an exciting moment for me. I was able to bring the school back to life after the crisis of the 1960s, and to attract as studio teachers some of the best-known and most creative architects of the moment.

Shortly after assuming my deanship I was selected to design the renovation and expansion of the Museum of Modern Art in New York City. I was happy being Dean of a great school with no plans to practice, but the opportunity to design a building for this iconic institution in Manhattan was irresistible.

This was also the opportunity I had dreamed of to design my office, considering my ideals and what I had learned about producing good, efficient, reliable work at Saarinen, DJMM, and Gruen. I also wanted an office of collaborators.

I asked Diana Balmori, my wife, who was teaching at SUNY, Oswego, and Fred Clarke—a young and bright designer that I had attracted to Gruen and was now teaching at Rice University—to join me in New Haven. I associated with Gruen Associates to do the construction documents.

The expansion of MoMA was a difficult problem. We had to design what was to be a new museum within existing structures and with very little money. Our design was supervised by the Board of Directors. Its president was Blanchette Rockefeller, a wonderful, very intelligent lady. On the Board there were some well-known architects such as Philip Johnson, Gordon Bunshaft, and Edward Larrabee Barnes. I am still very happy and proud of our design. It worked well, it was beautiful, and it was exciting to use. But it doesn't exist anymore. It was completely redone in the expansion of 2004, by Yoshio Taniguchi. Only the apartment tower remains of my design.

The design of MoMA lasted some seven years. Towards the end of this period I was invited by Olympia & York to participate in a competition to design the World Financial Center in lower Manhattan. We developed a scheme that responded to their needs and to the aesthetic preoccupations of the moment, and were selected.

The World Financial Center was a successful project and this established our firm as capable of handling large-scale, complex projects, of which we have since designed many.

In the early 1990s we were invited to participate in an international competition to design two towers for the company, Petronas, in Kuala Lumpur, Malaysia. We were asked to go to an interview with the Board of Directors of KLCC Berhad and the Prime Minister of Malaysia, Dr. Mahatir. During this interview, we were told that they wanted a Malaysian design but they could not explain what that meant.

I thought this was a key request and we endeavored to make the towers as Malaysian and as modern and exciting as possible. We were selected and later learned that we were the only firm to take this request seriously.

Another key international competition was for the design of the Salesforce Transit Center in San Francisco. This is a very complex and beautiful structure with a variety of dynamic spaces and a 1.82-hectare (4.5-acre) public park on its roof. We expect it to open in 2019. Next to it we designed a skyscraper for Salesforce scheduled to open in 2018. It is a beautiful tower that aspires to the sky. It will be the tallest structure in San Francisco and an appropriate symbol for this lovely city.

When I opened the firm, we employed as designers several students that showed great promise. Now, those designers that remain with us are principals in the firm and are able to shoulder greater responsibilities. In 2005, we changed the name of the firm to Pelli Clarke Pelli Architects to recognize the increased value and contributions of Fred Clarke (leading our New Haven office in projects all over the globe) and my son Rafael Pelli (who leads our New York office). The firm, I am confident, will produce many truly great designs.

Biography—Cesar Pelli FAIA, RIBA, JIA

Senior Principal

Cesar Pelli was born in Argentina where he earned a Diploma in Architecture from the Universidad Nacional de Tucumán. He came to the US with a scholarship to the University of Illinois in Urbana-Champaign. After obtaining a Master's Degree, he went to Bloomfield Hills, MI, to work in the offices of Eero Saarinen, serving as Project Designer for several buildings, including the TWA Terminal at JFK Airport in New York and Morse and Stiles Colleges at Yale University. After this apprenticeship, he was Director of Design at DJMM and, later, Partner for Design at Gruen Associates, both in Los Angeles. Throughout these years, he designed several award-winning projects, including the San Bernardino City Hall in San Bernardino, California; the Pacific Design Center in Los Angeles, California; and the US Embassy in Tokyo, Japan.

In 1977, Mr. Pelli became Dean of the Yale University School of Architecture and, shortly thereafter, founded Cesar Pelli & Associates. He resigned his post as Dean in 1984, but continues to lecture on architecture. Since the firm's establishment, Mr. Pelli has worked with his Principals to originate and direct the design of each of its projects. In 2005, the firm was renamed Pelli Clarke Pelli Architects in recognition of the increased role of the firm's principals.

Mr. Pelli has avoided formalistic preconceptions in his designs. He believes that buildings should be responsible citizens and that the aesthetic qualities of a building should grow from the specific characteristics of each project such as its location, its construction technology, and its purpose. In search of the most appropriate response to each project, his designs have covered a wide range of solutions and materials.

Mr. Pelli has written extensively on architectural issues. In 1999 he wrote *Observations for Young Architects,* published by The Monacelli Press. His work has been widely published and exhibited, with nine books and several issues of professional journals dedicated to his designs and theories. He has received fourteen Honorary Degrees, over 300 awards for design excellence and is a Fellow of the American Institute of Architects, a Member of the American Academy of Arts and Letters, the National Academy of Design, the International Academy of Architecture, and of l'Academie d'Architecture de France.

In 1995, the American Institute of Architects awarded Mr. Pelli the Gold Medal, in recognition of a lifetime of distinguished achievement in architecture. In 2004, Mr. Pelli was awarded the Aga Khan Award for Architecture for the design of the Petronas Towers, Kuala Lumpur, Malaysia.

CESAR PELLI HONORARY DEGREES

1990	Honorary Doctorate, Doctor of Humane Letters University of New Haven
1990	Honorary Doctorate, Doctor of Humane Letters Pratt Institute
1993	Honorary Doctorate Universidad Nacional de Tucumán, Argentina
1993	Honorary Doctorate Universidad de Mendoza, Argentina
1994	Honorary Doctorate, Doctor of Humane Letters Albertus Magnus College
1996	Honorary Doctorate, Honorary Doctor of Fine Arts Rodger Williams University
1998	Honorary Doctorate Universidad de Belgrano, Argentina
1999	Honorary Doctorate Universidad Empresarial Siglo 21, Argentina
2000	Honorary Doctorate Connecticut College
2000	Honorary Doctorate Universidad Nacional del Nordeste Argentina
2004	Honorary Doctorate, Doctor of Humane Letters University of Minnesota Duluth
2007	Honorary Doctorate, Doctor of Humane Letters University of Miami
2008	Honorary Doctorate, Doctor of Fine Art Yale University
2012	Honorary Doctorate, Doctor Honoris CaUS The National University of Cordoba
2014	Honorary Doctorate, Doctor of Humane Letters DePaul University

PROFESSIONAL CREDENTIALS

1980	*Fellow*, American Institute of Architects
1995	First Class Registered Architect, Japan

PROFESSIONAL AFFILIATIONS

1982	*Academician*, American Academy of Arts and Letters
1990	*Member*, National Academy of Design
1990	*Honorary Member*, Fundacion Miguel Lillo
1992	*Diploma al Merito*, Konex Foundation, Buenos Aires, Argentina
1993	*Diploma and Honorary Membership*, La Sociedad de Arquitectos Mexicanos
	Correspondent Member, French Academy of Architecture
1994	*Academician*, International Academy of Architecture
	Member, International Committee of the City Library of Viipuri
1996	*Honorary Fellowship*, Tokyo Society of Architects and Building Engineers
	Membre de l'Academie d'Architecture de France
	Member, Russian Academy of Architecture and Construction Sciences
	Honorary Member, Sociedad de Arquitectos de Cordoba
2002	*Honorary Member*, Order of Catalan Architects
2008	*Honorary Member*, Order of Catalan Architects

TEACHING EXPERIENCE

1950–1952	Title of Teaching Universidad Nacional de Tucumán
1968–1977	Visiting Professor University of California Los Angeles
1972–1974	Visiting Professor Yale University
1977–1984	Dean School of Architecture, Yale University
1987	Honorary Professor Universidad Nacional de Tucumán, Argentina
1996	Honorary Professor Universidad de Buenos Aires, Argentina
1999	The Eero Saarinen Visiting Professorship of Architectural Design Yale University

BOOKS

American Architecture of the 1980's. Washington, D.C.: The American Institute of Architects Press, 1990, 162–9, 218–25.

Anger, David. *Cesar Pelli (Architects: Artists Who Build).* North Mankato: Capstone Publishing, 1995.

Archer, B. J. *Houses for sale: Architects, Emilio Ambasz, Peter Eisenman, Vittorio Gregotti, Arata Isozaki, Charles Moore, Cesar Pelli, Cedric Price, Oswald Mathias Ungers.* New York: Rizzoli International Publications, 1980.

Architecture and Polyphony: Building in the Islamic World Today, The Aga Khan Award for Architecture. London: Thames & Hudson Ltd, 2004, 120–39.

Arnell, Bickford. *A Tower For Louisville: The Humana Competition.* New York: Rizzoli International Publications, 1985.

Baba, Shozo. *Can You Be An Architect Like One of Them?* Okokusha, Japan 2004, 188–95.

Binder, Georges (editor). *Tall Buildings of Asia & Australia.* The Images Publishing Group, Victoria, Australia 2001, 9, 152–3, 210, 213.

Pelli, Cesar. *Cesar Pelli Selected and Current Works.* With an introduction by Michael J. Crosbie. The Master Architect Series. Mulgrave, Victoria, Australia: The Images Publishing Group Pty Ltd, 1993.

Cesar Pelli. Essays by Esther McCoy, Cesar Pelli, John Pastier, Gavin Macrae-Gibson. Tokyo: A + U Publishing Co., Ltd., 1985.

Chen, John S. M. *Architecture in Pen and Ink.* New York: McGraw-Hill Education, 1994.

City + Architecture European Cities,London, 21st Century Exhibition Catalog: Junta De Andalucia, 2004, 94–8.

Columbus Area Chamber of Commerce, Inc. *A Look at Architecture Seventh Edition.* Columbus, Indiana: Visitors Center, 1998, 98–101.

Crosbie, Michael J. *Architecture of the Cape Cod Summer: The Work of Polhemus Savery DaSilva: New Classicists.* With a foreword by Cesar Pelli. Victoria, Australia: The Images Publishing Group, 2008.

Crosbie, Michael J. *Cesar Pelli: Recent Themes.* Basel, Switzerland: Birkhäuser, 1998.

Crosbie, Michael J. *Curtain Walls: Recent Developments by Cesar Pelli & Associates.* Basel, Switzerland: Birkhäuser, 2005.

Cyberspace: the World of Digital Architecture. Victoria, Australia: The Images Publishing Group, 2001. "National Museum of Contemporary Art," 188–21. F de Brea, Ana. *Total Latin American Architecture: Libretto of Modern Reflections & Contemporary Works.* With introduction by Cesar Pelli. New York: Actar Publishers, 2015.

Details in Architecture. Victoria, Australia: The Images Publishing Group, 2000, 42–7.

Ai Dingzheng and Li Shu, eds. *Cesar Pelli: Famous Foreign Architect Series, Number 2.* Beijing: China Architectural Publications, 1991.

Duda, Turan and Jeffrey Paine. *Individual to Collective: Duda/Paine Architects.* With a foreword by Cesar Pelli. Novato: ORO Editions, 2013.F

Expressing Structure: The Technology of Large-Scale Buildings. Fairweather, Virginia. Basel, Switzerland: Birkhäuser, 2004, 18–41, 116–23, 134–43.

Förster, Wolfgang. *Housing in the 20th and 21st Centuries.* New York, 2006, 143.

Gandelsonas, Mario and John Pastier. *Cesar Pelli: Buildings and Projects 1965–1990.* New York: Rizzoli International Publications, 1990.

Garreta, Adriana Alvarez. *Skyscrapers* Mexico: Books Factory, 2002, 30–5, 40–5, 96–101, 102–7, 308–15, 370–7, 406–13, 442–7, 560–5, 566–71.

Goldberger, Paul. *Cesar Pelli: Buildings and Projects, 1965–90.* New York: Rizzoli International Publications, 1991.

Gossel, Peter. *The A–Z of Modern Architecture.* Los Angeles: Taschen, 2007, 764–5.

Gray, Lee Edward and David Walters. *Pattern and Context, Essays on Cesar Pelli.* Charlotte, North Carolina, 1992.

Halfmann, Janet. *The Tallest Building.* New York: Kidhaven Press, 2004.

Knight, Richard. *Saarinen's Quest: A Memoir.* With a foreword by Cesar Pelli. Richmond, CA: William Stout Publishers, 2009.

Lee, Sungmin. *International Architecture Annual.* Seoul, Korea: Archiworld, 2005, 152–7.

Linton, Harold. *Portfolio Design.* 3rd ed. With a foreword by Cesar Pelli. New York: W. W. Norton & Company, 2004.

Linton, Harold. *Portfolio Design.* 4th ed. With a foreword by Cesar Pelli. New York: W. W. Norton & Company, 2012.

Macrae-Gibson, Gavin. *The Secret Life of Buildings An American Mythology for Modern Architecture.* London and Cambridge, Mass.: MIT Press, 1985, 52–73.

Malin, Nadav & Janke, Nicholas. *Battery Park City, The Solaire, Green by Design.* New York, New York: The Battery Park City Authority, 2005.

Mehta, Geeta and Deanna MacDonald. *New Japan Architecture: Recent Works by the World's Leading Architects.* With a preface by Cesar Pelli. Clarendon: Tuttle Publishing, 2015.

Molinari, Luca. *Atlas: North American Architecture Trends, 1990–2000.* (Sassuolo, Italy: Marazzi Gruppo Ceramiche, 2001) 36–41.

Nakamura, Toshio. *Cesar Pelli.* Tokyo: A + U Publishing Co., 1985.

Ojeda, Oscar Riera, ed. *National Airport Terminal: Cesar Pelli.* With an introduction by Paul Goldberger. Single Building Series—Process of an Architectural Work. Gloucester, Massachusetts: Rockport Publishers, 2000.

Ojeda, Oscar Riera, *The New American House.* Whitney Library of Design, New York, 1995, 76–87.

Passenger Terminal 2, Tokyo International Airport (Haneda). Japan: Shin kenchiku-Sha, 2005.

Pastier, John. *Cesar Pelli.* New York: Whitney Library of Design, 1980.

Pelli, Cesar. *The Charlottesville Tapes.* With an introduction by Jaquelin Robertson. New York: Rizzoli International Publications, 1985, 108–15.

Pelli, Cesar. *The Chicago Tapes.* With an introduction by Stanley Tigerman. New York: Rizzoli International Publications, 1987, 204–15.

Pelli, Cesar. *Observations for a Young Architect.* New York: The Monacelli Press, 1999.

Pelli, Cesar and Michael J. Crosbie. *Petronas Towers: The Architecture of High Construction.* Hoboken: Wiley-Academy Press, 2001.

Pelli, Cesar, ed. *Yale Seminars on Architecture, Volume 2.* New Haven, Yale University, 1981, 89–114.

Petrini, Catherine M. *The Petronas Towers.* New York: Blackbirch Press, 2004.

Porter, Tom & John Neale. *Architectural Supermodels.* Oxford, England: Architectural Press, 2000, 26, 28–29.1.

Preble, Duane and Sarah Preble. *Artforms.* "Space in Three Dimensions." New Jersey: Prentice Hall, 2002, 49.

Rapson, Ralph. *Ralph Rapson: Sketches and Drawings from Around the World.* With a foreword by Cesar Pelli. Afton: Afton Press, 2002.

Sailer, John. *The Great Stone Architects: Interviews With Philip Johnson, John Burgee, Michael Graves, Cesar Pelli, Helmut Jahn, John Portman and Der Scott.* River Edge: Tradelink Publishing Company, Inc., 1991.

Anna M. Sanko, ed., *New Haven's Cultural Landscape: Its Changing People and Places.* New Haven, Connecticut: Architectural Resource Center, 2001, 74.

Sardar, Ziauddin. *The Consumption of Kuala Lumpur.* London: Reaktion Books, Ltd., 2000, 39.

Searing, Helen. *New American Art Museums.* Catalogue of exhibition at the Whitney Museum, New York. Berkeley, California and London, University of California Press, 1983, 78–86.

Self, Ronnie. *The Architecture of Art Museums: A Decade of Design: 2000–2010.* Abingdon: Routledge, 2004.

Suzuki, Hiroyuki. *Sections Through a Practice.* Barreneche, Raul A., Editor. Designed by Bruce Mau Design, essays by Joseph Giovannini, Hiroyuki Suzuki. Ostfildern-Ruit, Germany: Hatje Cantz Verlag, 2004.

Terranova, Antonio. *Skyscrapers.* Whitestar Publishers, Italy (printed in Korea) 2003, Cover, 17, 190–3, 198–209, 244–59.

Alexander Tzonis, Liane LeFaivre, and Richard Diamond, eds. *Architecture in North America.* London: Thames and Hudson Ltd, 11995: 156–9; 248–51.

The National Museum of Art, Osaka. Nikkei Architecture Books, Ed. Japan: Royal Production, 2005.

Van Uffelen, Chris. *2:00:6 Die Stadien.* Germany: Verlagshaus Braun, 2006: 126, 135.

SELECTED MAJOR EXHIBITIONS

1992	Retrospective on Cesar Pelli College of Architecture Gallery, University of North Carolina-Charlotte
1994	Cesar Pelli: Architecture of Response Delphi Research Inc., Tokyo, Japan
1998–2000	At the End of the Century: One Hundred Years of Architecture Curated by The Museum of Contemporary Art—Los Angeles Tokyo, Mexico City, Cologne, Chicago, Los Angeles
2000–2002	Skyscrapers. The New Millenium Curated by Art Institute of Chicago, Chicago, Illinois San Francisco, Washington, D.C., New York Bilbao: The Transformation of a City Art Institute of Chicago, Chicago, Illinois
2000	Cesar Pelli: Building Designs 1965–2000 Yale School of Architecture, New Haven, Connecticut
2001–2002	Cesar Pelli Retrospective National Building Museum, Washington, D.C.
2005	Sections Through A Practice: Cesar Pelli & Associate Curated by the Philbrook Museum of Art, Tulsa, Oklahoma
2008	Una Vida en Arquitectura (A Life In Architecture) Curated by the Asociación Amigos del Centro Cultural Recoleta, Buenos Aires, Argentina
2008–2009	Vertical Cities: Hong Kong | New York Curated by The Skyscraper Museum, New York, New York
2011–2012	Pelli del croquis al listón (from sketch to ribbon cutting) Retrospective Exhibition— Pelli Clarke Pelli Architects University Museum for Arts and Science Universidad Nancional Autónoma de México, Mexico City, Mexico
2012	Architecture: Art, Science & Energy The Discovery Museum, Bridgeport, Connecticut

2013–2014 Practical Utopias: Global Urbanism in Hong Kong, Seoul, Shanghai, Singapore, and Tokyo
Curated by Jonathan D. Solomon, AIA
Center for Architecture, New York, New York

FILMS

2016 *American Masters. Eero Saarinen: The Architect Who Saw the Future*
Dir. Peter Rosen

2005 *The World's Tallest Architect: a documentary on Cesar Pelli*
Dir. Sebastian Neville

2000 *Skyscrapers: Going Up*
Dir. Kurt Sayenga

SELECTED VIDEOS

"Entrevista Cesar Pelli." Architects Association in Bizkaia and the Office of the Mayor of Bilbao. https://www.youtube.com/watch?v=HxtxYRQyX0Y. Uploaded 21 Jul. 2016. 3 minutes.

"Entrevista con Cesar Pelli." El Consejo Profesional de Arquitectura y Urbanismo (CPAU). https://vimeo.com/115975742. Uploaded 2015. 30 minutes.

"Arboleda—Entrevista a diseñador Cesar Pelli." Arboleda. https://www.youtube.com/watch?v=DPUGB0mnAJU. Uploaded 1 Jun. 2015. 4 minutes.

"Cesar Pelli 2012 AIANY President's Award." The American Institute of Architects NY Chapter, Center for Architecture, and Arbuckle Industries. .https://vimeo.com/52293547. Uploaded 27 Oct. 2012. 2 minutes.

"Spotlight on Design: Cesar Pelli." National Building Museum. https://www.youtube.com/watch?v=p8Ay_gtWr4I. Uploaded 23 Mar. 2012. 1 hour and 27 minutes.

"American Architecture NOW: Cesar Pelli." https://www.youtube.com/watch?v=pyZbB1mq5ik. Uploaded 5 Oct. 2011. 1 hour and 17 minutes.

"Pelli: Creador De Rascacielos." Otro Tema. https://www.youtube.com/watch?v=8QCim69XNAM. Uploaded 19 Feb. 2011. 23 minutes.

ARTICLES

"25 Innovative Glass Designers," *Glass Magazine*, April 2004, 46–52.
"A milestone in the making, Sidra Center," *Gulf Times*, March 8, 2007, 2.
"Achievements in Building," *Blueprints* 20, 2001, 2–11.
"AIA New England 2000 Design Awards," *AIA Connecticut News*, Winter 2001, 7.
Amelar, Sarah, "Neon Tigers," *Architectural Record,* December 2004, 104–9.
"An Art of Response," *Outukumpu Factor*, February 2004, 8–11.
Anderson, Luke, "The Value of Good Practice: Interview with Cesar Pelli of Pelli Clarke Pelli," *Paprika*, http://yalepaprika.com/the-value-of-good-practice-interview-with-cesar-pelli-of-pelli-clarke-pelli/.
Appelbaum, Alec, "Green Giant," *Metropolis,* October 2001, 58–62.
Aratani, Shinji, "Tailor-made Architecture," *New York Times* 571, 2002, 18–22.
"Architect selected for state of the art science center at Adriaen's Landing," *The Day*, September 25, 2004.
"Architects Design Art to Live In," *Washington Times*, September 19, 2006.
"Architecture of Response: Recent Works of Cesar Pelli," Space Design, October 1995, 5–60.
"ARIA a high note for MGM Mirage," *Gaming Today*, June 2, 2008.
"Atago Green Hills: Mori Tower and Forest Tower," *Contemporary Architecture*, January 2002: 57–66.
"Atago Green Hills: Mori Tower and Forest Tower," *Shinkenchiku*, November 2001: 184–7.
Baard, Eric, "The Towers Tomorrow," *Village Voice,* January 2, 2002: 46.
Babini, Pablo, "Realismo Mágico," *Gestion,* September/October, 2005: 14–19.
Beaton, Audrey, "Eye Catching" Museum by Pelli Under Way," *Architectural Record,* December 2004: 44.
Beirut, Michael, "Sections Through a Practice: Cesar Pelli & Associates," *Constructs*, Fall 2004: 17.
Benitez, Andres, "Pelli, El Maestro," *Capital*, May 5–18, 2006: 102–3.
Bertamini, Fulvio, "Interessi Privati," *Costruire,* October 2005: 16–21.
Besançon, Yves, "Costanera Center; Un Ícono Para Satiago," *Bora*, Mayo 2006: 58–61.
Besançon, Yves, and Ernesto Barreda, "Pelli Clarke Pelli Arquitects," *Bora*, número 7: 2006, 26–30.
Bharucha, Nauzer K, "Godrej to give prime realty in Mumbai," *TNN*, April 14, 2010.
"Big Urban Projects: Cesar Pelli & Associates: Connecticut Center for Science and Exploration, Hartford, Connecticut, US For Connecticut Center for Science and Exploration," *Mipim Architectural Review Future Project Awards 2005*, 2005: 72.
"Big Urban Projects: Cesar Pelli & Associates: Regional Events and Convention Center, Tulsa Oklahoma, US For City of Tulsa," *Mipim Architectural Review Future Project Awards 2005,* 2005: 71.
Binns, Jessica, "New Tower Augments Skyline in Philadelphia," *Civil Engineering,* May 2005: 31–3.
"Bloomberg: Office Design Amplifies Communication," *Eciffo* 47, Autumn 2005: 24–31.
Blum, Andrew, "UCSF's Mission Bay Campus Attracts Long List of Architects," *Architectural Record,* May 2005: 64.
Boehm, Mike, "Transbay designer will be Pelli," *Los Angeles Times*, May 21, 2008.
Borlenghi, Riccardo, "Le Cupole di Washington," *Il Nuovo Cantiere*, September 2000: 24–9.
Brake, Alan, "Pelli Crowns SF Skyline," *The Architect's Newspaper*, October 3, 2007, http://www.archpaper.com/e-board_rev.asp?News_ID=296.
Britt, Aaron, "Miami Advice," *Dwell,* July/August 2006: 116.
Brooks, Samantha, "One Beacon Court, NY," *Vacation Homes*, Fall 2004: 34.
Brown, Lindsay, "Post-mortem on the old Eaton's building: an interview with Cesar Pelli," *Ouno Design*, March 2, 2015, http://ounodesign.com/2015/03/02/cesar-pelli-eatons-building-nordstrom-vancouver/.
Broverman, Neal, "West Hollywood's Red Building Is Still Rising," *Curbed,* January 4, 2010.
"Bungalow didacto," *Arquitectura y Urbanismo* 16, no. 89, Abril/Maio 2000, 28–31.
Carlisle, Candace, "Three questions with famed architect Cesar Pelli," *Dallas Business Journal*, June 27, 2014, http://www.bizjournals.com/dallas/print-edition/2014/06/27/three-questions-with-famed-architect-cesar-pelli.html.
Casale, Rocky, "Now Booking: Mexico City Duo," *T, The New York Times Style Magazine,* October 9, 2009.
Castillo, Arielle, "Buildings Big & Small: Cesar Pelli Update," *Florida InsideOut*, May/June 2006, 50.
Catinella, Rita F, "Products: Metal Cladding & Treatments: An Unusual Roof of Italian Copper-Clad Tiles," *Architectural Record*, October 2004, 229.
Celaya, Claudia, "El BankBoston, un nuevo hito para la ciudad," *Arquitectura, Ingeniera, Planeamiento y Diseño*, 11 de setiembre de 2000, 6–7.
Celeste, Sofia, "Italy's Monument to Fashion," *The Boston Globe,* June 18, 2005, E1-E2.
"Central Planning," *Duke Magazine,* May-June 2008, Duke University.
"Cesar Pelli—Carnegie Hall Tower," *A+U*, Tokyo, April 1992, 110–17.
"Cesar Pelli & Associates," *Architects of the New Millennium*, Mulgrave, Australia: The Images Publishing Group Pty. Ltd., 2000, 54–5.

"Cesar Pelli & Associates: Lead By A Gentle Genius," *Columns*, May 22 to July 17, 2005, 2–5.
"César Pelli construirá la torre más alta de Sevilla," *Infodomus: Constucción Sostenible y Edificios Inteligentes* 5, January 2007, 13.
"Cesar Pelli," *A+U*, Tokyo, January 1993, 102–36.
"Cesar Pelli," *Octogon Arhitectura & Design*, 2000, 4–36.
"Cesar Pelli: Architectural Design which Serves the City," *A T*, Tokyo, July 1990, 7–30.
"Cesar Pelli: Connections and Contexts," *Vassar Views* 130, Spring 2002, 1–2.
"Cesar Pelli: Museum of Contemporary Art," *Zoo* 4, London: The Friary Press, January 2000, 116–7.
"Cesar Pelli: the Architect is Attempting to Touch the Heavens," *View*, September 2001, 87–91.
"César Pelli: Un arquitecto mayor," *Estilo Propio Revista* 2, April 2007.
Céspedes, Analya, "Cesar Pelli: El Oficio De Tocar El Cielo," *Vivienda Decoracíon*, Chile, April 1 2006, 62–5.
Chow, Phoebe, "Aga Khan Awards 2004" Subsection "Tower Power," *The Architectural Review*, January 2005, 62–83, 74–5.
Cirillo, Anna, "Vi racconto come sarà la mia piazza del silenzio," *La Repubblica*, July 30, 2004, 5.
"City Center, Las Vegas," *Premiere*, 2007.
Colegio Oficial de Arquitectos Vasco-Navarro, "Concurso de Ideas para la Ordenacion de la zona Abandoibarra del P.G.O.U. de Bilbao," *Arquitectos* 130, no. 93/4, 42–50.
Collyer, G. Stanley Jr., "A Tale of Two Cities, Miami and Dayton," *Competitions*, Summer 2004, 2–3.
Collyer, G. Stanley Jr., "Developer Competitions," *Competitions*, Summer 2004, 16–21.
Collyer, G. Stanley Jr., "Making The Right Connection," *Competitions*, Summer 2004, 22–31.
"Color Coordination: Pelli Unveils Red Building," *Architectural Record*, May 2006, 42.
"Con la altura de Cesar Pelli," *Doquier*, September 2005, 24–8.
"Connecticut Center for Science and Exploration, US-Hartford," *Wettbewerbe Aktuell*, Freiberg, Germany, March 2005, 33–34.
"Connecticut's Best Architecture," *Business New Haven*, December 26, 2005, Cover, 17–20.
Cooke, Julia, "Reforma Movement," *Metropolis*, October 2008.
Critchley, Jill, "Slate Provides an 'Elegant and Unique Skin' for Office Building," *Stone Work*, June 2001, 60–8.
Crosbie, Michael J, "New Catholic Center for Yale," *Faith & Form* XXXVIII, no. 4, 2005, 31.
Curtis, Wayne, "Deco, MiMo, and Up We Go" *Preservation*, July/August 2004, 29–32.
Dagnino, Tomás, "Con diversas exposiciones Comienza el mes Pelli," *El Cronista Arquitectura*, Miércoles 1 de noviembre de 2000, 1, 8.
Dagnino, Tomás, "Entrevista A Cesar Pelli," *Todo Obras*, Argentina; January 2006, 6–9.
David, Charles, "The Big Green Apple," *Multifamily Trends*, Washington D.C.: Urban Land Institute, 2001, Cover, 19.
Davis, Nancy M, "Custom Work Provides the Competitive Edge," *Glass Magazine*, April 2006, Cover, 40–2.
Davis, Nancy M, "Pelli's Sculptural Pillars: Steel Tubes Penetrate Skylights," *Glass Magazine*, September 2005, 86–7.
"Deconstructing the Pacific Design Center," *Frontiers*, April 22, 2008, 51, 52.
"Designer Spotlight: Cesar Pelli," *Revolution*, April 25, 2017, http://revolutionprecrafted.com/blog/designer-spotlight-cesar-pelli/.
"Dewan Filharmonik Petronas," *Architecture Malaysia*, May/June 2000, 32–3.
Donati, Maria Cristina, "Progetti: De Resident, Aja, Olanda," *Costruire in Laterizio*, March/April, 12–18.
Dorigati, Remo, "La vita del mare," *l'Arca*, Milano, Italy: l'Arca Edizioni spa, June 2000, 20–5.
"Duke Selects Pelli Clarke Pelli Architects as Master Designer for Central Campus," *Office of News and Communications: Duke University*, July 17, 2007.
Dunne, Diane Weaver, "Selecting Hartford's 'Wow' landmark," *Hartford Business Journal*, September 27, 2004.
"Edificio República," *Summa+23*, Buenos Aires, Febrero/Marzo 1997, 46–53.
"Octogono para la Fe," *El Cronista Arquitectura*, Capital Federal: Argentina, Miercoles, 22 de Marzo de 2000, 1, 6–7.
"Extra Edition: Cesar Pelli," *A+U*, July 1985.
"Extreme Assignments," *PDN Magazine*, October 2007, 46–55.
Fairley, Peter, "In The US, Architects Are Ramping Up The Design Power of Photovoltaics," *Architectural Record*, March 2004, 161–4.
Fanelli, Guillermina, "El Poder De Los Espacios Publicos," *Urbana* 2, May/June 2004, 38–9.
"Feature: Tall Buildings," *A+U*, Japan, July 2005, 12–13, 84–5, 114–15.
Fei, Michael C.Y., "On Practice: A Conversation with Cesar Pelli and Fred Clarke," *Dialogue*, March 2005, 82–95.
Fisher, Thomas, "Building Body Art: Three New Minneapolis Structures Show Off Their Skins," *Architecture*, March 2005, 58–61.
Forgey, Benjamin, "Cesar Pelli's Gift: A Capital Gateway," *The Washington Post*, 27 July 1997, G1, G7.
Fortmeyer, Russell, "The New Age of High-Tech Hospitals," *Architectural Record*, September 2007, 151–8.
"Frances Lehman Loeb Art Center, Vassar College," *A+U* 302, November 1995, 110–19.
Galbraith, Robert, "An Urban Renaissance is Transforming Milan," *International Herald Tribune*, July 11, 2007, 10.
"Gerald C. Ratner Athletic Center University of Chicago," *Athletic Business*, June 2004, 112.
"Gerald Ratner Athletic Center," *Modern Steel Construction*, April 2004, 35–7.
Gerfen, Katie, "Cesar Pelli & Associates: Connecticut Center for Science and Exploration, Hartford, Connecticut," *Architecture*, December 2004, 69.
Gilyard, Burl, "Speaking Volumes," *Presentations*, March 2002, 38–43.
Gintoff, Vladimir, "Spotlight: Cesar Pelli," *ArchDaily*, October 12, 2016. http://www.archdaily.com/555428/spotlight-cesar-pelli.
Goldberger, Paul, "ARCHITECTURE VIEW; Cesar Pelli Seeks the Perfect Skyscraper," *The New York Times*, January 15, 1989, http://www.nytimes.com/1989/01/15/arts/architecture-view-cesar-pelli-seeks-the-perfect-skyscraper.html.
Goldberger, Paul, "Shanghai on The Hudson," *The New Yorker*, August 2, 2004, 76–8.
Green, Joan De Natale, "Chatting with Cesar Pelli," *The Hartford Courant*, June 24, 2005, H1, H10.
Guazzone, Vicky, "Cesar Pelli: El éxito hace daño," *Noticias De La Semana*, October 6, 2015, http://noticias.perfil.com/2015/10/06/cesar-pelli-el-exito-hace-dano/.
"Hail Cesar," *Business New Haven*, November 1, 2004, 3.
Hall, Peter, "Behind The Curtain Wall," *Metropolis*, December 2004, 42.
Harlander, Thomas, "Starchitect Spotlight: Cesar Pelli," *Los Angeles Magazine*, August 31, 2015, http://www.lamag.com/citythinkblog/starchitect-spotlight-cesar-pelli/.
Hart, Sara, "Slender, Robust, and Very Tall," *Architectural Record*, November 2004, 36–41.
Herman, Eric, "Empire Blue headed to Brooklyn," *New York Daily News*, November 15, 2001.
Hinshaw, Mark, "Mission Statement," *Landscape Architecture*, January 2004, 76–83.
Hodgins, Paul, "Wave Theory," *Coast*, April 2006, 110–16.
"Hong Kong International Finance Centre," *Dialogue*, July 2004, 52–69.
"Honor Awards: Architecture; Kuala Lumpur City Centre, Phase 1," *Architectural Record*, May 2000, 107.
Hoppe, David, "White River Dream," *Nuvo*, August 9–16, 2001, 12–14.
Hughes, C.J, "Pelli Building Will Replace Flood-Damaged Iowa Theater," *Architectural Record*, October 21, 2010.

ARTICLES cont.
Ilia, Tony, "Pelli's Hotel-Casino on Las Vegas Strip will be Centerpiece of Massive Development," *Architectural Record,* May 2005, 66.
"In the Modern World: National Museum of Art, Osaka, Japan," *Dwell*, April/May 2005, 52.
Joubert, Claire, "Cesar's Palace," *Mpls St Paul*, May 2006, 84–6.
Jurado, Miguel, "Entrevista | Cesar Pelli," *Arq, Clarin Diaro de Arquitectura,* August 23, 2005, 8–9.
Kamin, Blair, "Chicago Comes Back," *Architectural Record,* May 2004, 109–13.
Keegan, Edward, "A City of Two Tales," *Architecture,* December 2003, 67–8.
Keegan, Edward, "Street Performance," *Architecture,* November 1996, 120–7, 192.
Kelly, Joseph Dennis III, "Philadelphia Grows Up With A Slew of High Rise Projects," *Architectural Record,* December 2005, 40.
Kelly, Joseph Dennis, "Postcards from the Edge," *Metropolis*, May 2004, 42–6.
Kelly, Joseph Dennis, "Unified Through Light," *Architectural Lighting,* March 2005, 40–3.
Kelly, Joseph II, "Correspondent's File: Philadelphia Sets a Path Toward Revitalization Through a Redefined Government Role," *Architectural Record,* October 2004, 73–8.
Kerner, Leighton, "The New Season" *Travel + Leisure,* November 2004, 173–8.
King, John, "Jury Names Favorite for Transbay Terminal, Tower," *SF Gate*, September 11, 2007.
King, John, "Transbay Terminal design contract OKd," *San Francisco Chronicle*, May 16, 2008, B3.
King, John, "Decade in review: Top 10 in S.F. architecture," *San Francisco Chronicle*, December 30, 2009.
Kline, Benjamin, "Benjamin and Marian Schuster Performing Arts Center," *Architectural Record*, October 2003, 134–7.
Knowles, David, "Cesar Pelli's Transbay Transit Tower, soon to be the tallest building west of the Mississippi, will reshape San Francisco's skyline," *Daily News*, April 6, 2013, http://www.nydailynews.com/news/national/cesar-pelli-transbay-transit-tower-soar-61-stories-san-francisco-article-1.1308926.
Kuchment, Anna, "The Sky's the Limit," *Newsweek*, March 17, 2008.
"La Torre de Repsol-YPF en Puerto Madero," *Todo Obras*, Argentina; January 2006, Cover, 10, 11.
"La Torre y la Diana," *International Architecture and Design Magazine, Arquine,* Spring 2006.
"Laboratori in Campagna," *Domus*, March 1971, 6–10.
Lackmeyer, Steve, "New Arena Leading Downtown Makeover," *NewsOK.com*, July 3, 2008.
Lacter, Mark, "Betting on Red," *Los Angeles,* April 1, 2008.
Laitinen, Denise, "Touching the Stars," *NFPA Journal*, May/June 2001, 64–7.
Lameiras, Maria M, "Dream a Little Dream," *Georgia Tech Alumni Magazine,* Summer 2000, 26–37.
Landecker, Heidi, "Scientific Community: Physics and Astronomy Building at the University of Washington/Seattle," *Architecture*, February 1995, 76–85, 107, 112–13.
Langdon, Philip, "Yale's Architectural Do-Overs," *The Hartford Courant*, March 23, 2008.
LeClaire, Jennifer, "With a Tight Budget, Construction Begins on Pelli's Miami Performing Arts Center," *Architectural Record*, April 2002, 38.
Leissner, Travis, "Healthcare's future arrives at Qatar," *Healthcare Design* 7, no. 8, October 2007, 59–63.
Lepri, Laure, "A Garibaldi-Varesine nasce un'altra Milano," *Real Estate,* November 2005, 38–9.
"Life of the Body," *University of Chicago Magazine*, December 2003, 32–9.
Linn, Charles, "Cesar Pelli's new Passenger Terminal at National Airport in Washington, D.C., eases the life of the world-weary traveler," *Architectural Record*, October 1997, 88–95.
Lopez, Carol Paredo, "Meeting the Challenge," *Paraplegia News*, April 2003, 42–6.
Lubell, Sam and James Murdock, "2004 Aga Khan Award for Architecture: Promoting Excellence in the Islamic World," *Architectural Record,* December 2004, 94–102.
Lubell, Sam, "Tall Building Capitals Still Scrape The Sky," *Architectural Record,* November 2004, 12–13.
Lynch, Sarah, "Pacific Design Center: Red Building," *California Home + Design,* June 2006, 91.
MacArthur, Ali, "Reaching for the Skies," *Focus*, August 2000, no. 93, 22–8.
Madia, Arq. Enrique H, "Observaciones para Arquitectos Jovenes," *Ibero Americana Internacional,* November 16, 2000, 10.
Mahler, Jonathan, "Gotham Rising," *Talk*, December 2001, 120–5, 148–52.
Martinez de la Cruz, Carmelina, "De Pipa y Guante: Renée & Henry Segerstrom Concert Hall," *SPOT: Moda Cultura y Motivaciones contemporáneas* 37, 42–5.
Martinez, Ezequiel, "César Pelli: El Señor Rascacielos," *La Revista de Clarin,* June 16, 1996, 14–25.
"Mathematics Building and Lecture Hall, Institute for Advanced Study," *A+U* 302, November 1995, 120–7.
Matsuura, Takayuki, "Close up Projects: National Museum of Art, Osaka: Introduction of Public Space", *Nikkei Architecture*, 27 December 2004, 8–17.
Mays, Vernon, "New South, New Square," *Architecture*, May 1993, 64–73.
Tom McGrath, ed., "The Best of Philly 2005: Best Work In Progress," *Philadelphia,* August 2005, 123.
McHugh, Sharon, "The final chapter for an architectural icon: Cesar Pelli's west coast Mecca for design nears completion," *World Architecture News*, March 7, 2011, http://www.worldarchitecturenews.com/index.php?fuseaction=wanappln.projectvi%ED%AF%80%ED%B2%AB.
McIntyre, Zoe, "Explore Architect Cesar Pelli's Breathtaking Skyscrapers," *The Culture Trip*, https://theculturetrip.com/south-america/argentina/articles/architect-cesar-pelli-height-above-all-else/.
McKee, Bradford, "A Beacon of Hope in a Time of World Conflict," *Competitions*, Spring 2003, 4–17.
"Medical Campus is United by Stone," *Stone World*, April 2002, 122–130.
Merkel, Jayne, "Building Consensus on Midtown West," *Oculus,* February/March 2001, 15–16.
Mezzolo, di Michela, "Città della moda, 100mila metri antismog," *Libero,* June 30, 2004, 35.
"Miami's New Performing Arts Center Struggles", *The Dallas Morning News*, January 3, 2008.
"Minneapolis Modern: Cesar Pelli's Minneapolis Central Library," *Food & Wine*, June, 2006, 156–61.
"Modernidad y Tradición, de sur a norte," *Summa+*, April 1991, 24–38.
Moholy-Nagy, Sibyl, "Cesar Pelli: Public Architect," *The Architectural Forum*, March 1970, 42–7.
Molina, Margot, "Una antorcha de cristal para Sevilla: El argentino César Pelli construirá una torre de 178 metros que será "respetuosa," con la Giralda," *El País*, January 25, 2007, 43.
Monestiroli, Teresa, "Cesar Pelli: 'Il futuro di Milano è verticale ma per diventare europea mancano gli spazi all'aperto,'" *la Repubblica Milano*, November, 6, 2013, http://milano.repubblica.it/cronaca/2013/11/06/news/milano_citt_intervista_architetto_incontri_architettura_politecnico_in_triennale_europa_spazi_cesar_pelli_creatore_della_t-70339976/.
Moran, Gisselle, "Cesar Pelli: Un icono de la arquitectura mundial," *Real Estate Market & Lifestyle* 20, 2005, 24–32.
Morino, Marco, "Una città per la moda," *Il Sole—24 Ore,* July 30, 2004, 18.
"Museum of Modern Art Extension, New York," GA Document, Tokyo, January 1985, 29–42.
"Museum, tower to become first downtown Austin LEED Building," *Concrete Monthly*, April 2008.
"National Art Museum, Osaka, Japan," *Yapi*, January 2005, 69–76.
"National Museum of Art Osaka," *Elle Decor*, October 2005, 76.
"National Museum of Contemporary Art," *Space* 16, April 2000, 34.

"NationsBank Corporate Center," *l'Arca* 31, 2001, 10–17.
Neild, Larry, "Project wins award and it's not even built," *Liverpool Daily Post,* October 5, 2007.
Neiswander, Judith, "Medical Marvel," *Architecture Minnesota*, November/December 2002, 40–3.
New Architecture, July 2000, 4.
"News Architecture," *100% Office* 4, 2004, 14.
Ngiom, Lim Teng, "Place in an Emerging Urbanscape," *Architecture Malaysia*, May/June 2000, 12–15.
Nuno, Mari Carmen, "Arquitecto de Altura," *Elle Decoracion*, September 2006, 22–4.
"Obra Maestra," *Vanidades*, September 16, 2003, 50–61.
"Observaciones sobre la arquitectura," *SCA Noticias*, January 2001, 8.
Ogasawara, Masatoyo, "Big Projects in Tokyo," *Casa Brutus,* January 2005, 224.
Olguin, Claudia, "Usos Mixtos," *Real Estate Market & Lifestyle* 20, 2005, 34–46.
Onniboni, Luca, "Cesar Pelli and his idea about Architecture," ArchiObjects.org, June 28, 2014, https://archiobjects.org/architecture-of-cesar-pelli/.
Origlia, Gabriela, "César Pelli: 'Los countries son malsanos, dividen a la población'," *La Nacion*, April 21, 2016, http://www.lanacion.com.ar/1891148-cesar-pelli-los-countries-son-malsanos-dividen-a-la-poblacion.
Otero, Luis & Alonso, Abraham, "Nueva Architectura: Los Mejores Arquitectos Del Siglo XXI," *Muy Intersante*, February 2006, 67–78.
"Outstanding Buildings," *AS&U*, November 2000, 308–309.1.
Panza, Pierluigi, "Una città della moda da 680 milioni di euro," *Corriere della Sera, Milano,* July 30, 2004, 49.
Pastier, John, "Tech Briefs: In Osaka, An Iconic Entry and Sculpture Mark The Spot of A Mostly Underground Museum," *Architectural Record,* May 2005, 281–3.
Pastore, Daniela, "Architettura della globalizzazione," Controspazio, June 2001, 4–29.
Patterson, Maureen, "A Tradition of Excellence," *Buildings*, September 1997, 40–44.
Patterson, Rob, "Science Project: U of H Expands With Science and Engineering Complex," *Texas Construction*, March 2005, 17–19.
Pearson, Clifford A, "What's Left Top Learn from Las Vegas," *Architectural Record,* May 2005, 194–7.
Pedersen, Martin C, "Office Space," *Metropolis,* November 2004, 96–7.
Pelletier, George, "Cesar Pelli: Building for the Future," *Florida,* July/August 2003, 76–81.
"Pelli Clarke Pelli Architects Design Green Neighborhood For Wuxi, China," *China Business Outlook*, October 2010.
"Pelli Clarke Pelli Explore New Shores," *World Architecture News*, February 11, 2010.
"Pelli diseñará el Campus Universitario de la UNSTA," *UNSTA Noticias*, July 2001, 3.
Pelli, Cesar, interview by Cristina Donati, "Le opinioni di Cesar Pelli su Canary Wharf e l'evoluzione dell'architettura moderna," *Controspazio*, May 1993, 23–7.
Pelli, Cesar and Bernard Hanson, "Art and Architects: An Interview with Cesar Pelli," *State of the Arts* 14, Summer 1984, 4–6.
Pelli, Cesar and Diana Balmori, "Latin American Influence on U.S. Architecture," *U.S. Information Agency Bulletin,* March 1979.
Pelli, Cesar and Paulhans Peters, "Skyscrapers in the US," *Baumeister,* Berlin, February 1984, 8–10, 17–24.
Pelli, Cesar and William Bailey, "Art and Architecture: The History and Future of Collaboration," *A+U,* Tokyo, May 1982, 108–9.
Pelli, Cesar and Andreas Papadakis, "Cesar Pelli: The Mega-Building in Context," *Architectural Design,* London, November/December 1988, 50–53.
Pelli, Cesar, "A Few Words on Philip Johnson's Buildings," *A+U* extra edition, Tokyo, May 1979, 79.
Pelli, Cesar, "Architectural Form and the Tradition of Building," *via 7: The Journal of the University of Pennsylvania School of Architecture.* Cambridge: University of Pennsylvania and the MIT Press, 1985: 145–60.
Pelli, Cesar, "Architectural Form and the Tradition of Building," *A+U* extra edition, Tokyo, July 1985, 26–32.
Pelli, Cesar, "Biennale House Project," *A+U,* Tokyo, November 1976, 109–16.
Pelli, Cesar, "Cesar Pelli & Associates: Canary Wharf Skyscraper," *Architectural Design,* London, November 1988, 40–9.
Pelli, Cesar, "Collaboration," *Japan Landscape* 34, 1995, 10–16.
Pelli, Cesar, "A Conversation with Cesar Pelli," New Haven Living, July 2013, 36–9.
Pelli, Cesar, "Defining Paradigm," *Perspecta 22: The Yale Architectural Journal*, 1986: 100–1.
Pelli, Cesar, "Designing with Colour," *Architectural Design* 120, 1996, 26–9.
Pelli, Cesar, "Excerpts from a Conversation," *Perspecta 19, The Yale Architectural Journal* 1983, 127–37, 184–5.
Pelli, Cesar, "Four Buildings Responsive to their Critical Surroundings," *A+U*, January, 1993, 104–5.
Pelli, Cesar, "Joseph Paxton's Crystal Palace," *A+U,* February 1980, 3–14.
Pelli, Cesar, *Korean Architects* 15, February 1997, 54–71.
Pelli, Cesar, "Nissan Motors Building," *A+U,* December 1972, 15–27.
Pelli, Cesar, "Pieces of the City," *Architectural Digest,* August 1988, 29–36.
Pelli, Cesar, "Sculpting Above the Trees in Mexico City," *Insite*, July 1994, 10–11.
Pelli, Cesar, "Sea Hawk Hotel & Resort," *Shinkenchiku*, June 1995, 285–95.
Pelli, Cesar, "Skyscrapers," *Perspecta 18, The Yale Architectural Journal,* 1982, 134–70.
Pelli, Cesar, "Statement," *A+U*, February, 1990, 63–4.
Pelli, Cesar, "The Challenge of the '90s," *Young Architects Forum,* 1991: 22–30.
Pelli, Cesar, "The Glass Box: Pelli Explains Why," *Architectural and Engineering News*, November 1969, 34–6.
Pelli, Cesar, "This is good but is it right?" Ben Farmer and Hentie Louw, eds., *Companion to Contemporary Architectural Thought*. London: Routledge Inc., 1993, 500–1.
Pelli, Cesar, "Thoughts about Louis I. Kahn," *A+U*, Tokyo, November 1983, 216.
Pelli, Cesar, "Thoughts on Supergraphics," *Approach,* Spring 1971, 12–31, 38–9.
Pelli, Cesar, "Today & Tomorrow," *San Francisco Bay Architects' Review,* Spring 1983, 12–15.
Pelli, Cesar, "Transparency-Physical and Perceptual" and "The Biennale House Project," *A+U*, November 1976, 74–86.
Pelli, Cesar, "When Does Architecture Apply Structure as an Element for Aesthetics?" *Architecture and Society*, November 1994, 47–50.
Pelli, Cesar, "Working in Asian and Other Countries Overseas," *Space Design*, October 1995, 8–9.
Pelli, Cesar, "Worldway Postal Center, Los Angeles International Airport," *Lotus 6*, 1969, 252–7.
Pelli, Cesar and Diana Balmori, "Eero Saarinen," *A+U* extra edition, June 1979, 15–18.
Pelli, Cesar and Diana Balmori, "Eero Saarinen," *GA 6*, 1971, 1–6.
Pelli, Cesar, "Comments on the World Trade Center," *Nikkei Architecture* 23, October 2001, 94.
Pelli, Cesar, "Connections," An excerpt from *Observations for Young Architects. NY Arts International Edition.5,* no.2, February 2000, 25–7.
Pelli, Cesar, "Eero Saarinen," *Architects on Architects,* 2002, 128–37.
Pelli, Cesar. Interview in *Gente* 1472, October 7, 1993, 64–5.
"Pelli-Hines Team Picked for Transbay," *Architectural Record*, December 2007, 35.
"Petronas Towers," *International Architecture Yearbook*, The Images Publishing Group Pty Ltd., 2000, 28–9.
Phocas, Marios C, "Tragwerke fur den Hochhausbau," Berlin: Ernst & Sohn, 2001, 237–43.
Phylina, "Matrix Experience, The Return of Experience," *Vision,* March 2006, 276–80.

ARTICLES cont.
"Physics and Astronomy Building, University of Washington," *A+U* 302, November 1995, 100–9.
"Physics and Astronomy Building, University of Washington/Seattle," *Architecture*, May 1994, 152–3.
Power, Mathew, "Going Places," *Choir&Organ* March/April 2004, 62–5.
Primeaux III, Henry, "BOK Center is a Dream Come True," *GTR & Union Boundary*, June 15, 2008.
Puleo, Tom, "New Science Center's Architect Brings Passion for State to Work," *Hartford Courant*, September 25, 2004.
R.K, "El Genio de Tucuman," *Nuestra*, March 17–23, 2000, 1, 4–7.
"Rafael Pelli: the Evolution of an Environmental Designer," *Designer/Builder*, January/February 2003, 24–36.
Ramstack, Tom, "Square 54 going up near GWU," *The Washington Times*, May 22, 2008, 8.
"Red Glass Helps Define PDC Campus," *Architect's Guide to Glass*, June 1, 2011, www.glassguides.com/index.php/archives/2148.
Reid, Alice, "A New National," *The Washington Post* Special Commemorative Issue, July 16, 1997, F1–16.
Reis, Michael, "Limestone defines Brooklyn Courthouse," *Stone World*, October 2003, 108–12.
Reiss, Gwen North, "Drawn to Perfection," *Preservation,* January/February 2001, 50, 52.
Rich, Motoko, "Aiming to Be the Next Big Amenity," *The New York Times*, November 13, 2003, F1, F13.
Rich, Sarah, "Moving Designs for San Francisco Transit Terminal Put the Light Back in Rail," *Fast Company*, April 28, 2010.
"Ritratto di un Gigante," *Il Magazine dell' Architettura*, Luglio-Agosto 2008, 26–30.
Robertson, Emma, "Cesar Pelli: 'One Aspires for the Sky'," *The Talks*, March 22, 2017, http://the-talks.com/interview/cesar-pelli/.
"Rosario, La ciudad de los parques," *Todo Obras*, January 2006, 12.
Russell, James S., "The New Workplace," *Architectural Record*, June 1992, 70–5.
Saldaña, Yolanda Bravo, "El Impulso Hacia La Verticalidad," *Obras,* Septembre 2004, 78–84.
Schultze, Franz, "Towers for Tomorrow," *Art in America,* May 2001, 160–1.
Schulz, Dana, "The Architecture of Cesar Pelli: How a Sense of Place Left a Lasting Mark on the NYC Skyline," *6sqft*, August, 14, 2014, https://www.6sqft.com/the-architecture-of-cesar-pelli-how-a-sense-of-place-left-a-lasting-mark-on-the-nyc-skyline/.
Schumacher, Thomas, "Looking at Four Star Architects Along With Airports That Make Their International Practices Possible: Books," *Architectural Record,* May 2005, 101–6.
"Sea Hawk Hotel & Resort," *Interior Spaces of Asia and the Pacific Rim*, 2001, 110.
"Sections Through a Practice: Cesar Pelli & Associates," *Azure*, March/April 2005, 127.
"Sections Through a Practice," *City*, Fall 2004, 27.
Shuster, Laurie A, "Pelli-Designed Library Moves Forward," *Civil Engineering,* July 2004, 14,15.
"Sidra to be an architectural marvel," *The Peninsula*, Qatar: March 8, 2007.
Singer, Paola, "Cesar Pelli's Nonchalant Architecture," *Surface*, May 10, 2016, http://www.surfacemag.com/articles/cesar-pelli-architecture/.
Skyhigh Living: Contemporary High-Rise Apartment and Mixed-Use Buildings, 2002, 12, 23, 96–7.
Smith, Dakota, "Red Building Cladding Spotted, Primary Colors Congregate," *Curbed L.A*, November 10, 2010, http://la.curbed.com/archives/2010/11/red_building_cladding_spotted_primary_colors_co.
Smith, Dakota, "Red Rising," *Curbed L.A*, March 1, 2011, la.curbed.com/archives/2011/03/red_rising.php 5/5.
Solomon, Nancy B. AIA, "Exotic Woods Gain Popularity in the U.S," *Architectural Record*, November 2004, 223–30.
"Special Feature: Cesar Pelli," *A+U*, November 1976, 27–120.
"Special Feature: The Recent Works of Cesar Pelli," *A+U*, February 1990, 63–148.
"Special: Super Tall Buildings of the World," *Archiworld*, 2005/07, 58–111.
Speck, Lawrence, "Campuses," *Texas' Best Places: a Special Feature of Texas Architect*, September/October 2002, 4–5.
Stamp, Jimmy, "Pelli Clarke Pelli to Green the Embarcadero," February 4, 2008.
Stephens, Suzanne, "Bloomberg Headquarters," *Architectural Record,* March 2006, 138–43.
Stern, William F, "Raising the Bar: Cesar Pelli's Science Engineering Research and Classroom complex sets a new standard at the University of Houston," *Cite: The Architecture and Design Review of Houston* 68, Fall, 2006, 26–9.
Stinnard, Michell "Stone Adds Visual Interest at Yale," *Stone World*, April 2006, 82–92.
Stone, Brad, "Ambitious Downtown Transit Project Is at Hand," *The New York Times*, January 3, 2010.
Strauss, Mark, "New Jersey's Waterfront: Doing It Right," *Oculus,* July 2004, 32–34.
Stucchi, Silvano, "Herring Hall, Rice University, Houston, Texas," *Industria delle Costruzione,* February 1986, 34–41.
Stucchi, Silvano, "The World Financial Center in New York," *l'Industria delle Costruzione,* November 1988, 38–49.
"Stunning Resort Casino Designed by Cesar Pelli Includes Fine Art Program," *Artdaily.org*, June 11, 2008.
Stutz, Howard, "City Center's Centerpiece hotel-casino dubbed 'Aria'," *Las Vegas Review Journal*, May 20, 2008, 1D, 4D.
Tailler, A. Garcia Herrera, "Madrid's Muscle," *Techniques & Architecture*, June/July 2005, 24–31.
Takahama, Valerie, "Cesar Pelli," *Orange County Register*, September 15, 2006.
Tarricone, Paul, "Headquarters Goes Horizontal: The Talk of Toledo — Owens Corning World Headquarters," *Facilities Design & Management*, July 1997, 33–7.
Tasquer, Rolando Moya, Evelia Peralta, and Romulo Moya Peralta, "Houses of the World/Casas del Mundo," *Ecuador: TRAMA*, 2006, 112–15, 198.
Than, Su, "Tall Cool Ones: Asia's Towers of Power," *Face the East* 2, January/February 2000, 86–93.
"The 2004 Aga Khan Award For Architecture," Yapi, January 2005, 45–57.
"The Architecture Top Ten," *Time Online*, December 18, 2007.
Cameron, Kristi, Ariana Donalds, Mirielle Hyde, Alexandra Lange, Laurie Manfra, Mark Pedersen, and Julie Taraska, "The Bloomberg Experience," *Metropolis*, November 2005, 81–126.
"The Connecticut Center for Science & Exploration Design Competition" *Concept, Architecture & Concept; International Magazine of Competition*, 2005, 1–2.
"The Sky's the Limit," Canary, London: The Conde Nast Publications Ltd, 2001, 23–6.
"The Vertical Challenge," *Azure*, March/April 2005, 68.
Thomas, Ralph, "Cesar Pelli in the City of Towers," *Architectural Record*, www.archrecord.com/Intrview/Pelli/Pelli1.asp.
Thomas, Ralph, "Doing the Right Thing," *Perspective*, April/May 2000, 22–30.
"Torres Petronas," *Architector: Construir Segun Las Reglas*, November 2000, 5–10.
"Towers and Skyscrapers," *L'Arca Plus*, 1997, 14–19, 76–93, 102–109.
"Transit Project Could Transform City and More From the Bay Area," *The New York Times*, January 2, 2010.
Trauthwein, Christina, "Sea Worthy," *Architectural Lighting*, March/April 2000, 60–3.
"Travel With a Difference," *HSBC*, 2001, 46–47.
Trescott, Jacqueline, "Landing First-Class Art," *Washington Post*, June 18, 1996, B1, B6.
"Tulsa: New Opportunities," *Convention South*, March 2008.
Turner, Nicola, "Walking on Water," *World Architecture* 87, June 2000, 56–9.
"US Courthouse," *New York Construction Review*, 2003, 109.
"US Embassy, Tokyo," *Japan Architect*, November 1976, 102–8, 202.

Urata, Michiyo, "Sea Hawk Hotel & Resort," *Nikkei Architecture*, June 12, 1995, 38–50.
Verga, Gianni, "Mailand Wächst," *Bauwelt,* October 2004, 38–9.
Vigano, Bruno, "Cosmic Pillars: Interview with Cesar Pelli," *Habitat Ufficio* 78, February/March 1996, 28–35.
Vincent, Roger, "Sign of a market on fire," *Los Angeles Times,* March 29, 2007.
Von Hoffman, Nicholas, "Cesar Pelli: Creating an Architecture That Is Responsive to Function and Place," *Architectural Digest,* March 2005, 74–9.
Von Hoffman, Nicholas, "Cesar Pelli Architecture and Design," *Architectural Digest*, February 28, 2005, http://www.architecturaldigest.com/story/pelli-article-032005.
Walker, Alissa. "The Star-Studded Design of Vegas' $8.5 Billion CityCenter," *Fast Company*, November 30, 2009.
Walker, Tom, "Fear of heights unlikely to stop builders for long," *Atlanta Journal-Constitution*, May 5, 2002, Q1, Q6.
"WaterfrontToronto Unveils Bayside Plan In The East Bayfront," *Urban Toronto*, August 19, 2010.
Welton, Michael, "Cesar Pelli's California Cathedrals," *Huffington Post*, March 24, 2011, http://www.huffingtonpost.com/j-michael-welton/cesar-pellis-california-cathedrals_b_839848.html.
"Westward: Queens West," *Oculus*, July 2004, 43.
Will, Tracy, "Mayo Clinic Rochester's New Front Door," *Mayo Today*, November 2001, 4–7.
Wiseman, Carter, "Flights and Fancy," *ARTnews*, June 1997, 116–21.
Worland, Gayle, "Pelli returns to reflect on his shining MMOCA design," *Wisconsin State Journal*, April 5, 2016, http://host.madison.com/wsj/entertainment/arts-and-theatre/pelli-returns-to-reflect-on-his-shining-mmoca-design/article_ba5ad61b-4957-5cf7-8ddd-1b5d2aedc9f3.html.
Wright, Gordon, "Pelli Brings His Vision to Tulsa with Events Center," *Building Design & Construction*, November 2004, 5.
"Yale Under Construction," *Yale Alumni Magazine*, January/February 2006, 28–39.
Daniel A. Yanson ed., "Retrospectiva: Arq. Cesar Pelli," *Construyendo* 20, August 2000, 11–15.
Daniel A. Yanson ed., "Retrospectiva: Arq. Cesar Pelli," *Construyendo* 21, September 2000, 7–11.
Daniel A. Yanson ed., "Retrospectiva: Arq. Cesar Pelli," *Construyendo* 22, October 2000, 4–7.
Daniel A. Yanson ed., "Retrospectiva: Arq. Cesar Pelli," *Construyendo* 23, November 2000, 5–9.
Daniel A. Yanson ed., "Retrospectiva: Arq. Cesar Pelli," *Construyendo* 24, December 2000, 3–7.
Daniel A. Yanson ed., "Retrospectiva: Arq. Cesar Pelli," *Construyendo* 25, January 2001, 3–7.
Daniel A. Yanson ed., "Retrospectiva: Arq. Cesar Pelli," *Construyendo* 26, February 2001, 3–7.
Daniel A. Yanson ed., "Retrospectiva: Arq. Cesar Pelli," *Construyendo* 27, March 2001, 3–7.
Daniel A. Yanson ed., "Retrospectiva: Arq. Cesar Pelli," *Costos & Constuccion* 35, November 2001, 6–9.
Zachmann, Will, "Charging the Battery," *Environmental Design + Construction*, March/April 2002, 33–6.

DESIGN AWARDS

1966 First Design Award
Urban Nucleus, Sunset Mountain Park
Progressive Architecture

1968 Citation
COMSAT Laboratories
Progressive Architecture

1968 Honor Award
Teledyne Labs
American Institute of Steel Construction

1969 Merit Award
Third Street Tunnel Extension
AIA Southern California

1969 First Prize
U.N. City
International Architectural Competition

1969 Honor Award
Worldway Postal Center
AIA Southern California

1974 Merit Award
Wells Fargo Building
AIA Bay Area

1974 William E. Lehman Award for Architectural Excellence
Western Electric Building

1975 Honor Award
Federal Office Building
AIA Southern California

1975 Honor Award
San Bernardino City Hall
AIA Southern California

1975 Merit Award
The Commons and Courthouse Center
AIA Southern California

1975 Merit Award
Wells Fargo Building
AIA Southern California

1976 Citation
Fox Hills Mall
AIA Southern California

1976 Honor Award
Pacific Design Center—Blue Building
AIA Southern California

1977 Citation
Rainbow Center Mall and Winter Garden
Progressive Architecture

1978 Arnold W. Brunner Memorial Prize
Cesar Pelli
American Academy/Institute of Arts and Letters

1984 Certificate of Commendation
Cesar Pelli
City of Los Angeles

1984 Restoration and Expansion Award
Museum of Modern Art Gallery and Residential Tower
Building Owners and Managers Association of Greater New York

1984 Certificate
American Society of Interior Designers

1985 Award
Cesar Pelli
Industrial Design Society of America

1985 Design Award
Herring Hall
AIA Connecticut

1985 Award of Excellence
Museum of Modern Art Gallery and Residential Tower
Urban Land Institute

1985 Certificate of Merit
World Financial Center
The Municipal Art Society of New York

1986 Chicago Award
Cesar Pelli
AIA Illinois/Architectural Record

DESIGN AWARDS cont.

1986 Outstanding Architect Award
Cesar Pelli
Minnesota Real Estate Journal

1986 Honor Award
Crile Clinic Building
AIA

1986 Honor Award
Herring Hall
AIA

1987 UN Federico Villarreal Le Corbusier Plaque
Cesar Pelli

1987 Design Award
Ley Student Center
AIA Connecticut

1987 Design Award
Pacific Design Center—Green Building
Progressive Architecture

1987 Associate
National Academy of Design

1988 Domino's Top 30 Architects
Cesar Pelli

1988 Unbuilt Project Award
Columbus Circle
AIA Connecticut

1988 Excellence in Design Award
Museum of Modern Art Gallery and Residential Tower
AIA New York State

1988 Beautification Award, Landmark Award
Pacific Design Center—Green Building
West Los Angeles Chamber of Commerce

1988 Award
Cesar Pelli & Associates
Connecticut Commission on the Arts

1988 Outstanding Achievement Award in Architecture
Cesar Pelli & Associates
Port Authority Hispanic Society

1988 Best Project, Grand Winner
World Financial Center Winter Garden
Interiorscape Magazine Award

1989 Building of the Year Award (under 100,000 square feet [9,290 square meters])
Century Executive Park Master Plan and Office Building
Connecticut Building Owners and Managers Association

1989 Excellence in Masonry Award
Century Executive Park Master Plan and Office Building
Masonry Institute of Connecticut

1989 Domino's Top 30 Architects
Cesar Pelli

1989 Award
Herring Hall
Brick Institute of America

1989 Award
Wells Fargo Center
Minnesota Chapter of the National Association of Industrial and Office Parks

1989 Award for Excellence for the Outstanding Large Scale Office Building
Wells Fargo Center
Urban Land Institute

1989 Merit Award
Pacific Design Center—Green Building
AIA Connecticut

1989 Firm Award
Cesar Pelli & Associates
AIA

1990 Unbuilt Projects Award
Miglin-Beitler Tower
AIA Connecticut

1990 Award of Excellence
Wells Fargo Center
AIA Connecticut

1990 Award of Excellence
Pacific Design Center—Green Building
American Institute of Steel Construction

1990 Award of Excellence
Pacific Design Center—Green Building
NAHB National Commercial Builders Council and Building Design & Construction

1990 Award of Excellence
World Financial Center
AIA Connecticut

1990 Design Award
World Financial Center
Society of American Registered Architects

1990 Design 100 Editorial Award
Yerba Buena Tower
Metropolitan Review Magazine

1991 Design Award
Boyer Center for Molecular Medicine
AIA Connecticut

1991 Design Award
Carnegie Hall Tower
AIA Connecticut

1991 First Place Winner
Carnegie Hall Tower
Masonry Institute of New York City and Long Island

1991 Honor Award
Plaza Tower
AIA Orange County

1991 Design for Excellence/Certificate of Merit
Plaza Tower
Southern California Edison

1991 Design Award
St. Lukes Medical Tower
Modern Healthcare/AIA

1991 Selected as one of the 10 most influential living American architects
AIA

1992 Award of Merit
181 West Madison
Chicago Lighting Institute

1992 Top Honors: Best New Structure in Downtown
777 Tower
Downtown Breakfast Club

1992 Commendation, Structural Steel Design Awards Scheme
Canary Wharf Tower
The British Constructional Steelwork Association

1992 Special Citation
Carnegie Hall Tower
The City Club of New York

1992 Design of the Year Award
Cleveland Marriott Hotel, Society Center
Services for Independent Living

1992 Award of Merit
Miglin-Beitler Tower
Chicago Lighting Institute

1992 Award of Merit
Plaza Tower
Illuminating Engineering Society of North America

1992 Award, Architecture
Plaza Tower
Los Angeles Beautiful

1992 Bard Honor Award
World Financial Center
The City Club of New York

1993 Best High Rise Commercial
777 Tower
Los Angeles Business Council

1993 Excellence in Architecture Award
Carnegie Hall Tower
AIA New England

1993 Merit Finalists, Benedictus Award Competition
Founders Hall, NationsBank Corporate Center
AIA/ACSA Council on Architectural Research, the International Union of Architects and the Du Pont Company

1993 Merit Award for University Building
Institute for Advanced Study
International Masonry Institute/New Jersey Masonry Center

1993 Honor Award
Reagan National Airport, North Terminal
Community Appearance Alliance

1993 Merit Finalists, Benedictus Award Competition
World Financial Center
AIA/ACSA Council on Architectural Research, the International Union of Architects and the Du Pont Company

1993 Honor Award
Private Residence
American Wood Council

1994 Beautification Award
777 Tower
Los Angeles Business Council

1994 Honor Award
Carnegie Hall Tower
AIA

1994 Excellence in Design Award
Carnegie Hall Tower
AIA New York State

1994 Vitruvio Award
Edificio Republica
Argentina Cultural Affairs Bureau and CAYC

1994 Honor Award
Frances Lehman Loeb Art Center
AIA Westchester/Mid-Hudson

1994 Certificate of Merit
Frances Lehman Loeb Art Center
State of New York Executive Chamber

1994 Merit Award
Institute for Advanced Study
AIA New England

1994 Winner CRSI Design Awards XII
NationsBank Corporate Center
Concrete Reinforcing Steel Institute

1994 Winner
NationsBank Corporate Center
Consulting Engineers Council of Texas

1994 Citation
NationsBank Corporate Center
International Association of Lighting Designers

1994 Certificate of Honor
NationsBank Corporate Center
Structural Engineers Association of Illinois

1994 Office Building of the Year Award
Wells Fargo Center
Building Owners and Managers Association

1994 1994 Building of the Year
St. Luke's Medical Tower
Houston Building Owners and Managers Association

1995 Gold Metal
Cesar Pelli
AIA

1995 Award
Institute for Advanced Study
AIA/Brick Institute of America

1995 Charles Bulfinch Award
Institute for Advanced Study
AIA/Brick Institute of America

1995 Lumen Citation Award
NationsBank Corporate Center
New York Section of the Illuminating Engineering Society

1996 Office Building of the Year
777 Tower
Building Owners and Managers Association

1996 Merit Design Award
Aronoff Center for the Arts
AIA Cincinnati

1996 Design Award
Frances Lehman Loeb Art Center
AIA Connecticut

1996 Award
Frances Lehman Loeb Art Center
Preservation League of New York State

1996 Vintage Award
Humanities and Social Sciences Building Unit 1 at the University of California/Riverside
AIA Inland California Chapter/American Planning Association California Chapter

1996 Office Building of the Year
NationsBank Corporate Center
Building Owners and Managers Association

1996 Award for Design Excellence
Physics and Astronomy Building at the University of Washington/Seattle
Architectural Precast Association

1996 Achievement Award
Cesar Pelli
University of Illinois Alumni Association

1996 Award
Cesar Pelli
Academia Nacional de Arquitectura/Sociedad de Arquitectos

1997 Certificate of Merit
1900 K Street
Associated Builders and Contractors

1997 Design Award
Aronoff Center for the Arts
AIA Connecticut

1997 Honor Award
Aronoff Center for the Arts
US Institute for Theatre Technology

1997 Finalist
Reagan National Airport, North Terminal
Masonry Institute

DESIGN AWARDS cont.

1997 Design Award
NTT Shinjuku Headquarters
AIA Connecticut

1997 Award of Merit, Paul Waterbury Award of Excellence
One Market
International Illuminating Society

1997 Lumen Citation Award
One Market
New York Section of the Illuminating Engineering Society

1997 Certificate
Owens Corning World Headquarters
AIA/DuPont Benedictus Award

1997 Drawing Award
Pacific Design Center—Green Building
AIA Connecticut

1997 Certificate of Engineering Excellence
Petronas Towers
New York Association of Consulting Engineers

1997 Award of Merit
Petronas Towers
Structural Engineers Association of Illinois

1997 Certificate of Honor
Petronas Towers
Structural Engineers Association of Illinois

1997 Award
Physics and Astronomy Building at the University of Washington/Seattle
AIA/Brick in Architecture

1997 First Place Honor Award
Victor Yacktman Children's Pavilion of Lutheran General Hospital
American Society of Interior Designers

1997 First Place
Yacktman Pavilion at Lutheran General Hospital
12th Annual American Society of Interior Designers/Houston Chronicle Interior Design Awards

1998 Premio FV-Ferrum
Edificio Republica
VII Bienal Internacional de Arquitectura de Buenos Aires

1998 Design Award
Reagan National Airport, North Terminal
AIA Connecticut

1998 First Place
Reagan National Airport, North Terminal
Ceilings and Interior Systems Construction Association

1998 Lumen Award
Reagan National Airport, North Terminal
New York Section of the Illuminating Engineering Society

1998 Certificate of Merit
US Federal Courthouse, Brooklyn NY
AIA/Justice Facilities Review

1998 Merit Award
Yacktman Pavilion at Lutheran General Hospital
Illinois Chapter of the American Society of Landscape Architects

1999 Best New Office Development
Investment Building
Washington Business Journal

1999 Design Award
Kuala Lumpur City Centre, Phase 1
AIA Connecticut

1999 Award for Excellence
Lerner Research Institute
The Cleveland Engineering Society, Design & Construction Division

1999 Honor Award
Reagan National Airport, North Terminal
AIA New England

1999 Lumen Award
Petronas Towers
New York Section of the Illuminating Engineering Society

1999 Honorary Prize
Cesar Pelli
Colegio de Arquitectos de la Provincia de Cordoba

2000 Honor Award
Kuala Lumpur City Centre, Phase 1
AIA New England

2000 Honor Award
Kuala Lumpur City Centre, Phase 1
AIA

2000 Honor Award
Reagan National Airport, North Terminal
Design for Transportation National Awards, US Department of Transportation

2000 Professional of the Year
Cesar Pelli
Revista Architector, Buenos Aires, Argentina

2001 Mention
BankBoston
Marble Architectural Award: Oceania, Central and South America

2001 Winner—Large Renovation
Greenwich Library
Build Connecticut Awards

2001 President's Award
Mystic Aquarium
Metal Construction Association Merit Awards

2001 Corporate Partnership Award
Cesar Pelli & Associates
New Haven Public Education Fund

2001 Award of Achievement
Taussig Cancer Center
Northern Ohio Live

2002 Certificate of Excellence
25 Canada Square
The Concrete Society

2002 Golden Trowel Awards, Winner—J. DeLuca Memorial Award
Greenwich Library Addition and Renovation
International Masonry Institute

2002 Craftmanship Award
Investment Building
Washington Building Congress

2002 Best Architecture
Investment Building
Washington Business Journal

2002 Winner—Large Renovation
Payne Whitney Gymnasium
Build Connecticut Awards

2002 Lucy G. Moses Preservation Project Award
World Financial Center
New York Landmarks Conservancy

2003 Award for Excellence
Atago Green Hills
Urban Land Institute

2003 Barrier-Free America Award
Reagan National Airport, North Terminal
Paralyzed Veterans of America

2003 25 Year Award
Pacific Design Center—Blue Building
AIA Los Angeles

2003 Build Ohio Award
Schuster Performing Arts Center
Association of General Contractors

2004 Design Award
Center for Drama and Film
AIA Connecticut

2004 Engineering Excellence Honor Award
Gerald Ratner Athletics Center
American Council of Engineering Companies

2004 Engineering Award of Excellence
Gerald Ratner Athletics Center
American Institute of Steel Construction

2004 Eminent Conceptor Award
Gerald Ratner Athletics Center
Consulting Engineers Council of Illinois

2004 Engineering Excellence Award
Gerald Ratner Athletics Center
Consulting Engineers Council of Illinois

2004 Honor Award for Excellence
Gonda Practice Integration Building, The Mayo Clinic
Minnesota Concrete and Masonry Contractors Association

2004 Craft Award
Gonda Practice Integration Building, The Mayo Clinic
International Union of Bricklayers and Allied Craftsworkers Craft Award

2004 Pinnacle Award of Merit
Gonda Practice Integration Building, The Mayo Clinic
Marble Institute of America

2004 Best of 2004
Overture Center for the Arts
Midwest Construction

2004 Aga Khan Award for Architecture
Petronas Towers

2004 Build America Award
Schuster Performing Arts Center
Association of General Contractors

2004 Top Ten Green Project
The Solaire
AIA/Committee on the Environment

2004 Award, Certificate of Merit
Two International Finance Centre
Hong Kong Quality Building

2004 Excellence in Structural Engineering Award
Weber Music Hall
National Council of Structural Engineers Associations

2004 Bybee Prize
Cesar Pelli
The Building Stone Institute

2004 "Mayor Notable de Tucumán"
Cesar Pelli
Provincia de Tucumán

2005 Award for Excellence
731 Lexington Avenue/One Beacon Court
Urban Land Institute

2005 Distinguished Leadership Award
Cesar Pelli
Connecticut Architecture Foundation

2005 Award of Merit—Out of Area
Malone Engineering Center
Concrete Industry Board Roger H. Corbetta Awards Program

2005 Louis Sullivan Award
Cesar Pelli
International Union of Bricklayers and Allied Craftworkers

2005 Award
Greenwich Library
Connecticut Award for Excellence in Public Library Architecture

2005 Design Award
National Museum of Art, Osaka
AIA Connecticut

2005 Annual Award
US Federal Courthouse, Brooklyn NY
Concrete Industry Board Roger H. Corbetta Awards Program

2006 Award
Cesar Pelli
Farmington Canal Rail to Trail Association

2006 Project Award
Cira Centre
March of Dimes

2006 American Architecture Award
Cira Centre
The Chicago Athenaeum

2006 Design Award
Minneapolis Central Library
AIA Connecticut

2006 Golden Trowel Award of Excellence
Science, Engineering & Classroom Building
Associate Masonary Contractors of Houston

2006 Building Brooklyn Award, Public Works
US Federal Courthouse, Brooklyn NY
Brooklyn Chamber of Commerce

2006 National Leadership Award
Cesar Pelli
Merage Foundation for the American Dream

2006 Lifetime Achievement
Cesar Pelli
Cemex Building Award

2007 Terrazzo Honor Award
Adrienne Arsht Center for the Performing Arts of Miami-Dade County
National Terrazzo & Mosaic Association

2007 Lifetime Achievement Award
Cesar Pelli
Stars of Design

2007 Lumen Award Citation
Children's Reading Room, Minneapolis Central Library
New York Section of the Illuminating Engineering Society

2007 Honorable Mention
Renée and Henry Segerstrom Concert Hall and Samueli Theater
AIA Connecticut

2007 American Legacy Award
Cesar Pelli
ACE Mentor Program

2008 Pinnacle Award, Commercial Exterior
Adrienne Arsht Center for the Performing Arts of Miami-Dade County
Marble Institute of America

2008 American Architecture Award
Adrienne Arsht Center for the Performing Arts of Miami-Dade County
The Chicago Athenaeum

DESIGN AWARDS cont.

2008 Lynn S. Beedle Award
Cesar Pelli
Council on Tall Buildings and Urban Habitat

2008 Premio Trayectoria Profesional
Cesar Pelli
Premio Fiabci Argentina a la Excelencia Inmobiliaria

2008 Illinois Medal in Architecture
Cesar Pelli
University of Illinois at Urbana Champaign, School of Architecture

2008 Design Award
Malone Engineering Center
AIA Connecticut

2008 International Architecture Award
Edificio Caja Sol
The Chicago Athenaeum

2008 Design Award
Overture Center for the Arts
AIA Connecticut

2008 American Architecture Award
Overture Center for the Arts
The Chicago Athenaeum

2008 Award for Excellence
Overture Center for the Arts
Urban Land Institute

2008 Award of Excellence
Renée and Henry Segerstrom Concert Hall and Samueli Theater
Edwin F. Guth Memorial Award for Interior Lighting

2008 Award of Merit
Renée and Henry Segerstrom Concert Hall and Samueli Theater
International Association of Lighting Designers

2008 Lumen Award of Excellence
Renee and Henry Segerstrom Concert Hall and Samueli Theater
Illuminating Engineering Society

2008 Grand Prize
The Visionaire
Green Building Competition for New York City

2009 Project of the Year
Adrienne Arsht Center for the Performing Arts of Miami-Dade County
Urban Land Institute, Southeast Florida/Caribbean District Council

2009 Innovative Design in Engineering and Architecture with Structural Steel (IDEAS2) Award
BOK Center
American Institute of Steel Construction

2009 Excellence Award
MGM CityCenter
Novum Design

2009 Library Building Award
Minneapolis Central Library
American Institute of Architects/American Library Association

2009 Housing Honor
The Visionaire
AIA New York and Boston Society of Architects Building Type Awards

2009 Design Award
Thomas E. Golden Jr. Center
AIA Connecticut

2010 Design Award (Metal Accessories)
ARIA Resort & Casino
Metal Architecture Magazine

2010 American Architecture Award
ARIA Resort & Casino
The Chicago Athenaeum

2010 Medalla del Bicentenario
Cesar Pelli
Cuidad de Buenos Aires

2010 American Architecture Award
CityCenter
The Chicago Athenaeum

2010 Architecture Merit Award
Renée and Henry Segerstrom Concert Hall and Samueli Theater
US Institute for Theatre Technology

2010 Merit Award
Salesforce Transit Center and Salesforce Tower
AIA New York Chapter

2011 Design Award
BOK Center
AIA New England

2011 Distinguished Achievement Award in Architecture
Cesar Pelli
US Institute for Theatre Technology, Inc.

2011 Masters Award
Charles Benson Bear '39 Recreation and Athletic Center
Master Builders of Iowa (MBI)

2011 Green Development Award
Ocean Financial Center
South East Asia Property Awards

2011 Best New Development or Renovation—Public Building
Overture Center for the Arts
Commercial Design Awards, In Business Magazine

2011 Design Award
Tokyo American Club
AIA Connecticut

2011 Team of the Year Award
Pacific Design Center—Red Building
AIA Los Angeles

2012 American Architecture Award
BOK Center
The Chicago Athenaeum

2012 Konex de Brillante
Cesar Pelli
Fundación Konex

2012 Konex de Platino en la disciplina Arquitectura: Quinquenio 2007–2011
Cesar Pelli
Fundación Konex

2012 Best Commercial High Rise Development Singapore
Ocean Financial Center
Asia Pacific Property Awards 2012–2013

2012 Best Office Architecture Singapore
Ocean Financial Center
Asia Pacific Property Awards 2012–2013

2012 Best Office Development Singapore
Ocean Financial Center
Asia Pacific Property Awards 2012–2013

2012 Green Building Award Merit Award and New Building Category (Building Under Construction) Asia Pacific
Ocean Financial Center
Green Building Council Hong Kong

2012 World's Best Commercial High Rise Development
Ocean Financial Center
International Property Awards 2012–2013

2012 Pinnacle Award—Commercial Interior—Merit Award
Ocean Financial Center
Marble Institute of America

2012 Global Award of Excellence
The Avenue
Urban Land Institute

2012 Premio Mención Asprima
Torre Iberdrola
Asprima (Asociación de Promotores Inmobiliarios de Madrid)

2012 Emporis Skyscraper Award Top 10 (8th Place)
UniCredit Headquarters, Porta Nuova Garibaldi
Emporis

2012 Highly Commended award for China, Mixed-use Architecture
Wuhan Riverview Plaza
International Property Awards

2012 Highly Commended award for China, Retail Architecture
Wuhan Riverview Plaza
International Property Awards

2012 5 Star award for China, High-rise Architecture
Wuhan Riverview Plaza
International Property Awards

2012 President's Award, Heritage Ball honoree
Cesar Pelli
AIA New York

2012 Merit Award
Hillhouse Avenue Pedestrian Bridges
AIA Connecticut

2013 BCA Construction Excellence Award
Ocean Financial Center
Building & Construction Authority

2013 Largest Vertical Garden (Green Wall)
Ocean Financial Center
Guinness World Records

2013 Workplace Safety & Health Performance Award
Ocean Financial Center
Ministry of Manpower, Workplace Safety & Health

2013 Excellence Award
Ocean Financial Center
National Parks Board Singapore, Skyrise Greenery Awards (SGA)

2013 AL Lighting and Design Awards Best Use of Daylighting
St. Katharine Drexel Chapel
Architectural Lighting Magazine

2013 Lumen Citation
St. Katharine Drexel Chapel
Illuminating Engineering Society

2013 5 Star Award for China, High-rise Architecture
The Landmark
International Property Award

2013 5 Star Award for China, Mixed-Use Architecture
The Landmark
International Property Award

2013 Highly Commended Award for Chile, High-rise Architecture
Torre Costanera
International Property Awards

2013 5 Star Award for Chile, Office Architecture
Torre Costanera
International Property Awards

2013 Design Award—Built Merit Award
Torre Iberdrola
AIA Connecticut

2013 Lumen Award of Merit
Torre Iberdrola
Illuminating Engineering Society

2014 Award of Merit, Residential, Multi-Family
1214 Fifth Avenue
AIA New York State

2014 Finalist, Best Tall Building Asia & Australia
Abeno Harukas
Council on Tall Buildings and Urban Habitat

2014 Louis I. Kahn Citation
Bill and Melinda Gates Computer Science Complex
American School & University, The Architectural Portfolio

2014 Golden Towel Award—Honorable Mention
Bill and Melinda Gates Computer Science Complex
Central Texas Masonry Contractors Association

2014 Golden Towel Award for Sol LeWitt Sculpture
Bill and Melinda Gates Computer Science Complex
Central Texas Masonry Contractors Association

2014 Innovative Design in Engineering and Architecture with Structural Steel (IDEAS2) Merit Award
Brookfield Place Entry Pavilion
American Institute of Steel Construction

2014 Citation
Cooperative Arts and Humanities High School
AIA Connecticut

2014 Best Innovative Green Building (Gold)
Ocean Financial Centre
MIPIM Asia Awards

2014 Los Angeles Architectural Award
Pacific Design Center—Red Building
Los Angeles Business Council

2014 Citation
St. Katharine Drexel Chapel
AIA Connecticut

2014 Honorable Mention
The Theatre School
AIA Connecticut

2014 Merit Award, Owners' Choice
The Theatre School
Chicago Building Congress

2014 Outstanding Design
The Theatre School
American School & University, The Architectural Portfolio

2014 Merit Award
North Point
Green Building Award

2014 Lifetime Achievement Award
Cesar Pelli
The Arts Council of Greater New Haven

2015 Best in Class (K–12)
Choate Rosemary Hall, Lanphier Center
Brick in Architecture

2015 Honor Award—Religious Architecture: New Facilities
St. Katharine Drexel Chapel
Faith & Form; The Interfaith Forum on Religion, Art, and Architecture

2015 Lumen Award of Excellence
The Pavilion at Brookfield Place (Kugler Ning Lighting Design)
New York Section of Illuminating Engineering Society

2015 Honor Award for Distinguished Building category
The Theatre School
AIA Chicago

2015 Honor Award
The Theatre School
US Institute for Theatre Technology, Inc.

DESIGN AWARDS cont.

2016 Healthcare Best Project
Buerger Center for Advanced Pediatric Care, Children's Hospital of Philadelphia
ENR Mid-Atlantic Region

2016 Silver Award for the Project Leadership Award
Chemistry and Biomolecular Engineering and Chemistry Building
Construction Owners Association of America

2016 Award of Excellence
Center for Innovation in Medical Professions
Cleveland Engineering Society

2016 Bilbao Bizkaia Architecture Prize
Cesar Pelli
Architects Association in Bizkaia and the Office of the Mayor of Bilbao

2016 International Architecture Award
Yale-NUS
The Chicago Athenaeum: Museum of Architecture and Design and The European Centre for Architecture Art Design and Urban Studies

2016 Best Residential High-Rise Award
One West End
US Property Awards

2017 The National Best of the Best Winner—Healthcare
Buerger Center for Advanced Pediatric Care, Children's Hospital of Philadelphia
ENR

2017 Award of Excellence
Hancher Auditorium
International Association of Lighting Designers

2017 Award of Merit
Buerger Center for Advanced Pediatric Care, Children's Hospital of Philadelphia
Healthcare Design Awards

2017 Willard Rouse Award
FMC Tower at Cira Centre South
Urban Land Institute—Philadelphia

2017 Award of Merit in Higher Education/Research—Mid-Atlantic
The Roberts Center for Pediatric Research
ENR

2017 Honor Award
The George S. and Dolores Doré Eccles Theater
AIA Connecticut Design Awards

2017 Honor Award
Lanphier Center for Mathematics and Computer Science
AIA Connecticut Design Awards

2017 Award Winner—Office Architecture
McKinney & Olive
Americas Property Awards

2017 Innovation Award
McKinney & Olive
Urban Land Institute—North Texas

2017 Best Residential/Mixed-Use/Office Space Project
FMC Tower at Cira Centre South
Construction Excellence Awards from the General Building Contractors Association

2017 Best Clinical Health Project
The Roberts Center for Pediatric Research
Construction Excellence Awards from the General Building Contractors Association

Image Credits

INTRODUCTORY PAGES

© Tim Griffith/ESTO II;
© Jeff Goldberg/ESTO V;
© Tim Hursley/ESTO VI;
© courtesy of PCPA XII (left, middle, right), XIV (top, bottom left, bottom middle, bottom right), XV (top, bottom), XVI, XVII (top, middle, bottom), XVIII (top, middle, bottom), XX (top, bottom left, bottom right), XXI (top, middle, bottom), XXII (top left, top right, bottom), XXV (top, bottom);
© Nancy Lee Katz XXVI–XXVII

ESSAYS

Cesar Pelli's California Decade
© courtesy of PCPA XXVIII, XXXII;
© Balthazar Korab XXX–XXXI

Reflections of an Apprentice
© courtesy of PCPA 100, 104;
© Balthazar Korab 102

Celebrating Pelli
© courtesy of PCPA 208, 212;
© Gustavo Sosa Pinilla 210

My Father, My Mentor
© Jeff Goldberg/ESTO 370, 372–3;
© Cervin Robinson 374

Watching the Teacher Learn
© courtesy of PCPA 516–17;
© Mason Miller 518

Reflections
© Victoria Sambunaris 644

Acknowledgments
© courtesy of PCPA 667

PROJECTS

Abandoibarra Master Plan
© courtesy of PCPA 300, 302 (top, bottom left, bottom right), 304 (top, bottom), 305 (top, bottom), 306, 307, 308–9;
© Cesar Pelli 303;
© Jeff Goldberg/ESTO 310–11

Adrienne Arsht Center for the Performing Arts
© Jeff Goldberg/ESTO 390, 396 (top, bottom), 397, 398, 399, 400, 401 (top, bottom), 402–3, 405, 406, 407 (top, bottom), 408 (top), 409, 410–11, 412–13;
© courtesy of PCPA 392, 394, 395, 404, 408 (bottom);
© Cesar Pelli 393

ARIA Resort and Casino
© Jeff Goldberg/ESTO 464, 466–7, 469, 472 (top), 473, 474, 475, 476–7;
© Cesar Pelli 468;
© courtesy of PCPA 470, 471;
© Scott Frances 472 (bottom)

Aronoff Center for the Arts
© Jeff Goldberg/ESTO 184, 186 (bottom), 192, 193, 194, 195 (top, bottom);
© courtesy of PCPA 186 (top), 187, 188–9, 190, 191;
© J. Miles Wolf 196, 197

Biennale House
© courtesy of PCPA 80, 82, 83, 84 (top, bottom), 85 (top, bottom)

BOK Center
© Jeff Goldberg/ESTO 446, 448–9, 451, 453 (top), 454–5;
© courtesy of PCPA 448 (top, bottom), 452, 453 (bottom);
© Cesar Pelli 550 (top, bottom), 543

Carnegie Hall Tower
© Jeff Goldberg/ESTO 150, 152 (left), 153, 155;
© courtesy of PCPA 152 (right), 154 (left, top, bottom)

Cira Centre
© Jeff Goldberg/ESTO 346, 349, 351, 352–3;
© courtesy of PCPA 348;
© Cesar Pelli 350

COMSAT Laboratories
© courtesy of PCPA 18, 20, 21, 22 (top, middle, bottom), 23, 24, 25;
© Steven Hill 26–7

Connecticut Science Center
© Jeff Goldberg/ESTO 478, 480–1, 483, 485, 486, 488 (top left, top right, bottom), 489, 490–1;
© courtesy of PCPA 480, 487;
© Cesar Pelli 482, 484

Cooperative Arts and Humanities High School
© Jeff Goldberg/ESTO 492, 495, 497, 498, 499, 500–1;
© courtesy of PCPA 494 (top, bottom);
© Judy Sirota Rosenthal 496 (top, bottom)

Crile Clinic Building
© Jeff Goldberg/ESTO 118, 121, 122, 123;
© courtesy of PCPA 120 (top, bottom)

Edificio República
© Daniel Casoy Photography 214;
© courtesy of PCPA 216, 217 (top, middle, bottom), 218 (top);
© Gustavo Sosa Pinilla 218 (bottom), 220, 221;
© Cesar Pelli 219

Hancher
© Jeff Goldberg/ESTO 580, 582–3, 584 (top), 585 (top, bottom), 586, 587 (top, bottom), 588–9, 591, 592–3;
© courtesy of PCPA 584 (bottom), 590 (top, bottom)

Herring Hall
© courtesy of PCPA 94, 96 (bottom), 98 (top);
© Paul Hester Photography 96 (top), 99;
© Andrew Gordon Photography 97 (top, bottom)

Hillhouse Avenue Pedestrian Bridge
© Richard Barnes 510, 513;
© courtesy of PCPA 512;
© Wes Wright/courtesy of PCPA 513 (bottom left, bottom right)

International Finance Center
© Tim Griffith/ESTO 324, 327;
© courtesy of PCPA 328 (top, bottom), 329, 330–1, 331;
© Virgile Simon Bertrand 332–3

JPMorgan Chase Building
© Timothy Griffith/ESTO 278, 281, 282, 283;
© courtesy of PCPA 280 (left, right)

Kukui Gardens
© David Franzen/ESTO 28, 31 (top);
© courtesy of PCPA 30 (top, bottom), 31 (bottom), 32, 33

Malone Engineering Center
© Jeff Goldberg/ESTO 354, 358, 359, 360, 361, 362–3, 364, 366 (top, bottom), 367, 368–9;
© courtesy of PCPA 356 (top, bottom);
© Cesar Pelli 357

Maral Explanada
© Juanjo Martinez 594;
© courtesy of PCPA 596 (top, bottom), 597 (top, bottom)

Minneapolis Central Library
© Jeff Goldberg/ESTO 414, 416 (top), 417, 418–19, 420, 421, 422–3, 424–5, 427;
© courtesy of PCPA 416 (bottom), 424 (top, bottom);
© Paul Crosby 426

Museum of Modern Art Expansion and Tower
© Cervin Robinson 106, 112–13, 114, 117;
© courtesy of PCPA 108 (top, bottom left, bottom right), 109 (top, middle, bottom), 110 (top, bottom), 111 (top, bottom), 116, 117;
© Kenneth Champlin 115

National Museum of Art
© Jeff Goldberg/ESTO 334, 339, 340 (top), 341, 342, 243, 344–5;
© courtesy of PCPA 336, 338, 340 (bottom);
© Cesar Pelli 337 (top);
© Roberto Espejo/courtesy of PCPA 337 (bottom)

North Terminal, Reagan National Airport
© courtesy of PCPA 240, 242, 243, 248–9 (top and middle), 255 (bottom), 264 (top);
© Cesar Pelli 244–5 (top and bottom);
© Jeff Goldberg/ESTO 246–7, 248 (bottom), 249 (bottom), 250–1, 252–3, 254, 256, 257, 258, 259, 260, 261, 262–3, 263 (top), 264 (bottom), 264–5, 266 (left), 266 (right), 267 (left), 268 (top, bottom), 269 (top, bottom), 270–1;
© Kenneth Champlin 255 (top);
© Isaac Campbell 267 (right)

NTT Headquarters
© Mitsuo Matsuoka 198, 202, 203, 207;
© courtesy of PCPA 200 (top, bottom), 201;
© Kaneaki Monma 204, 206;
© Tohru Waki 205

One Canada Square Tower and Docklands Light Railway Station
© courtesy of PCPA 156, 159, 160 (top, bottom), 161 (top, middle, bottom), 162 (top, bottom), 163;
© Miller Hare Limited 164–5

Overture Center for the Arts
© Jeff Goldberg/ESTO 428, 432–3, 435, 436 (top), 437 (top), 438 (top, bottom), 439 (left, right), 440, 441, 442, 443 (top, bottom), 444, 445;
© Cesar Pelli 430, 431;
© courtesy of PCPA 434 (top, bottom), 436 (bottom), 437 (bottom)

Pacific Design Center
© Michael LeRoy 44;
© Cesar Pelli 46 (bottom), 47 (top, bottom);
© courtesy of PCPA 46 (top), 48, 49, 50 (top, bottom), 51, 52 (top), 53, 54, 55, 59 (top, bottom);
© Adrian Velicescu 52 (bottom);
© Jeff Goldberg/ESTO 56–7, 58, 60 (bottom), 61, 62–3;
© Jeffrey Milstein 60 (top)

Petronas Towers
© Jeff Goldberg/ESTO 222, 230, 231, 232, 236, 238, 239;
© courtesy of PCPA 224, 226, 227, 228, 233, 234 (bottom left);
© Kenneth Champlin and Associates 225;
© Cesar Pelli 229;
© Fred Byfield 234 (top);
© John Apicella 235, 237

Plaza Tower
© John Connell Photography 166, 169, 170, 171;
© courtesy of PCPA 168

Porta Nuova Garibaldi and UniCredit Headquarters
© courtesy of PCPA 554, 556 (top, bottom left, bottom right), 557 (bottom left, bottom right), 562;
© Gabriel Bekerman Arquitectos 557;
© Stefano Gusmeroli 558–9;
© Jeff Goldberg/ESTO 560, 561, 563, 564–5, 566–7

Private Residence
© Scott Frances/ESTO 172, 174–5, 178, 179, 180, 182 (top), 183;
© courtesy of PCPA 176 (top, middle), 181, 182 (bottom left, bottom right);
© Rafael Pelli 176;
© Cesar Pelli 177

Rainbow Center Winter Garden
© Norman McGrath 86, 88, 90, 91, 92, 93;
© courtesy of PCPA 89 (top, bottom)

Renée and Henry Segerstrom Concert Hall and Samueli Theater
© Tim Hursley/ESTO 376, 378–9, 380–1, 382 (top), 383, 385, 388, 388–9;
© courtesy of PCPA 378 (left), 382 (bottom), 384, 386, 387

Salesforce Tower
© Steelblue 620, 622–3, 625, 628–9;
© Cesar Pelli 624;
© Gregory Vasquez 626–7;
© courtesy of PCPA 626 (left)

Salesforce Transit Center
© Steelblue 630, 634, 635, 642–3;
© courtesy of PCPA 632–3 (top), 632 (bottom), 637 (top, bottom left), 638–9, 641 (bottom);
© Gregory Vasquez 636 (top);
© Vittoria Zupicich 636 (bottom), 637 (bottom right), 640–1, 641 (top)

San Bernardino City Hall
© Balthazar Korab 64, 66, 70–1;
© courtesy of PCPA 67 (top, bottom), 68 (top, bottom), 69

Schuster Performing Arts Center
© Jeff Goldberg/ESTO 294, 297, 298, 299;
© courtesy of PCPA 296 (top, bottom)

South Coast Repertory
© Jeff Goldberg/ESTO 272, 275 (top), 276–7;
© courtesy of PCPA 274 (top, bottom), 275 (bottom)

St. Katharine Drexel Chapel, Xavier University of Lousiana
© Jeff Goldberg/ESTO 520, 522, 523, 524, 525, 527, 528–9, (top), 530, 532, 533, 534–5
© courtesy of PCPA 522 (top), 526, 531 (top, bottom)

Sunset Mountain Park
© courtesy of PCPA 2, 4–5, 6, 7, 8–9

Teledyne Labs
© Julius Shulman 10, 12 (top; bottom), 13 (top), 16–17;
© courtesy of PCPA 13 (bottom), 14–15

The Theatre School, DePaul University
© Jeff Goldberg/ESTO 536, 538, 539, 540–1, 542, 543, 544 (bottom), 545, 546 (top, bottom), 547, 548 (top, bottom), 549 (top, bottom), 550, 551, 552–3;
© courtesy of PCPA 540, 544 (top)

Torre Banco Macro
© Gustavo Pinilla 616, 618 (bottom left), 619;
© courtesy of PCPA 618 (top left, top right)

Torre Costanera
© Jeff Goldberg/ESTO 568, 572, 575, 576, 577, 578–9;
© Pablo Blanco 570–1;
© courtesy of PCPA 573, 574

Torre Iberdrola
© Jeff Goldberg/ESTO 312, 315, 316, 318–19, 322–3;
© courtesy of Iberdrola AIE 314;
© courtesy of PCPA 314 (bottom), 320;
© Cesar Pelli 317;
© Josep Ma. Molinos/Wenzel 321

Torre Libertad
© Jeff Goldberg/ESTO 502, 504 (top), 505, 507, 508–9;
© courtesy of PCPA 504 (bottom), 506 (left, right)

Torre Sevilla
© courtesy of PCPA 606, 609, 610, 611, 612 (top, bottom), 613, 615;
© Cesar Pelli 608;
© Axel Zemborain/courtesy of PCPA 614

Torre YPF
© Gustavo Sosa Pinilla 456, 459, 461, 462–3;
© courtesy of PCPA 458;
© Cesar Pelli 460

UN City
© courtesy of PCPA 34, 36, 37, 38–9, 40, 41, 42–3

US Embassy
© courtesy of PCPA 72, 75 (top, bottom), 76 (bottom), 77, 78–9;
© Masao Arai/The Japan Architect 74–5;
© Mitsuo Matsuoka/The Japan Architect 76 (top)

Weber Music Hall
© courtesy of PCPA 284, 286, 287, 289;
© Jeff Goldberg/ESTO 288–9, 290–1, 292, 293

Wells Fargo Center
© George Heinrich 140;
© courtesy of PCPA 142, 146, 148 (right);
© Steven Bergerson Photography 143;
© Balthazar & Christian Korab 144, 145, 147, 148 (left), 149

Wintrust Arena
© Steelblue 598, 600 (top), 604–5;
© courtesy of PCPA 600 (bottom), 601, 602–3 (top, bottom)

World Financial Center
© Timothy Hursley Photography 124;
© courtesy of PCPA 126 (top, bottom), 128,129, 130–1, 132 (top, bottom), 134 (bottom);
© Jon Pickard 127;
© Jeff Goldberg/ESTO 131, 133, 134 (top), 135, 138–9;
© M. Paul Freidberg & Partners 136;
© Jeff Perkell 137

Acknowledgments

I am very fortunate to have designed buildings all around the world. I wish to thank all of the clients, associate architects, Pelli Clarke Pelli Architects, designers, and consultants involved in the featured projects. I'm very honored and proud of the work that we produced over the course of the last forty years. I also wish to thank Michael Crosbie with whom I have worked numerous times, who wrote the compelling text about my life and work.

To my son Rafael Pelli, who I have worked with for over twenty-five years, most recently as a partner. I'm very proud of all that you have accomplished. To my partner Fred Clarke who started the firm with me—thank you for your invaluable creativity and business acumen. To Principals of my firm—William Butler, David Chen, Mitchell Hirsch, Gregg Jones, Mariko Masuoka, Mark Shoemaker—who I have collaborated with extensively since the early years of the firm. Thank you for contributing your talent and expertise to the success of the firm and the projects we designed.

To Pablo Mandel for his design expertise, Images Publishing for publishing this book, Janet Yoder for coordinating and managing the entire process, Ken Carlson for his work on bringing the older photos to life, Melissa Kraby and Zac Zuber-Zander for their work in compiling and organizing the end matter, and to the readers who take the time to read this book.

—Cesar Pelli

Firm Partners, Principals, and Senior Associate Principals, from left to right: Mark R. Shoemaker, Gregg E. Jones, Mitchell A. Hirsch, William E. Butler, Mariko Masuoka, Fred W. Clarke, Darin C. Cooke, Susana La Porta Drago, Rafael Pelli, Cesar Pelli, Edward Dionne, David P. Chen.

Book Contributors

Cesar Pelli, FAIA, founded the firm in 1977, the year he became dean of the Yale University School of Architecture. He has designed buildings around the globe, and his work has won numerous awards internationally. In 1995, the American Institute of Architects bestowed upon Pelli the AIA Gold Medal—the Institute's highest honor. Pelli has written extensively on architectural issues, authoring the book in 1999, and has lectured at architecture schools, professional and public gatherings, and at symposia around the world.

Michael J. Crosbie, FAIA, is Professor of Architecture at the University of Hartford and editor-in-chief of *Faith & Form: The Interfaith Journal on Religion, Art, and Architecture*. Dr. Crosbie is the author of or contributor to more than forty books on architecture, design, and practice and has written hundreds of articles published internationally. He lectures on architecture throughout the US and abroad. A registered architect, Dr. Crosbie was the Walton Visiting Critic at The Catholic University of America School of Architecture and Planning in 2015.

John Pastier has worked in the fields of architecture, city planning, and design journalism since the 1960s. He was the founding architecture critic for the *Los Angeles Times* and has contributed to numerous publications. In 1980, he wrote the first monograph on Cesar Pelli's work. He has taught at the University of California at Berkeley, the University of California at Los Angeles, the University of Texas at Austin, McGill University, and the University of Washington.

John J. Casbarian, FAIA, is co-founding partner of the internationally-recognized, award-winning firm Taft Architects. A fellow of the American Academy in Rome, he is also dean emeritus, Harry K. and Albert K. Smith Professor, and director of External Programs at Rice University's School of Architecture. In 2002, he founded and continues to direct the Rice School of Architecture Paris program. He worked for Gruen Associates, in Los Angeles, under Cesar Pelli from 1969 to 1970.

Berto González Montaner is an architect, adjunct professor at FADU-UBA (Facultad de Arquitectura Diseño y Urbanismo, Universidad de Buenos Aires), managing editor for the ARQ-Architecture supplement, *Diario Clarin*, and host of television show "Crónicas Urbanas," currently on the air on Canal (á).

Rafael Pelli, FAIA, is a partner in Pelli Clarke Pelli Architects and directs the firm's New York office, established in 2000. He has focused on sustainable design in the firm's work and has made significant achievements in this realm, producing architecture recognized with numerous design awards. He has lectured widely on the firm's commitment to sustainable building design and has served on a number of boards promoting the design and construction of sustainable architecture.

Fred W. Clarke, FAIA, is a co-founder of the firm. As Senior Design Principal, he directs all of the firm's projects in the New Haven office and Asian studios. A career-long teacher and writer, Clarke has been a faculty member at Yale University, Rice University, and the University of California at Los Angeles and has written on urbanism, sustainability, public art and architecture, and tall-building design. He has served on numerous design juries and panels internationally.